W9-BMH-509

EX LIBRIS
Randy Manning

The Color Encyclopedia of Ornamental Grasses

The ornamental grass teaching display at Longwood Gardens, Kennett Square, Pennsylvania, provides a glimpse of the varied world of textures, forms, sizes, and colors to be found among the grasses.

The Color Encyclopedia of Ornamental Grasses

Sedges, Rushes, Restios, Cat-tails, and Selected Bamboos

RICK DARKE

Timber Press
Portland, Oregon

Part title page illustration of zebra grass, *Miscanthus sinensis* 'Zebrinus', is from a 1909 Storrs and Harrison Company nursery catalog.

Published in 1999 by
Timber Press, Inc.
The Haseltine Building
133 S.W. Second Avenue, Suite 450
Portland, Oregon 97204

Fifth printing 2002

Printed in Hong Kong
Jacket and text designed by Susan Applegate

Cataloging-in-Publication Data

Darke, Rick.
The color encyclopedia of ornamental grasses: sedges, rushes, restios, cat-tails, and selected bamboos/Rick Darke.
p. cm.
Includes bibliographical references (p.) and index.
ISBN 0-88192-464-4
1. Ornamental grasses—Encyclopedias. 2. Ornamental grasses—Pictorial works. I. Title.
SB431.7.D363 1999
635.9'349—DC21 98-23440
CIP

Contents

Foreword

GRASSES are plants that throughout time have greatly benefited the inhabitants of the earth and the land itself. Grasses provide food for our bodies and for our souls. They create food and shelter for many animals. The grain crops have provided sustenance that has allowed civilizations to develop and survive. Grasses are pioneer plants. They are the first to grow in disturbed and destroyed nature. Their diversity in appearance and in growing regions is unequaled. Grasses are found on all continents to the reaches of Antarctica; where nothing else will grow, one will find a grass. And now grasses are finally being recognized for their phenomenal contribution to landscaping. For every niche of our lives there is a grass that harmonizes and further beautifies the space.

Limited use of ornamental grasses in the garden can be traced back to Victorian times. Even in the late fifteenth century, the master painter and nature illustrator Albrecht Dürer painted *Das Grosse Rasenstück* (the large meadow section). His composition depicts fine-textured grasses with broad-leaf plantain and the serrated-leaved dandelion. Columbines are complemented by the gently arching bows of blue meadowgrass. It is a truly inspiring depiction of nature, and an image I have long carried with me.

In the early part of the twentieth century several horticulturists worked to introduce a new diversity of plants for our landscapes and gardens. Now, a new generation has discovered the limitless beauty of ornamental grasses. Rick Darke has recognized the many positive attributes of this vast plant group. He has spent years precisely documenting his observations and *The Color Encyclopedia of Ornamental Grasses* is a reflection of his dedication to the grasses. He is an accomplished photographer and presents his findings in a very informative manner. This book contains the most up-to-date taxonomy of the grasses and will be an excellent reference for both the amateur and the professional gardener.

This book is part of a larger celebration of the coming of age of our native flora, the growing recognition of our North American plants. The hope is to inspire a new generation of impressionist landscape designers to use grasses for the beauty they contribute through all seasons, a beauty that is distinguished by the colors and textures that only grasses can provide.

Ornamental grasses are key plants for the natural landscape. From the Atlantic to the Pacific, from the lakes of Minnesota to the theme parks of Florida, ornamental grasses are taking the country by storm. This has been a life-long goal of mine, and it is truly gratifying to witness the recognition of grasses.

The garden of the future will host many native plants; grasses will play a very important role because of their diversity and adaptability. The door is open to a more varied and natural approach to landscape design. I envision a broadening of landscape designs away from the straight-lined, evenly spaced planting to one of fluid, dynamic, and constantly changing beauty. Rick Darke provides us with a guide and a reference for our future gardens. I challenge everyone to take a look at the diversity grasses can provide.

Kurt Bluemel
June 1997

Preface

> In the laying out of lawns and artistic gardens, a few of the many beautiful hardy grasses should not be overlooked. Their stateliness, tropic luxuriance, and soft colors harmoniously punctuate the prevailing green, while their graceful, sinuous yielding to every wind gives animation to gardened landscapes too apt to look "fixed."
>
> Spring 1909 Catalog
> The Storrs and Harrison Company
> Painesville, Ohio

THE TURNING of a century inspires both reflection and speculation. Looking back at ornamental grasses and their role in gardens over the past 100 years, it is easy to see that much has changed. Whereas turn-of-the-century gardeners had perhaps a dozen perennial grasses to choose from, today's gardeners have hundreds. Ornamental grasses now embody a huge array of textures, forms, sizes, colors, flowering times, and cultural adaptations. This exhilarating increase in diversity has resulted from the efforts of botanists, breeders, and nurseries in nearly all parts of the globe and seems certain to continue. The unprecedented popularity grasses now enjoy can be attributed partly to this development; however, there are other factors fueling the current enthusiasm that are sure to influence the place grasses will hold in tomorrow's gardens.

As we enter not just a new century but a new millennium, we are doing more than expanding the plant palette—we are redefining the garden. Landscape gardening, that unique confluence of art and science, is searching for a model that will provide an opportunity for creative expression and a reverent link to the larger ecology. Gardens must be at once inspiring and conserving, high-spirited and low maintenance. They must reflect and sustain the rhythms of our lives and our homes, and they must speak to us eloquently of the sun and seasons. Delightfully, grasses are sympathetic to all these ideals.

This book is intended for gardeners in a wide range of situations and climates, and draws from the experience and creativity of great gardens and gardeners around the world. It begins with an exploration of the unique aesthetics and appeal of ornamental grasses. A review of the families of ornamental grasses explains botanical characteristics important to gardeners. A chapter on names helps to simplify the complex, often confusing world of botanical and horticultural nomenclature and taxonomy. A survey of grasses in their native habitats analyzes ecological and visual patterns that can be of practical and inspirational value to gardeners. The design section features the imaginative use of grasses in myriad fine gardens, and a chapter on growing and maintaining grasses explains how to support such creations.

Gardeners usually speak of "ornamental grasses" in the broad sense, including not only the true grasses, but also related families of grasslike plants, such as sedges and rushes. Following this tradition, this book provides a detailed treatment of the perennial grasses (Poaceae), sedges (Cyperaceae), rushes (Juncaceae), restios (Restionaceae), and cat-tails (Typhaceae) available to modern gardeners, as well as selected bamboos (Poaceae).

Acknowledgments

SO MANY people have contributed to my understanding of the grasses and to the making of this book. Among them are friend and former professor Dick Lighty, an early advocate for grasses who has for many years shared his knowledge and insight; Bill Frederick, another friend who long ago saw the beauty in grasses and who has taught me much about reconciling a passion for plants with the greater art of the garden; Kurt Bluemel, who shared with me (and countless others) his incredible energies, knowledge, and enthusiasm for ornamental grasses, and who provided personal introductions to Ernst Pagels, Hans Simon, Hermann Müssel, Anke Mattern, and others in Germany who have been vital to the richness of the modern garden ornamental grass palette; Masato Yokoi and Barry Yinger, whose understandings of Japanese ornamental grasses are unparalleled; Wolfang Oehme, who tirelessly took me to innumerable gardens to see grasses growing, fueled by sheer enthusiasm and a trunkful of bananas; Tony Avent of Plant Delights Nursery, Raleigh, North Carolina; Dale Hendricks of North Creek Nurseries, Landenberg, Pennsylvania; Neil Diboll of Prairie Nursery, Westfield, Wisconsin; Randy Baldwin of San Marcos Nursery, Santa Barbara, California; Harlan Hamernik of Bluebird Nursery, Clarkson, Nebraska; Dan Heims of Terra Nova Nursery, Portland, Oregon; Richard Simon and Martha Simon Pindale of Bluemount Nursery, Monkton, Maryland; Carl Schoenfeld and John Fairey of Yucca Do Nursery, Waller, Texas; John Greenlee of Greenlee Nursery, Pomona, California; Don Jacobs of Eco Gardens, Decatur, Georgia; Janet Rademacher of Mountain States Nursery, Glendale, Arizona; Kim Hawks of Niche Gardens, Chapel Hill, North Carolina; Adrian and Alan Bloom of Bressingham Gardens, Bressingham, Diss, Norfolk, England; Roger Grounds of Apple Court, Hordle, Lymington, Hampshire, England; Steve and Katsy Schmidt of American Ornamental Perennials, Eagle Creek, Oregon; Dan Hinkley of Heronswood Nursery, Kingston, Washington; Greg Spiechert of Crystal Palace Perennials, St. John, Indiana; Gerry Kopf of Bald Eagle Nursery, Fulton, Illinois; and many other nursery professionals who are working tirelessly to provide us with the best plants for our gardens.

I am also grateful to a several other individuals who helped in various ways with this project, including Whitney Adams, Jim Aitken, Yoko Arakawa, Mary Barkworth, who provided critical assistance with *Stipa*, Carol Bornstein, Roberto Burle

Marx, Cole Burrell, Gordon Collier, Mervyn Feesey, Hermann Fuchs, Galen Gates, Roger Gettig, Jacqueline and Eric Gratz, Gary Hammer, Penelope Hobhouse, Surrey Jacobs, Louise Lacey, Alan Leslie, Christopher Lloyd, Ron Lutsko, Mark Moskowitz, Kathy Musial, Nichole O'Neill, Karen Offutt, Roger Raiche, Thomas and Martina Reinhardt, Ann Rhoads, Claire Sawyers, George Schenk, Cassian Schmidt, Jack Schuler, Shigeto Tsukie, Jim Waddick, Dick Weaver, Chris Woods, and Pauline Volmer.

The following people contributed photographs to this book: Tony Avent, Gordon Collier, Dan Heims, Dale Hendricks, Nichole O'Neill, Hideaki Tatsumi, and Melinda Zoehrer. All other photographs were taken by the author using a Nikon FM2 camera and almost entirely with 35 mm Kodachrome ASA 64 film, in diverse gardens large and small. I am deeply grateful to these places and institutions: Bellevue Botanic Garden, Washington; Berlin-Dahlem Botanic Garden, Germany; Beth Chatto Gardens, Colchester, England; Brooklyn Botanic Garden, New York; Chanticleer, Wayne, Pennsylvania; Chicago Botanic Garden, Illinois; Christchurch Botanical Garden, New Zealand; The Coach House, England; Fazenda Vargem Grande, Areias, Brazil; Firefly Farm, Landenberg, Pennsylvania; Great Dixter, East Sussex, England; The Grove Park Inn, Asheville, North Carolina; Hamburg Botanical Garden, Germany; Hof Botanical Garden, Germany; Huntington Botanical Gardens, San Marino, California; Jardin de Aclimatacion de La Orotava, Tenerife, Canary Islands; Little Thakeham, Storrington, England; Longwood Gardens, Kennett Square, Pennsylvania; Mitchell Park Conservatory, Milwaukee, Wisconsin; Mt. Cuba Center, Greenville, Delaware; Munich Botanical Garden, Germany; National Botanical Garden, Kirstenbosch, Cape Town, South Africa; New York Botanical Garden; Palmengarten, Frankfurt, Germany; Rakusai Bamboo Garden, Kyoto, Japan; Royal Botanic Garden, Edinburgh, Scotland; Royal Botanic Gardens, Kew, England; Royal Horticultural Society Wisley Garden, Surrey, England; Santa Barbara Botanic Garden, California; Scott Arboretum, Swarthmore, Pennsylvania; Shaw Arboretum, Missouri Botanical Garden, St. Louis; Springwood, Kennett Square, Pennsylvania; Stonecrop, Cold Spring, New York; University of California, Berkeley, Botanical Garden; University of Washington Center for Urban Horticulture, Seattle; U.S. National Arboretum, Washington, D.C.; Wave Hill, Bronx, New York; Willowwood Arboretum, Morristown, New Jersey; Winterthur Museum and Gardens, Delaware.

All black and white illustrations, unless individually credited otherwise, were adapted, using Adobe Photoshop and PageMaker programs, from USDA Miscellaneous Publication No. 200, the classic 1951 revision of the *Manual of the Grasses of the United States* by A. S. Hitchcock and Agnes Chase.

A very special thanks to Longwood Gardens director Fred Roberts and to the staff of this wonderful institution, which provided me extraordinary opportunities to learn and share for more than two decades. At Longwood I was able to conduct long-term research trials of ornamental grasses and to observe public reaction to new plants. I also had the critical use of one of the finest horticultural libraries in the world. My work with international plant introduction for Longwood afforded the uncommon chance to observe most of the plants in this book first-hand and to become acquainted with a devoted, eclectic community of ornamental grass enthusiasts in gardens all over the world.

Thanks also to Jerry Darke, who provided generous counsel and endured endless questions about the digital technologies without which this book would not have been produced, and to Melinda Zoehrer, who compiled the bibliography, has been my reader, my encouragement, and, though she might appear at the end of any alphabetical summary, has long been at the top of my list.

Various ornamental grasses including melic grass, *Melica ciliata,* blue oat grass, *Helictotrichon sempervirens,* and different cultivars of *Miscanthus sinensis* in the Wild Garden at Wave Hill, New York, contribute to a richly textured, beautifully balanced ensemble.

For Marjorie D. Darke,
who encouraged me toward
the study of living landscapes,

And for Melinda,
who knows to greet
the morning light with laughter.

A sweep of common reed, *Phragmites australis,* epitomizes the graceful movement of grasses in the wind. The slender stalks retain their pliancy even at –5°F (–21°C) on a snowy February day in Pennsylvania.

CHAPTER 1

The Beauty of Grasses

THE AESTHETIC appeal of ornamental grasses is quite distinct from that of most garden perennials. Instead of brightly colored, broad-petaled flowers, grasses offer a wealth of beauty and interest derived from translucency, line, form, texture, scale, seasonal change, sound, and movement. Their colors, though generally less saturated, are softly sophisticated, subtle, and varied. An awareness and understanding of these unique attributes greatly contribute to success and pleasure when gardening with ornamental grasses.

Sound and Movement

Grasses are the first to tell of every caressing summer breeze. Their lissome stalks and flowers flutter and bow, dancing before every spring gale, every autumn storm, every winter wind. Supple and sinuous in their yielding, they paint portraits of the wind. As they move, they sing in tones ranging from a low rustle to a staccato rattle. This sound and movement add immeasurably to the vibrancy of the garden and to its resonance with the larger landscape. Such movement can also be enjoyed from a window looking out to the garden, where it may also serve as a subtle beckoning outdoors.

Light and Translucency

Ornamental grasses surpass all other garden plants in their luminous qualities. The flowers and foliage are highly translucent and are often most dramatic when back-lit or side-lit by the sun. The low angle of sunlight in late autumn and winter accentuates this radiant effect, bringing a welcome vibrancy to the landscape at times when typical flowering plants are at their lowest ebb.

Narrow plumes of feather reed grass, *Calamagrostis ×acutiflora* 'Karl Foerster', are resplendent in the midsummer sun.

Two photos of a field of common annual foxtails, *Setaria* species, dramatize the translucency of grasses in angled sunlight.

Left: The grasses, seen in a flat, direct light coming from over the photographer's shoulder, appear dull, and their detail is indistinguishable. The scene lacks a sense of depth or contrast.

Below: The same view, seen later in the day when the sun has shifted and is now illuminating the grasses from the side. The angled sunlight reveals beautiful detail even in these simple foxtails, which are now set off brilliantly against shadows.

Sunlight plays on grasses in much the same way it plays on flowing water or a fountain spray. In this November scene inside the conservatory at Longwood Gardens, container-grown *Miscanthus* shares sunstreams with a fountain.

Natural back-lighting causes the foliage of Japanese blood-grass, *Imperata cylindrica* 'Red Baron', to flicker like flames, set in a groundcover of black *Ophiopogon* at Brookside Gardens, Maryland.

The Quality of Line

Most grasses, no matter what size, shape, or color, add a strong linear presence to the garden because of the parallel arrangement of their many fine stems and long, narrow leaves. The quality of line varies considerably. The foliage of some grasses is strongly vertical, others hold their leaves at sharp angles, and still others have lax and flowing foliage.

Porcupine grass, *Miscanthus sinensis* 'Strictus', is aptly named. The quill-like leaves project at sharp angles.

Form, Texture, and Scale

Characteristics of form, texture, and scale become of much greater importance when working with plants whose primary strength is not flower color, and ornamental grasses include a wide variation in all three. The shapes of grasses include tightly tufted mounds, neatly symmetrical fountains, vertical uprights, and irregular cascades. Grasses often change form considerably over the course of a garden year, as leafy basal rosettes give rise to variously shaped floral displays. Form also varies with different cultural conditions. A grass that grows strictly upright in full sun may be loose and arching if sited in shade. Although grasses share a linear nature, they encompass a wide range of textures from ultra-fine to coarse. Grasses also vary in scale from miniatures only 12 in. (30 cm) tall in full flower to giants that attain 15 ft. (4.6 m) tall in a single growing season.

The rounded form of *Miscanthus sinensis* 'Gracillimus' has made it a favorite of gardeners since Victorian days. The fine texture of this large grass demonstrates that size and texture can be independent of one another.

The irregular, almost explosive form of this Korean feather reed grass, *Calamagrostis brachytricha*, is part of its unique appeal. Form often varies under different cultural conditions. This grass tends to be loose and irregular in shaded situations and more erect in sunnier spots.

Below and at bottom: These photos of the grass display at Longwood Gardens show how dramatically the texture and form of grasses can change within a growing season.

In May, tufted hair grass, *Deschampsia cespitosa* 'Schottland', forms spiky regular mounds in the foreground while the coarser foliage of feather reed grass, *Calamagrostis ×acutiflora* 'Karl Foerster', is loosely cascading.

By early August, these plants have transformed themselves. The clumps of tufted hair grass have coalesced into a cloud-form of finely diffuse flowers, and the feather reed grass has become an erect wall of narrow plumes.

Huge specimens of giant reed, *Arundo donax,* tower over cannas lining the Flower Garden Walk at Longwood Gardens in October. Growing nearly 15 ft. (4.5 m) tall by the end of a season, this giant is among the largest of the grasses. Its texture is almost as coarse as corn.

Foliage and Flower Color

The leaves and flowers of grasses each have their distinct ranges of color. Spring and summer foliage colors include myriad greens, from dark forest to lime and from gray-green to blue-green, as well as powder blue, red, and bright yellow. Variegated foliage adds cream-white and snow-white to the choice, as well as occasional suffusions of rose-pink during cool days at the beginning and end of the growing season. Autumn augments the summer spectrum with an array of golds, oranges, and burgundies that weather to a sublime selection of winter hues from fawn though chestnut and russet. Flower colors are not as varied as foliage colors, but still include stunning whites, pinks, purples, burnished coppers, and blackish browns. These colors are often enhanced by morning fogs and frosts. Also, the flowers of many grasses remain fluffy and full even after seed-set and drying. Their translucent parts are often imbued with the varied tones of sunrise and sunset.

The spring foliage of golden millet, *Milium effusum* 'Aureum', is a vivid chartreuse, matching the color strength of May flowers in this Connecticut garden.

Foliage colors of grasses have a long-lasting presence in the garden, remaining satisfying as various flowers come and go. The rich sea-blue of this fescue, *Festuca glauca* 'Meerblau', will continue long after the surrounding heaths and heathers in this Berlin garden have ceased blooming.

The cool days of spring and fall sometimes bring suffusions of pink to the foliage of variegated grasses, such as Feesey's ribbon grass, *Phalaris arundinacea* 'Feesey'.

The rich autumn foliage tones of grasses parallel those of eastern deciduous forests. The green summer leaves of *Miscanthus* 'Purpurascens' become a kaleidoscope of deep salmon, orange, and red at Longwood Gardens in late September.

Color is sometimes found in unexpected places. Although the flowers of large blue fescue, *Festuca amethystina* 'Superba', are not especially colorful, the flower stalks turn a deep amethyst in early June.

The inflorescences of many grasses undergo striking changes of color, form, and structure over time, contributing a unique beauty to each month. Three photos illustrate the transformation of *Miscanthus* from initial flowering through final seed dispersal and senescence.

Left: The newly opened flowers of *M. sinensis* var. *condensatus* 'Cabaret' show many warm tones at this stage, including the dangling yellow pollen sacs. The flowers of some *Miscanthus* cultivars are reddish when first opening.

All *Miscanthus* species and cultivars go through a drying stage and, to different degrees, take on a silvery appearance. Shown here is *M. sinensis* 'Malepartus' after the flowers have dried to a peak of snowy translucency and the seeds are maturing.

Miscanthus sinensis 'Gracillimus' in late February, after all the seeds have been dispersed and winter storms have reduced the inflorescence to a stunning filigree.

The rice harvest is a ubiquitous autumn sight throughout Japan. Native to Southeast Asia, rice (*Oriza sativa,* an annual member of the grass family) has been cultivated for human consumption for more than 7000 years. It is the major food source for nearly half the world's population.

CHAPTER 2

The Families of Grasses and Their Relatives

THE TERM *ornamental grasses* usually includes the true grasses, as well as related families of grasslike plants. This book includes the perennial grasses and bamboos (grass family, Poaceae), sedges (sedge family, Cyperaceae), rushes (rush family Juncaceae), restios (restio family, Restionaceae), and cat-tails (cat-tail family, Typhaceae).

One characteristic these families have in common, besides their typically narrow grasslike foliage, is that they all belong to a subgroup of flowering plants called monocotyledons. The name of this subgroup refers to its members having one (mono) seed-leaf (cotyledon). The leaf veins of monocotyledons are typically parallel to one another, and the leaf margins are most often smooth, without any obvious teeth or notches. With a few exceptions, such as bamboos, most monocotyledons are also herbaceous, meaning they do not develop woody tissues. Members of the opposing group of flowering plants called dicotyledons have two seed-leaves, netted leaf veins, and leaf margins that are frequently toothed or cut, and are frequently woody.

It is not necessary to know all the complex botanical characteristics of the various families to appreciate the beauty of ornamental grasses or to successfully use them in the garden; however, a basic familiarity with family features helps develop the eye for detail and makes plant identification easier. An acquaintance with the social, economic, and ecological context of grasses enriches the gardener's understanding of how the plants grown fit into the larger living world.

The Grass Family, Poaceae

The true grasses belong to a family known either as the Poaceae or the Gramineae. Both names are correct. Modern rules of botanical nomenclature use the standard ending *-aceae* to designate plant families. Family names are made by adding this standard ending to a genus selected as the "type" (typical) for the family. The family name Poaceae is derived from *Poa*, the genus that includes the blue grasses. Gramineae is an older name for the grass family that has been conserved as an alternate by an international agreement among plant taxonomists. As further example, the sunflower family is known as either the Asteraceae (derived from the genus *Aster*) or the Compositae, a conserved name with a non-standard ending. The name used is a matter of individual choice. This book uses Poaceae for the grass family.

Size and Distribution

Comprised of more than 600 genera and more than 9000 species, the grass family is one of the largest, most successful flowering plant families. The orchid family, Orchidaceae, is larger, having a similar number of genera and nearly 19,000 species, and the sunflower family, Asteraceae, is the largest with more than 900 genera and 19,000 species.

The grass family is truly cosmopolitan, with the widest distribution of the flowering plants. Grasses grow on every continent and are a part of all the major biomes of the terrestrial world. They occur natively from the Arctic Circle through the temperate and tropical zones to Antarctica, growing from mountain tops to seashores. Most grasses are sun-loving. They are the dominant plants in most open habitats, and, except for the bamboos, are relatively scarce in dense forests.

Economic Importance

Though not the largest family, the grasses are economically the most important. Civilization of the human race is directly attributable to the development of agricultural practices, which from the beginning have been most dependent upon grasses. Grasses are the primary food source for humans as well as for wild and domestic grazing animals. All the cereal grains are members of the grass family, including rice, oats, wheat, rye, barley, corn (maize in Europe), and sorghum. Sugarcane, a grass, provides most of the world's sugar, and grasses are also the source of aromatic and culinary oils. The making of beer, rye, whiskey, and other alcoholic beverages is dependent upon various grass crops. Pioneers crossing the

North American continent built their houses of prairie grass sods, and people in many parts of the world still use grasses for thatching the roofs of their houses. Bamboos provide construction materials, such as framing and scaffolding, and are used in the production of furniture and fencing. Grasses are also an important source of reeds for musical instruments. The manicured grassy lawn, though questionable from an ecological standpoint, is still a ubiquitous tradition of great economic importance to many cultures around the world.

Human Impact on Grasses

Although the domestication of grasses came very late in their evolutionary development and late in the development of the human species, the modern interdependency of grasses and humankind is pervasive and complex. Grasses are supremely adapted physiologically as colonizers and are able to thrive under a wide array of challenging habitat conditions. Their seeds are produced in copious quantities and are equipped with generous energy reserves that allow them to germinate and establish seedlings under very difficult circumstances. Their fibrous roots are extremely efficient and can withstand great droughts. The low-growing points of grasses allow them to sustain continual damage to top growth by grazing animals, fires, or other destructive events without serious damage. Neil Diboll, founder of Wisconsin's Prairie Nursery, has observed that "the price of a global economy is a global ecology," and certainly economic forces are the prime motivation for the increasing ecological destabilization that is characteristic of the present age. This destabilization has been both good and bad for grasses. While humankind has nearly destroyed originally vast, stable native grass habitats, such as the North American prairie, it has simultaneously created a huge amount of disturbed, open habitat favorable to grasses (see photo next page). Though this has led to large-scale displacement of grasses, it has not been quite as threatening to them as it has been to other less resilient plant groups. For example, modern circumstances favor the grasses over the orchids, which generally occur in and are critically dependent upon stable habitats.

Life Cycles

The grass family is mostly herbaceous except for the bamboos, and its members are either annuals or perennials. Annuals, such as corn (maize), wheat, and rice, complete their life cycle from seed to seed in one year. Most ornamental species are perennials that live and set seed for years.

Roots

The initial, primary root produced by the grass seedling is usually short-lived. It is commonly supplanted by roots arising from lower portions of the stem, called adventitious roots. These secondary roots form the bulk of the fibrous roots that are typical of grasses. These mature root systems are extremely efficient and often quite extensive, penetrating deep into the soil and enabling the grass plant to survive long-term dry periods.

Stems

Grass stems are technically called culms. They are composed of solid joints, called nodes, separated by segments called internodes. Nodes are the points of attachment for leaves (Figure 2-1). Typically, culms are herbaceous and cylindrical, with hollow internodes. The internodes of some grasses, such as corn (maize), sugarcane, and those of the bamboo genus *Chusquea,* are solid and pithy. Though the culms of some grasses are slightly flattened in cross section, none are three-angled like the sedges. The woody character of bamboo culms results from the cells being impregnated with the hardening substances lignin and silica; however, even the largest tropical bamboos are not capable of the secondary thickening that is typical of woody trees.

Leaves

The leaves of grasses arise from alternate nodes, forming two ranks or rows ascending the culm. They are commonly composed of three parts: the sheath, blade, and ligule (Figure 2-2). Originating at a node, the sheath surrounds the culm and usually has overlapping margins. The blade is the flattened part of the leaf beginning at the top of the sheath and growing away from the culm. Leaf blades are typically narrow, with parallel veins and one larger median vein called a midrib. The

Locally native switch grass, *Panicum virgatum,* finds refuge in power line clearings in southern New Jersey. Although the North American original prairies have been nearly obliterated, open habitats favorable to grasses are commonplace today due to roadsides, utility rights of way, and myriad interstices of our modern built environment.

margins of grass blades are usually smooth; however, some are edged with minute teeth that can cause serious cuts. The ligule is a thin membranous ridge or small row of hairs located at the juncture of the sheath and blade on the side facing the culm. The function of the ligule is uncertain, although it may serve to keep rain from entering the sheath. The variation in ligules is often very important in the botanical identification of grasses. It is of lesser value to gardeners in distinguishing between cultivated varieties of ornamental grasses.

Growth

Most flowering plants have growing points or meristems located at the tips of their stems and branches. Terminal growth of a stem or branch ceases if the meristem is destroyed. Grasses are unusual in having two types of meristems, one at the base of each leaf and another just above each node on the culm. These meristems allow the stems and leaves of grasses to continue to elongate even if their tips are grazed, cut, burned, or otherwise destroyed. The meristems at the nodes are also capable of one-sided growth and make it possible for the stems of grasses to right themselves after being trampled or flattened by storms.

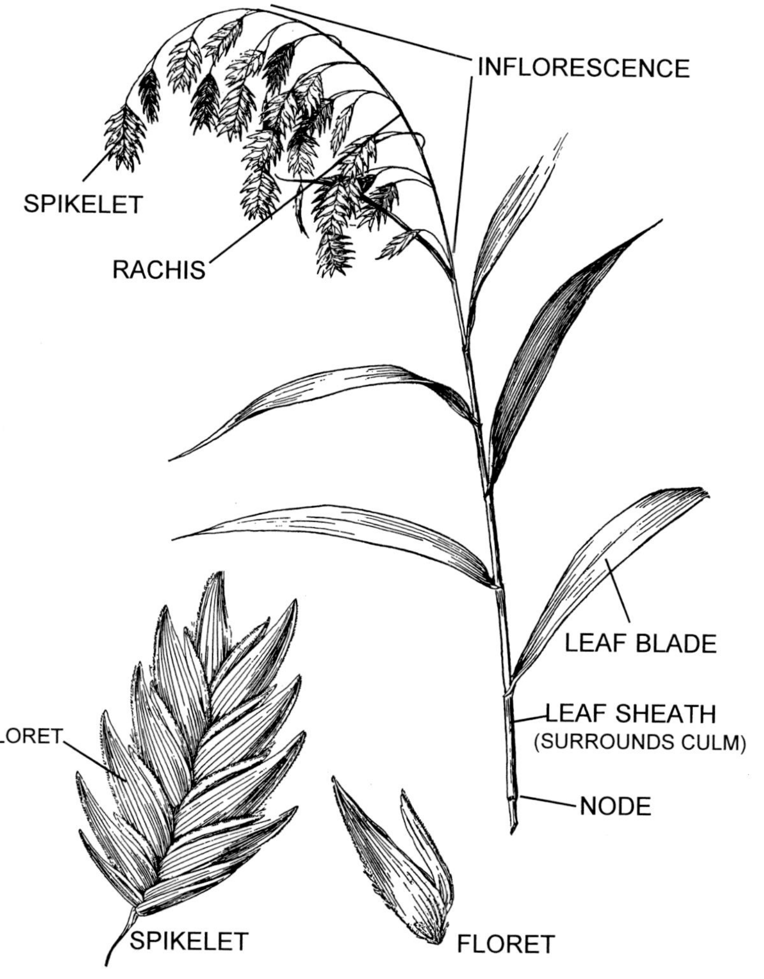

Figure 2-1. A culm (stem) of wild-oats, *Chasmanthium latifolium*. Each leaf is attached to the culm at a node. Each leaf sheath surrounds the culm up to the point where the leaf blade diverges.

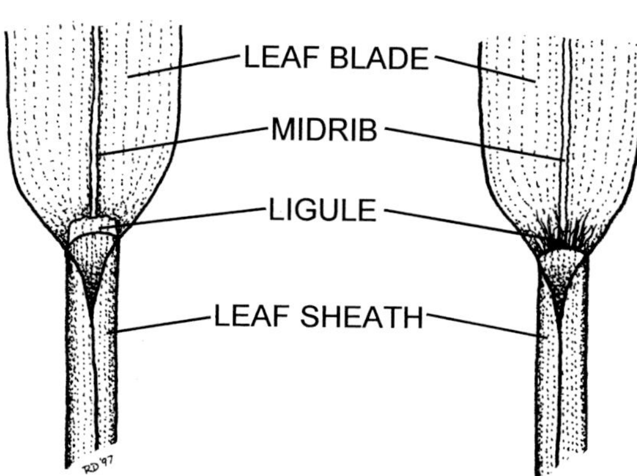

Figure 2-2. Ligules are usually present in grass leaves. They are located at the juncture of the leaf sheath and blade on the side facing the culm. The ligule may be a thin membranous ridge (left) or a small row of hairs (right). (R. Darke)

Grasses spread from their bases by various types of lateral shoots, often called tillers. These lateral shoots are formed in the axils of the lowest leaves. In some grasses, the lateral shoots grow vertically within the leaf sheaths, resulting in the tufted (caespitose) habit of growth typical of grasses, such as tufted hair grass, *Deschampsia cespitosa*. In other grasses, the lateral shoots do not elongate vertically but grow through the side of the leaf sheath and form rhizomes or stolons. Both rhizomes and stolons are capable of producing new shoots at their nodes, resulting in spreading habits of growth. Giant reed, *Arundo donax*, is an example of a grass that spreads by rhizomes (Figure 2-3). Buffalo grass, *Buchloe dactyloides*, spreads by stolons, as do many common turf grasses (Figure 2-4).

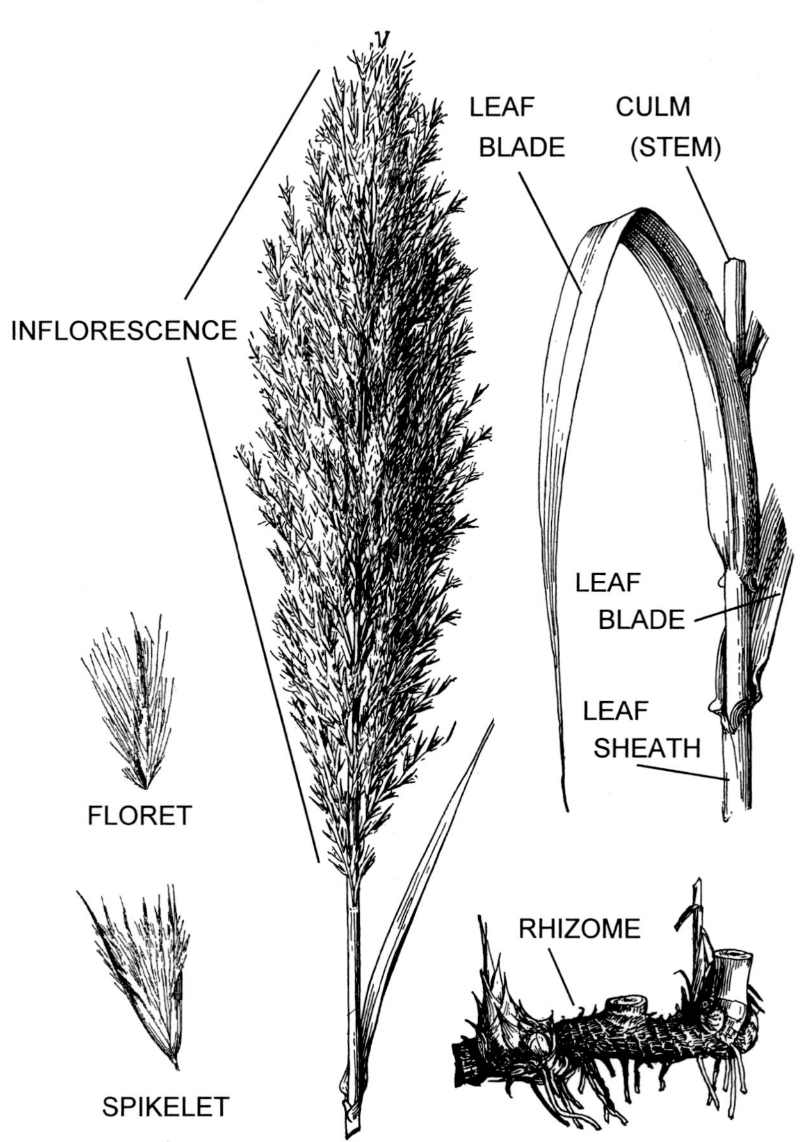

Figure 2-3. Giant reed, *Arundo donax*, spreads by stout rhizomes, which produce new shoots at each node.

Figure 2-4. Buffalo grass, *Buchloe dactyloides*, spreads by stolons, which produce new plants at each node.

Flowers and Inflorescences

The floral beauty of grasses can be credited to their delicately complex flower clusters, called inflorescences. The individual flowers of grasses are typically inconspicuous and greenish. Being wind-pollinated, grasses have had no reason to develop the colorful broad-petaled flowers that are so attractive to insects and most gardeners. Judging from the ecological and geographic prosperity of the grasses, this strategy has proved efficient and highly successful. Grasses are considered to be among the most highly evolved plants on earth, and their evolution has been characterized by reduction of certain features. Compared to most flowering plants, the floral parts of grasses are greatly reduced in size or are sometimes entirely lacking. While some of the floral detail of grasses is visible to the naked eye, many of the finer points necessary for technical identification require the use of a hand lens or microscope.

In place of sepals or petals, each flower has only two small scalelike structures called lodicules (Figure 2-5). An ovary is present, enclosing a single ovule that develops into the seed. In grasses the ripened ovary and seed together are called a grain or caryopsis. Inside each grain is a mass of endosperm, which is an energy reserve in the form of starch, and the embryonic grass plant, called the germ. Two short stalks called styles project from the top of the ovary. Each style ends in a feathery stigma that is adapted to receive the wind-borne pollen grains. The flower also includes three stamens, each consisting of a threadlike stalk called the filament, to which is attached a pollen-producing appendage called the anther. The flower is usually enclosed and protected by two small bracts. The lower, outer bract is called the lemma, and the upper, inner bract is called the palea. The grass flower, together with the lemma and palea, is called a floret.

The soil has been removed to show the spreading rhizomes of variegated manna grass, *Glyceria maxima* 'Variegata'.

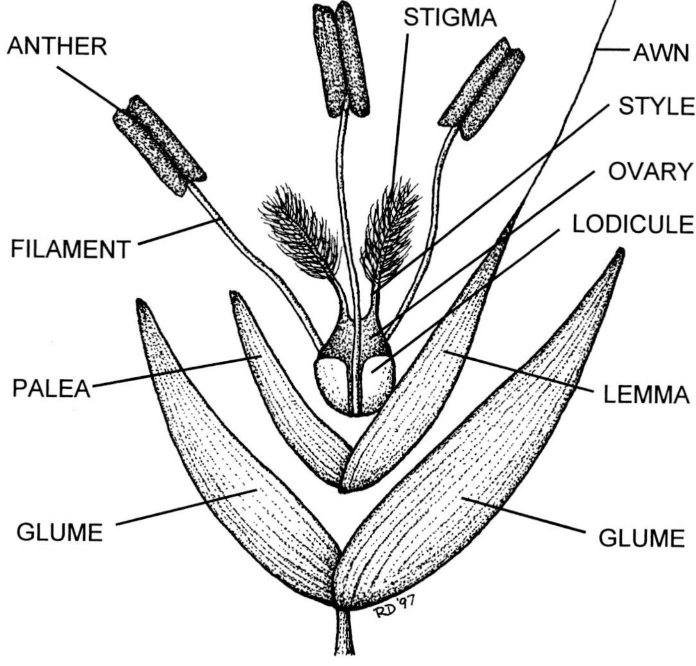

Figure 2-5. A single-flowered grass spikelet, vertically expanded for purposes of illustration. (R. Darke)

The individual flowers of grasses are often difficult to distinguish because they are partly concealed within various parts of the spikelets. Tiny red anthers hanging from threadlike filaments and feathery pink stigmas are clearly visible in this close-up of big bluestem, *Andropogon gerardii*.

Awns are bristlelike or needlelike appendages that extend from the glumes or lemmas of grass spikelets. The awns of needle grass, *Stipa barbata*, are exceptional, reaching a length of nearly 7 1/2 in. (19 cm). Their translucency can be quite dramatic as demonstrated by this photo at Foggy Bottom, the garden of Adrian Bloom in Bressingham, England.

A spikelet consists of one or more florets attached to a small central axis, together with two basal bracts called glumes. The glumes or lemmas sometimes end in long bristlelike structures called awns (Figure 2-5). There may also be various types of hairs or bristles associated with spikelets. Together with awns, these structures are responsible for the dramatic translucent effects of grass flowers. The basic pattern of spikelets consisting of two glumes and one to many florets is quite consistent among the grasses; however, modifications in the size, shape, sexual complement, or number of parts, or the inclusion of additional structures results in seemingly endless variations that make grasses difficult to identify using technical methods. Further discussion of these methods is beyond the scope of this book; however, for interested readers, several books on grass structure and identification are included in the bibliography. Fortunately, it is possible to distinguish most ornamental species and cultivated varieties from one another without a thorough mastery of structural details. It is helpful, though, to be able to recognize a spikelet and to be aware of the variation in structure and form of inflorescences.

There are three simple types of inflorescence that occur among the grasses: spikes, racemes, and panicles (Figure 2-6). Most inflorescences have a readily apparent main axis, called a rachis. A simple spike is an inflorescence having individual spikelets without stalks, attached directly to the rachis. Wheat, *Triticum aestivum*, and bottle-brush grass, *Hystrix patula*, are ex-

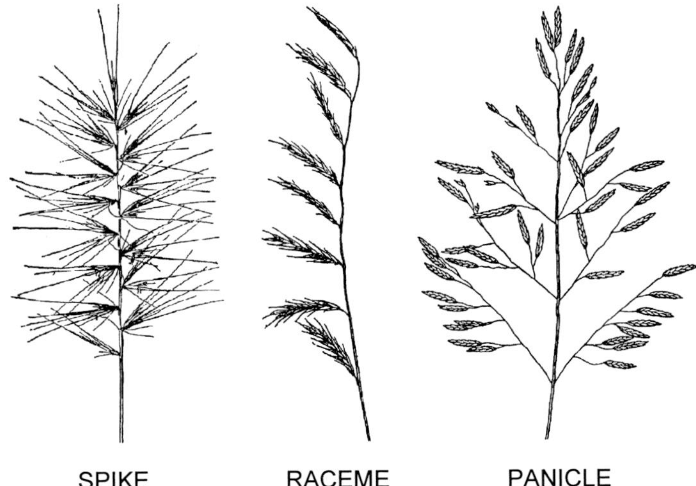

Figure 2-6. Typical simple inflorescences of grasses.

amples of simple spikes; however, this type of inflorescence is uncommon. In a simple raceme individual spikelets are attached to the rachis by short stalks. The annual semaphore grass, *Pleuropogon californicus,* is one of relatively few examples of a simple raceme. In a simple panicle the spikelets are attached at the ends of stalks that branch from the rachis. The genus *Panicum* is characterized by this type of inflorescence, which is by far the most common among grasses. Panicles are generally of two types: open and closed. The branching of open panicles is loose and airy, as in the examples of purple love grass, *Eragrostis spectabilis* (Figure 2-7), and wild-oats, *Chasmanthium latifolium* (Figure 2-1). The branches of closed panicles are usually upright and held close to the rachis, as in giant reed, *Arundo donax* (Figure 2-3). The panicles of many grasses undergo a striking metamorphosis as they develop, appearing quite open when flowering and then stiffening to a closed form upon setting seed and drying. Indian grass, *Sorghastrum nutans* (see photos on following pages), and feather reed grass, *Calamagrostis ×acutiflora,* are examples of such change in form.

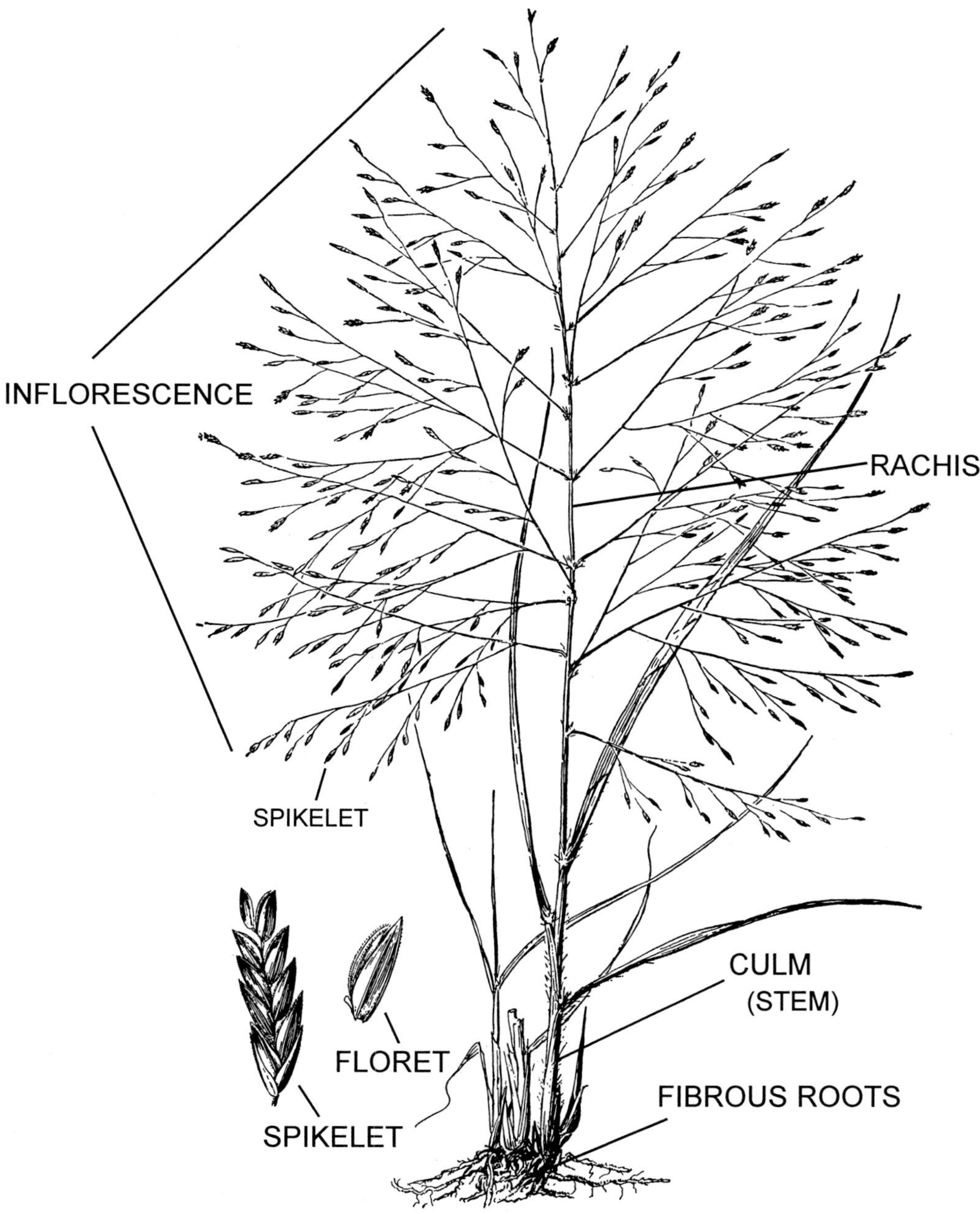

Figure 2-7. The inflorescence of purple love grass, *Eragrostis spectabilis,* is an open panicle.

The color and form of the inflorescences of many grasses change considerably from the time flowering begins through the setting and maturing of seed, as illustrated by four photos of Indian grass, *Sorghastrum nutans,* from August to November.

On 14 August bright yellow anthers and light yellow feathery stigmas can be seen extended from the copper tones of the awned spikelets.

By 8 September the anthers and stigmas have completed their task of pollen production and reception, and are no longer evident. The copper-colored panicle is still open and is especially lax due to the weight of a morning mist. The mist also accentuates backlighting of the delicate parts.

On 12 October the copper color has muted, and the panicles have become narrow and mostly closed as their branches have folded against the main axis.

By 3 November the seeds are ripe and dispersing. The culms have straightened to a nearly upright position and the panicles appear quite slender. Numerous tiny hairs attached to the surface parts of the spikelets add to the translucent effects.

The inflorescences of many grasses are not representative of any of the three simple types but rather are combinations of one or more types, referred to as compound inflorescences. For example, the compound inflorescence of side-oats grama, *Bouteloua curtipendula,* is a raceme of spikes (Figure 2-8). The feathery inflorescences of the genus *Miscanthus* are panicles of racemes (Figure 2-9).

Although the inflorescences of most grasses are located at the top of the culm, those of some species arise from multiple nodes along the culm (Figure 2-10). Also, although the inflorescences of most grass species consist of spikelets with bisexual florets, some, such as wild rice, *Zizania aquatica,* have male and female spikelets separated in different portions of the inflorescence. A few others, such as pampas grass, *Cortaderia selloana,* and buffalo grass, *Buchloe dactyloides* (Figure 2-3, showing male plants only), have inflorescences consisting entirely of male spikelets on one plant and entirely female inflorescences on another. These are called dioecious species. While complex and sometimes confusing, many such combinations are essential to the graceful, diverse beauty of grasses.

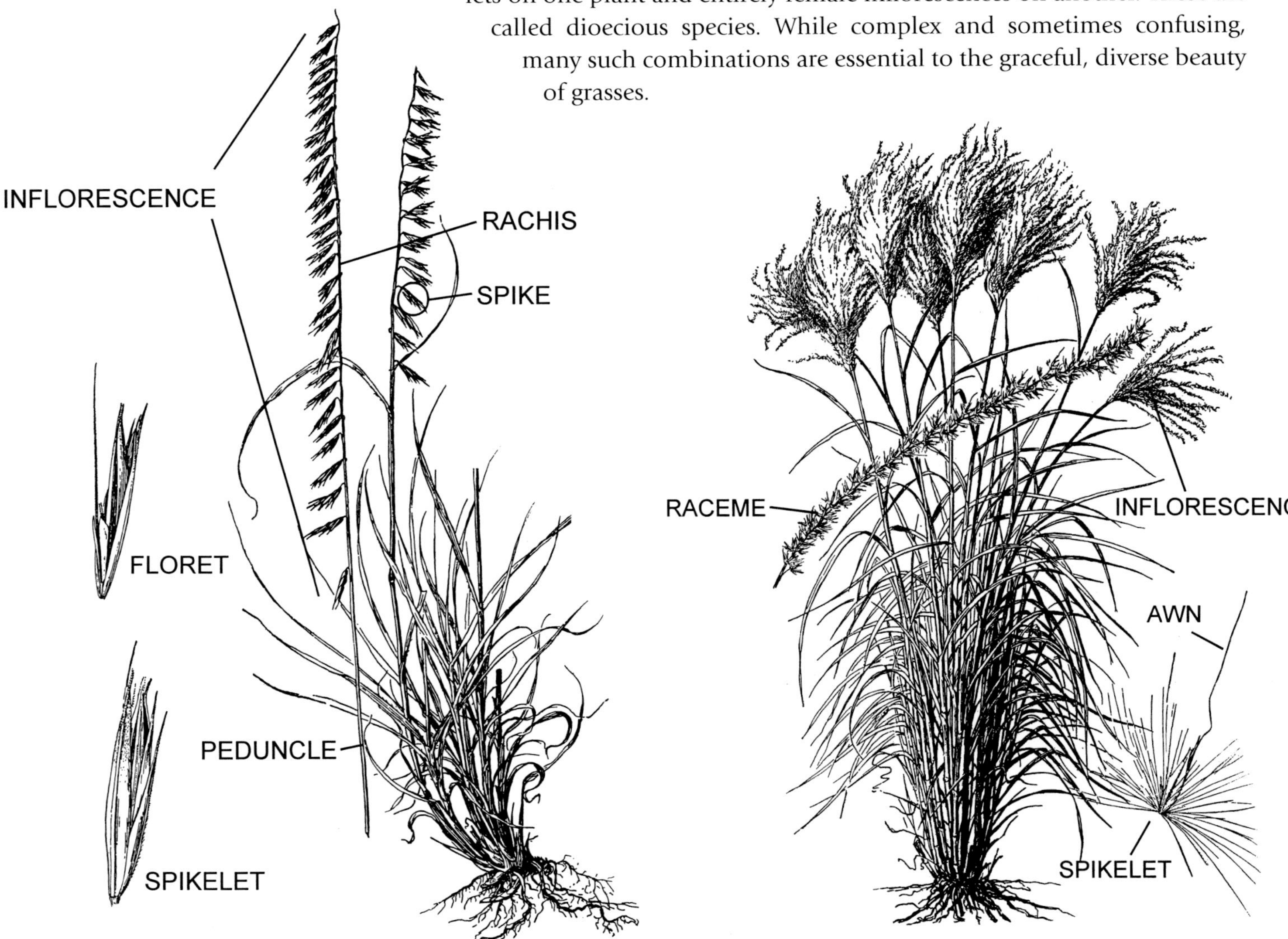

Figure 2-8. The compound inflorescence of side-oats grama, *Bouteloua curtipendula,* is a one-sided raceme of spikes. Each spike contains multiple spikelets. The peduncle is a mostly leafless extension of the culm, supporting the inflorescence.

Figure 2-9. The inflorescences of *Miscanthus sinensis* are compound panicles consisting of numerous pencil-thin racemes. Fine hairs extending from the base of each spikelet contribute to the feathery appearance of flower clusters.

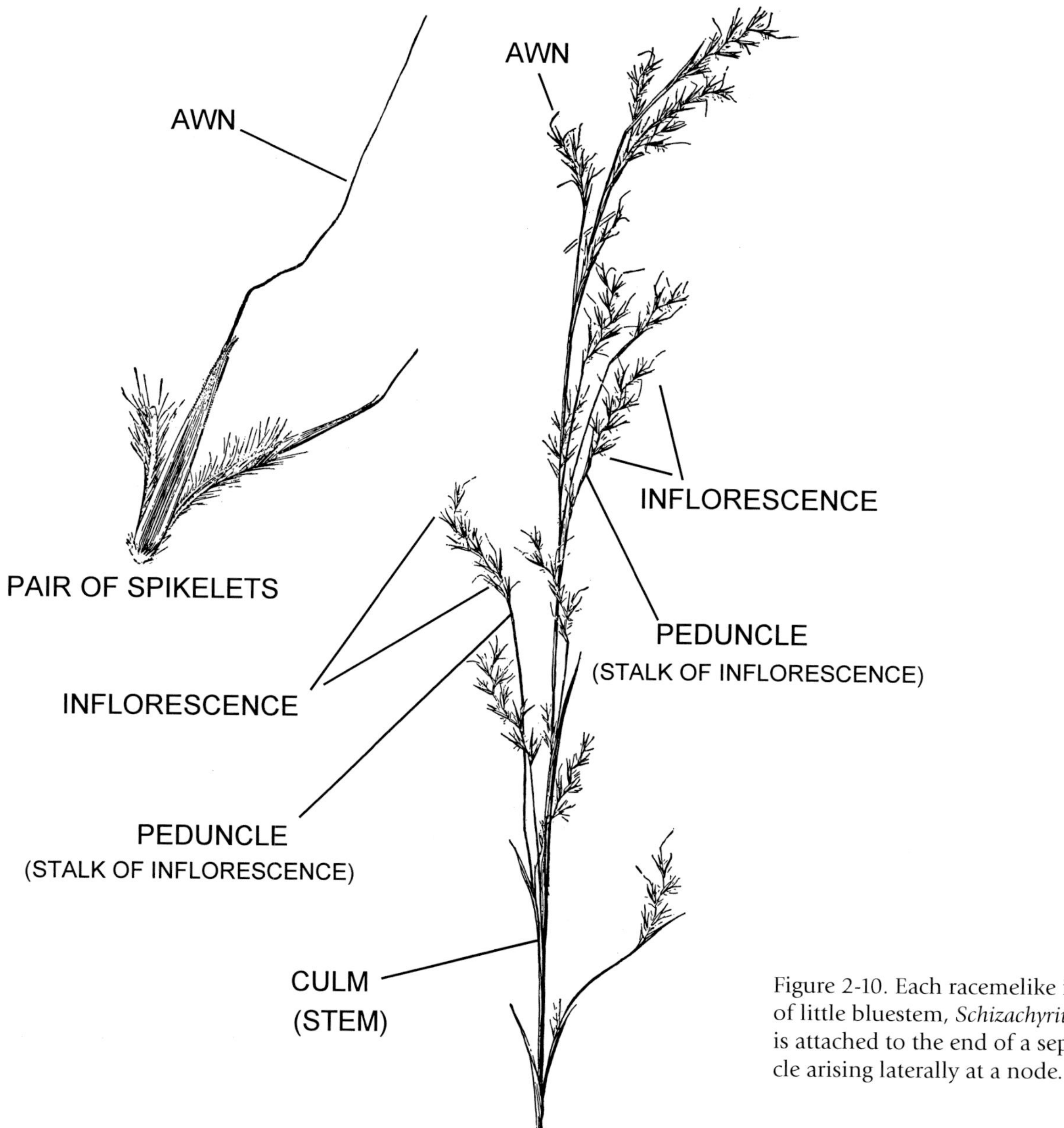

Figure 2-10. Each racemelike inflorescence of little bluestem, *Schizachyrium scoparium*, is attached to the end of a separate peduncle arising laterally at a node.

The Sedge Family, Cyperaceae

Sedges are fewer than grasses; however, they are still a relatively large family of approximately 115 genera and 3600 species, nearly all of which are perennial. The botanical name of the family is derived from the genus *Cyperus*. Like grasses, sedges are a cosmopolitan group. They are found in most parts of the world but are especially common in wet or moist habitats in temperate and subarctic zones, where they play an important role in soil stabilization. Most sedges are sun-loving, but there are also many species native to shady wooded environments.

Sedges are unimportant as food sources for humans or domesticated animals;

however, there are a few edible sedges as well as several species employed for other economic purposes. The Chinese water chestnut, *Eleocharis dulcis*, is cultivated for its edible tubers, as is the chufa or earth-almond, *Cyperus esculentus* var. *sativus*. The stems of Egyptian paper-reed or papyrus, *C. papyrus*, were the raw materials used to make the papyrus paper of classical antiquity. The bulrush, *Schoenoplectus tabernaemontani*, and various other sedge family members are used in basketwork, mat weaving, and the making of chair seats. Aromatic oils from the roots of galingale, *C. longus*, are used in perfumery. The fluffy heads of cotton grass, *Eriophorum* species, have been used in pillow stuffing.

Besides fibrous roots, most sedges have either rhizomes or stolons from which new plants are produced. Some sedges are tufted in their growth; others form spreading mats. Several stem and leaf characters make it possible to distinguish sedges from grasses. The stems of sedges are solidly filled with pith and lack nodes. They are triangular in cross section, spawning the popular maxim "sedges have edges." The leaves are arranged in three rows, and their sheaths are usually fused around the stem. The leaf blades of sedges are grasslike, but ligules are usually absent or very much reduced. The foliage of many sedges is evergreen or semi-

Curly white stigmas project from female flowers grouped in separate spikes in the inflorescence of Bowles' golden sedge, *Carex elata* 'Aurea'. The male flower spikes are located above the females and are dark brown with pendent, lighter brown anthers.

The female flower spikes of *Carex lupulina* dwarf a dime. Each female flower is enclosed in an inflated sac called a utricle, with tiny stigmas protruding from the apex. The male flowers are grouped in a separate, narrow spike higher up on the rachis of the inflorescence, visible here above the dime.

evergreen, ranging in color from greens to near-yellow, blue, and reddish browns. The leaves of many cultivated varieties are dramatically variegated.

Sedges are wind-pollinated, and the individual flowers are generally inconspicuous, without recognizable sepals or petals. The flowers are often but not always grouped in spikelets. The flowers or spikelets may be arranged in various spikes, umbels, or panicles, but sedges never develop the large open panicles or dense, plumelike panicles common to the grasses. Reduced leaves or bracts are often present at the base of the sedge inflorescence. In the genus *Rhynchospora* these bracts are attractively suffused white. Some sedge family members have bisexual flowers, although many, including the large genus *Carex*, have male and female flowers grouped in separate spikes within the inflorescence of a single plant. The female flowers of *Carex* are commonly enclosed in a saclike structure called a utricle or perigynium. These structures are enlarged and curiously attractive in Gray's sedge, *C. grayi*. There are sedges with nearly black flowers, such as *C. nudata*, and truly red flowers, such as *C. baccans*; however, the flowers and inflorescences of most sedges are subtle greens and off-whites, and they rarely produce the dramatic luminous effects of true grasses.

The rich red of the crimson-seeded sedge, *Carex baccans*, is due to the color of the utricles enclosing the maturing ovaries and seeds.

The Rush Family, Juncaceae

Though found worldwide, the rushes are a small family of only 10 genera and less than 400 species. Most are perennial herbs, growing primarily in wet or damp habitats in cool temperate and subarctic regions. Annual species are uncommon. The family is of minor economic importance as the source of various fibers and binding materials. *Prionium*, the only shrubby genus in the rush family, includes the South African palmiet, *P. palmitum*, the leaves of which are the source of a strong fiber called palmite. The sea rush, *Juncus maritimus*, is the source of the binding material known as juncio, and stems of the common or soft rush, *J. effusus*, are used in the making of baskets, chair seats, and various types of mats, including Japanese tatami.

Perennial herbaceous rushes usually have hairy roots and horizontal or erect rhizomes. The stems are erect, cylindrical, and solid. The leaves are mostly basal and are sometimes reduced to sheaths only. Like grasses and sedges, rushes are wind-pollinated and their flowers are quite small and subtle in coloration. They are most often green, brown, or near-black, but are occasionally white to cream-yellow. Though tiny, the flowers bear a close structural resemblance to lily flowers, having six similar tepals arranged in two whorls. Most rushes have bisexual flowers, each with six stamens and an ovary with three stigmas. Some have male and female flowers on separate plants. The numerous small flowers are arranged in panicles, clustered heads, or corymbs.

The inflorescences of common rush, *Juncus effusus*, are subtly attractive. The leaves are very similar in appearance to the cylindrical stems. The split stems of this species are widely used in mat-making in Asian countries.

Only two genera are important to ornamental horticulture, *Juncus*, the rushes, and *Luzula*, the woodrushes. Both are perennial herbs. Rushes prefer wet sunny habitats and tend to be summer-flowering. Their leaves typically arise from the base of the clump and are cylindrical, resembling the stems. Woodrushes are native to moist or dry shaded habitats, blooming in spring or very early summer. Usually evergreen, their leaves are also mostly basal, but their blades are flat, usually with conspicuously hairy margins.

The Restio Family, Restionaceae

Relatively unfamiliar to the gardening world, the restio family is almost entirely restricted to the Southern Hemisphere, occurring natively in Australia, Tasmania, New Zealand, Southeast Asia, Malaysia, Madagascar, Chile, and Africa. The family is comprised of approximately 38 genera and more than 400 species of perennial herbs, of which at least 300 are native to the Cape floral region of southern Africa. The climate in this region is Mediterranean, having cool, moist winters and hot, dry summers. The soils are typically sandy and very low in nutrients. The characteristic vegetation of the Cape is a fine scrub called fynbos, and in this restios often replace true grasses.

Closely related to the rushes, restios are most often rushlike in appearance, although some have much-branched stems (see photo next page) and bear a strong superficial resemblance to horsetails. They range in height from about 8 in. (20 cm) to more than 10 ft. (3 m). Restios rarely develop functional leaf blades. Photosynthesis takes place in the green stems, which may be solid or hollow, but usually have conspicuous nodes. Leaf sheaths are frequently present at the nodes and are often tan, gold, or cinnamon-brown colored and highly ornamental from a gardening perspective. Many restios are tufted and tussock-forming; others have slowly creeping rhizomes. Their roots may be fleshy or thin and wiry. The small, individual, wind-pollinated flowers are unisexual, with males and females occurring on separate plants. The flowers are green or brown in color and are typically grouped in spikelets, which in turn comprise loose inflorescences. Each spikelet is partly enclosed by a conspicuous, sheathlike bract that is often brown or amber-colored. Male and female plants of the same species are often quite different in appearance from one another, making identification and classification of this family more difficult than many.

Chondropetalum tectorum belongs to the restio family, Restionaceae; however, its minute brown flowers and cylindrical green stems could easily lead even an experienced botanist to mistake it for one of the rushes.

The stems of some restio family members are unbranched and quite rushlike; however, others, such as *Elegia capensis*, are finely branched and more like horsetails in appearance. The stunning translucent effects of this intricate branching can sometimes rival that of true grasses, as shown here at the National Botanical Garden, Kirstenbosch, Cape Town, South Africa.

The restio family is of no economic importance as a food source; however, a few species have long been important for thatching. Roofs thatched with *Thamnochortus insignis*, called *dakriet* in South Africa, may last more than twenty years, and a renewed interest in traditional architecture has led to a flourishing thatching industry in the African Cape. The beautiful stems and seed-heads of many restio family members are also important to the international cut-flower trade.

Many restios have great ornamental appeal, rivaling the graceful luminosity of the true grasses. Although few, if any, restios are winter-hardy in cold-temperate climates, they hold great ornamental promise for gardens throughout the world's Mediterranean regions and as subjects of glasshouse or warm-season container display. The reason restios are so little-known to horticulture has been, until recently, a difficulty in propagation. Restios do not like to have their roots disturbed and are ideally propagated by seed; however, germination rates for all but a few have been abysmally low using standard methods. Breakthrough research at the National Botanical Institute, Kirstenbosch, in Cape Town, South Africa, now offers a solution. By studying the native fynbos, which is a fire ecology, Kirstenbosch researchers determined that the smoke attendant with natural fires is a cue for the seed germination of many restios. They were able to produce similar results through controlled smoke treatment of seeds, raising germination rates to high levels that provide a necessary tool for conservation work and a promise that a great diversity of these uniquely beautiful plants will finally become part of the world's gardening palette.

The Cat-tail Family, Typhaceae

The cat-tail family is small, comprised of only one genus, *Typha*, and fewer than 15 species, yet it is commonly represented in freshwater habitats throughout the world. Herbaceous perennials, cat-tails prefer shallow water, growing to 8 ft. (2.4 m) in height and spreading by rhizomes to form large colonies in swamps, ponds, and river and lake edges. They provide important nesting materials and cover for wetland birds.

Cat-tails are of minor economic importance; however, the mature leaves have been used for matting, thatching, and caning. The thick rhizomes are edible and high in starch, and are a potential food source. Native peoples have used the fluffy seed-heads as a substitute for down. The value of cat-tails as filtering agents in polluted wetlands areas is of increasing importance. See *Typha* in Chapter 7 for further descriptive information.

The common cat-tail, *Typha latifolia*, is strongly rhizomatous, forming large colonies in shallow freshwater habitats. Male and female flowers form separate sections on each inflorescence. At the top, male flowers produce pollen and quickly begin to weather away, leaving just the central stalk. The female flowers below mature into a velvety-brown cylinder containing innumerable seeds that are eventually dispersed by the wind.

Chionochloa rubra in early October in its native habitat on New Zealand's South Island.

CHAPTER 3

The Names of Grasses

THE SO-CALLED common names of plants are many and varied, often evolving independently in distinct human communities. Many of these are vernacular names that are common, or standard, only within each community. Vernacular names frequently preserve information special to the cultures or regions that gave them birth.

Today, the global scale of technologies allows communication across communities. Thus, to use common names, such communication would undoubtedly benefit from some degree of standardization. Certainly horticultural literature is littered with redundant common names whose minor variations evolved from habitual carelessness rather than meaningful cultural tradition. Yet too much standardization can result in a loss of regional information and linguistic diversity. This is how, among eastern North American birding enthusiasts who use standardized common names, Baltimore has lost its oriole (it is now, through standardization, the northern oriole).

Grasses that have been of historic use to humans tend to have many common or vernacular names, often because they have been widespread in cultivation or native range. Many others have no precise names; they have been simply recognized as "grass," until they were brought into gardens. This book attempts to provide existing common or vernacular names for each grass and often provides multiple names believed to be reasonable and useful. Transliterations of Japanese vernacular names are given for many grasses native to Japan.

The System of Botanical Names

The system of botanical names (also called scientific names) was evolved to provide a precise, standard way of communicating about plants that is respectfully independent of cultural and regional tradition. Botanical names are Latinized names deliberately removed from the flux of any modern, living language. It is not correct to call them Latin names, since they are often derived from other language, such as Greek. Botanical nomenclature as we know it dates to 1753, when Swedish naturalist Carolus Linnaeus published his system of two-part names. In universal use by the scientific community, this Linnaean system is easily adopted by gardeners and is often a necessity when discussing ornamental grasses.

The botanical names of plants are governed by the *International Code of Botanical Nomenclature* (ICBN). The Code regulates various nomenclatural terms used to organize the plant kingdom into progressively narrower categories. The principal terms, in descending rank, are division, class, order, family, genus (plural: genera), and species (plural: species). A group of plants at any rank is called a taxon (plural: taxa). The grass family Poaceae is a taxon, as is wild-oats, *Chasmanthium latifolium*. Taxonomy is the study of the classification of taxa. When inserted in text, botanical names of the various taxa below the level of genus should be set off by a typographic device, such as italic font or underlining.

A **family** is a group of genera whose members resemble one another in several respects. Some families are large, and some very small. The grass family, Poaceae, contains more than 600 genera and more than 9000 species, while the cat-tail family, Typhaceae, contains only one genus, *Typha*, and fewer than 15 species (see Chapter 2 for further details). A **genus** is made up of closely related and similar plant species. The generic name is always capitalized, as in *Calamagrostis*. A **species** is an assemblage of plants that are similar in several characteristics. Cross-fertilization between plants of the same species produces seedlings that retain the distinguishing characteristics of the species. When referring to a single, perhaps unknown, species in a genus, it is acceptable to use the abbreviation sp. after the genus name, as in *Calamagrostis* sp. When multiple species of the same genus are referred to, the abbreviation spp. is correct, as in *Calamagrostis* spp.

The Code states that each plant species must have a binomial (two-word) name consisting of the genus followed by the **specific epithet** (species designation), which is normally not capitalized. These two parts together make up the species name of a plant. In the case of *Miscanthus sinensis*, *Miscanthus* is the genus, *sinensis* is the specific epithet, and *Miscanthus sinensis* (or *M. sinensis*) is the full name of the species. This precision may seem confusing because, in casual use, gardeners often use the word *species* when they are referring to the specific epithet. It may help to ask yourself, "Does *sinensis* really describe a plant species? (The answer is no. You need both parts of the species name: *Miscanthus sinensis.*)

Hybrids between different species occur infrequently in native ecosystems but are commonly produced through horticultural techniques. There are relatively few hybrids among ornamental grasses, but one widely known is *Calamagrostis ×acutiflora,* a cross between *C. epigejos* and *C. arundinacea*. The multiplication symbol (×) is used to indicate the hybrid nature of a plant.

Not to be confused with cultivated variety (see "Names of Cultivated Plants" later in this chapter), a **botanical variety** (abbreviated var.) is a nomenclatural rank below species. A variety differs from individual plants of the same species in one or very few characteristics. For example, the flowers may be different in color or the leaves different in shape. Varietal names are never capitalized and are always italicized or underlined. The abbreviation var. is neither italicized nor underlined.

The Code allows the formation of intermediate nomenclatural ranks by adding the prefix **sub-** to various taxa. Some examples are subfamily, subgenus, and subspecies (abbreviated subsp. or, alternately, ssp.). The latter term is the one most used in ornamental grasses. It and its abbreviations are not italicized or underlined. An example of a grass with defined subspecies is *Molinia caerulea*. The typical subspecies is *M. caerulea* subsp. *caerulea*. Note that the name of this first subspecies is a repeat of the specific epithet. This is always the case, according to nomenclatural code. The second subspecies is *M. caerulea* subsp. *arundinacea*. If

Widely planted for its upright stance and uniformity, Karl Foerster's feather reed grass is a vegetatively propagated selection of *Calamagrostis ×acutiflora*, which is a hybrid of *C. epigejos* and *C. arundinacea*.

no subspecies name is given, it is understood that the name refers to the typical (first) subspecies. For example, *M. caerulea* is understood to mean *M. caerulea* subsp. *caerulea*.

Authors of Botanical Names and Name Changes

All valid botanical names of plants have authors. Citing the names of authors is often unnecessary and impractical in gardening texts or magazines; however, author citations can be of critical importance when communicating precisely about a complex group of plants, such as the grasses.

The Code requires botanists to adhere to precise requirements when authoring names of plants. When naming a plant for the first time, a specimen must be collected, pressed, dried, and preserved in an herbarium along with a proper description of the plant. The new plant name must be properly published along with the description, a reference to the location of the specimen, and the name of the author. In this way, the author's name provides a direct link back to the plant, should confusion arise. This system of authorship is applicable to the various nomenclatural ranks including family, genus, and specific epithet. In precise works the author's name, usually in a standard abbreviation, is cited following the botanical name. For example, *Alopecurus* L. is Linnaeus's name for the genus of foxtail grasses.

Authors are obliged to determine that the plant they have found has not already been named, a task that is easier today than it was in Linnaeus's time. Occasionally and inadvertently, different names have been assigned to the same plant by different authors. When such errors are discovered, nomenclatural rules of priority require that the earliest validly published name be preserved as the correct one, and that the later names be consigned to synonymy. For example, botanists have now determined that the name *Andropogon elliottii* Chapman is a synonym for *A. gyrans* Ashe. Unfortunately, a botanical name may be in wide use for many years before it is found to be a synonym. Changes in long-established names are at the least inconvenient and are often seriously confusing since it may be many subsequent years before a change is reflected in printed literature.

Confusion also arises when the same name is, in error, applied to different plants by different authors. For example, the name *Carex stricta* was assigned by the botanist Jean Baptiste Lamarck to a North American native sedge. Another botanist named Samuel Goodenough used *C. stricta* for a European native sedge. In this case, the authors' names are necessary to confirm the identity of the species in question: *C. stricta* Lamarck is a different plant than *C. stricta* Goodenough. Nomenclatural rules preserve the former name for the American species, while the latter name has become a synonym for *C. elata* Allioni. The author citation of *C. stricta* Goodenough, *non* Lamarck, points out that the name in question is Goodenough's, not Lamarck's.

Name changes can also result from reclassification. Modern systems of plant classification aim to express the genetic relationships and evolutionary pathways of plants. In the past, information used to classify plants was often dependent on relatively unsophisticated technology and superficial observations. With the current ability to look into the very genetic makeup of living organisms, new information is becoming known that suggests changes in the way plants are classified, and this often means names are modified or changed. For example, newly interpreted data may reveal that a species formerly included in one genus really belongs in another. The botanist Harris O. Yates determined that the grass known as *Uniola latifolia* Michaux was logically a member of the genus *Chasmanthium*. The rules of nomenclature require that the specific epithet (*latifolia*) be re-used as part of the new combination *C. latifolium* (Michaux) Yates. Note that the original author's name is retained in parentheses followed by the transferring author.

The "Correct" Names of Grasses

The Code does not determine how data concerning the classification of plants must be interpreted, it merely sets forth rules and procedures for the construction of the names. For this reason, there is sometimes no clear answer to the question, "What is the correct name of this grass?" Since living organisms do not always fit into rigidly defined categories, there is sometimes disagreement among botanists how broadly the various nomenclatural ranks should be interpreted. For example, a particular group of plants that appears to constitute a subspecies to one classifying botanist might be judged a species by another. The purple moor grasses, *Molinia caerulea* (Linnaeus) Moench, are an example of this situation. Many botanists see the differences between the shorter and taller purple moor grasses as warranting recognition only as subspecies, in which case the shorter plants are named *M. caerulea* subsp. *caerulea* (Linnaeus) Moench, and the taller plants *M. caer-*

Although Elliott's broom-sedge has been known for many years as *Andropogon elliottii*, botanists have determined that the correct scientific name for this species is *A. gyrans.*

Wild-oats, *Chasmanthium latifolium*, was originally named *Uniola latifolia* by Andre Michaux. Although this species bears an obvious relation to sea-oats, *U. paniculata*, botanist Harris O. Yates felt it was distinct enough to be segregated from the genus *Uniola* and placed in *Chasmanthium*.

ulea subsp. *arundinacea* (Schrank) H. Paul. Other botanists have considered the taller plants worthy of recognition as a species, *M. arundinacea* Schrank. In such situations, the "correct" name is perhaps the one believed correct by most informed botanists.

This book attempts to follow the most current, carefully researched nomenclature for ornamental grasses. The names have been compiled from the most recent world floras, journal articles, and checklists available, including the USDA National PLANTS Database, currently online. Synonyms are included in individual encyclopedia entries in Chapter 7, and the Index of Synonyms provides cross-references to current names.

Names of Cultivated Plants

Horticulturists are often concerned with differences between plants that are not adequately distinguished by the preceding botanical ranks. The term *cultivar,* derived from cultivated variety, was coined to serve this purpose. The naming of cultivars is governed by the *International Code of Nomenclature for Cultivated Plants* (ICNCP), which supplements the *International Code of Botanical Nomenclature.*

A **cultivar** is a group of plants under cultivation selected for one or more distinct characteristics that are uniform, stable, and capable of being retained through appropriate means of propagation. Cultivars may arise by selection from variant individuals in the wild or in cultivation, or through deliberate or accidental hybridization. Cultivar names are always capitalized and, unlike botanical names, are never italicized or underlined; however, they must be enclosed in single quotation marks. Cultivar names are always placed at the end of the botanical name, as in *Miscanthus sinensis* 'Morning Light'. It is acceptable to drop author citations from botanical names when cultivar names follow. Also, in popular use, it is allowable (though not necessarily good practice) to drop the species epithet from the botanical name of a cultivar if there is no likelihood of confusion. For example, *M. sinensis* 'Morning Light' may be abbreviated to *M.* 'Morning Light' since the cultivar name 'Morning Light' has only been assigned to the species *M. sinensis.* If the species origin of a cultivar is not known, the cultivar name follows the genus, as in *M.* 'Giganteus'.

The use of cultivar names is a relatively recent convention. The first edition of the ICNCP appeared in 1953. Many early cultivar names originated as Latinized names coined in an era when the distinction between horticultural nomenclature and botanical nomenclature was unclear. 'Gracillimus' is such a name, as are 'Aurea', 'Variegata', and 'Rubra'. As of 1959, the ICNCP requires that all cultivar names must be from words in a modern language; they may not be Latinized. Thus, 'Morning Light' is an acceptable name, whereas 'Gracillimus Variegatus' is not. Also, the 1995 edition of the ICNCP no longer permits the use of translations of cultivar names. For example, the German cultivar *Miscanthus sinensis* 'Silberfeder' should not be translated to English and called *M. sinensis* 'Silver Feather'. Despite the ICNCP, this practice is common in commerce and for this reason, translations are provided in parentheses following the correct names in the encyclopedia entries of this book.

The ICNCP also includes a rule of priority requiring that the earliest valid cultivar name be preserved as the correct one. For example, the earliest established cultivar name for Bowles' golden sedge is *Carex elata* 'Aurea'. Several publications have incorrectly listed this plant as *C. elata* 'Bowles Golden', a later appellation that at best may be considered a synonym.

Contrary to popular misconception, cultivars are not, by definition, comprised of genetically identical plants (clones). They may be, in which case they are best referred to as clonal cultivars. An example is *Miscanthus sinensis* 'Goldfeder'. This cultivar must be vegetatively propagated if new plants are to retain all distinguishing characteristics, which include golden-variegated foliage. Cultivars may also be a group of plants whose one distinguishing characteristic, perhaps a certain narrowness of leaf, can be maintained through seed reproduction. Some seed-produced cultivars are maintained by selecting seedlings that meet the descriptive criteria of the cultivar and rejecting uncharacteristic seedlings. The widely popular *M. sinensis* 'Gracillimus' is an example of a cultivar that is often maintained by seed. It has been grown in Western gardens for more than a century, defined by its narrow leaves, rounded form, and late-season reddish inflorescences. Most seedlings of 'Gracillimus' (unless pollinated by other cultivars) are uniform in these characteristics, even though they are not genetically identical. Over decades, some nurseries have grown 'Gracillimus' from seed, rejecting occasional variants, and other nurseries have produced genetically uniform new plants by vegetative division. This can be confirmed by ordering *M. sinensis* 'Gracillimus' from 10 sources. The plants should all look essentially alike, but a keen eye is able to notice minor differences.

Gertrude Jekyll included *Miscanthus sinensis* 'Gracillimus', which she knew as *Eulalia gracillima,* in her design for the gardens at Hestercombe. Popular since Edwardian times, this cultivar exhibits slight variation due to seed propagation over decades. Unless specified as such in their descriptions, cultivars are not necessarily comprised of vegetatively identical clones.

Twilight tones of a Japanese autumn illuminate plumes of susuki, *Miscanthus sinensis,* growing natively on Mt. Hakone, while Mt. Fuji fades to a distant silhouette. In Japanese culture, miscanthus plumes and Japanese maple leaves are the two most popular symbols of the native landscape in autumn.

CHAPTER 4

Learning from Grasses in Native Habitats

MEMBERS of the grass family (Poaceae) are the principal component in more than one-fifth of the earth's cover of vegetation. Grasses grow natively on all the continents, are present in almost all ecological associations, and are the dominant vegetation in many, such as savannas, plains, steppes, and prairies. Grasses are an integral part of the contrast and harmony of textures, forms, colors, and illumination special to so many regional landscapes around the world. Studying the habitat preferences and natural patterns of grasses and their relatives increases an understanding of their cultural needs and provides a wealth of inspiration for integrating grasses into landscape designs. One of the best ways to begin studying plants in native habitats is to consult regional floras, which are often illustrated. Although floras are primarily oriented toward description and identification, they often include detailed information about native range and habitat preferences.

Literal millions of Hachijo susuki, *Miscanthus sinensis* var. *condensatus,* inhabit Japan's coastal lowlands, in huge masses reminiscent of *Phragmites australis* in North America and other continents. Grasses are naturally gregarious—they occur most often in huge sweeps and masses, in sunny habitats from mountain summits to the edge of the sea. They are scarce in dense forests.

The seasonal cycle of native warm-season grasses in the eastern North American landscape is illustrated by three photos of broom-sedge, *Andropogon virginicus*, little bluestem, *Schizachyrium scoparium*, and Indian grass, *Sorghastrum nutans*, covering a steeply sloped clearing between the edge of a deciduous forest and a moist meadow.

The landscape is still mostly green in late August, and the grasses are just beginning to flower.

Opposite, top: By late October the grasses have finished flowering and set seed. Their foliage, a rich mix of straw, salmon, and russet colors, complements the gold and red tones lingering in the autumn foliage of deciduous trees. The dark frame of the oak adds dramatic foreground contrast.

Opposite, bottom: A January snow cover reveals the grasses now to be the most colorful aspect of a winter landscape that is otherwise a study in dark browns, grays, and blacks.

Unidentified grasses and restios commingle with chartreuse *Leucodendron* shrubs on a windy, boulder-strewn slope high in the Bainskloof Pass of southern Africa. The drama of the scene owes much to the contrast between the fine-textured, supple grasses and the fixed, bold forms of the rocks. The attractive interweaving of grasses and shrubs is common in many native landscapes around the world.

A Wisconsin prairie remnant in June reveals the dramatic mixture of grasses and forbs that was a frequent feature of the once-vast American prairie. The broad, bold leaves of prairie dock, *Silphium terebinthinaceum,* and compass plant, *Silphium laciniatum,* are set in a matrix of the fine linear foliage of big bluestem, *Andropogon gerardii,* and Indian grass, *Sorghastrum nutans.*

A sunset in coastal Maryland highlights the textural interplay of huge sweeps of common reed, *Phragmites australis,* set against a broad, smooth surface of water. Many grasses including *Miscanthus* species and cultivars thrive in such moist or wet, full-sun environments.

Royal ferns, *Osmunda regalis,* in autumn color share a rocky river edge with switch grass, *Panicum virgatum,* and big bluestem, *Andropogon gerardii,* along the Goshen Pass in Virginia. Although true grasses are generally sun-loving and ferns usually prefer shade, there are instances like this where their habitats overlap, making for a rich mix of colors, textures, and forms.

Brilliant red patches of lowbush blueberry, *Vaccinium angustifolium*, are set off by a subtly colored matrix of grasses in this view of West Virginia heath barrens in mid-October. The landscape would be less interesting if it were entirely clothed in red, no matter how brilliant. The role of grasses as an aesthetic counterpoint to bright foliage or flowers is often underestimated.

Tan seed-heads of bottle-brush grass, *Hystrix patula*, overtop the brick-red fall foliage of fragrant sumac, *Rhus aromatica*, in a rocky, oak-hickory forest in West Virginia. Though most grasses are sun-loving, a few, such as *Hystrix*, are adapted to dry shade, presenting interesting possibilities for woodland gardens.

Many sedges prefer sunny wet or moist habitats. Three-way sedge, *Dulichium arundinaceum*, ventures into shallow waters in the New Jersey pine barrens, attractively contrasting with the orbicular leaves of the native fragrant waterlily, *Nymphaea odorata*. This combination is easily reprised in a small garden pool or container.

Tussock sedge, *Carex stricta,* is one of many sedges adapted to moist shady environments. Its fine, grassy texture is a natural foil for the bold foliage of the native skunk-cabbage, *Symplocarpus foetidus,* along a small creek in northern Delaware in early May.

Among the world's most beautiful sedges, Fraser's sedge, *Cymophyllus fraserianus,* is native to moist woodland slopes with rich organic soils, mostly on the western side of the Appalachian mountains in eastern North America. It is rare in its natural habitat and in gardens. Careful study of native environments is critical to both the horticultural introduction and *in-situ* conservation of such floral gems.

Side-angled sunlight illuminates the graceful, arching foliage of *Miscanthus sinensis* 'Morning Light' for visitors strolling paths in the Bellevue Botanic Garden in Washington State.

CHAPTER 5

Designing with Grasses

ORNAMENTAL grasses are a stunningly versatile group, offering myriad possibilities in the garden limited only by the imagination of the designer. The vast modern palette includes species and cultivated varieties suited for use as specimens, accents, groundcovers, masses, hedges, container subjects, and a host of other purposes.

Grasses are often most effective in garden designs that allow them to interplay with other perennials, annuals, biennials, trees, and shrubs. When first using grasses a common impulse is to segregate them; however, this rarely results in a satisfying design. Just as a border composed solely of flowering perennials can be colorfully bland, a garden collection of different grasses is often equally lacking in dimension and balance. Designs that utilize a variety of plant types are not only aesthetically richer, they are often the soundest strategy for making gardens capable of providing year-round interest while minimizing labor and consumption of natural resources.

The setting rays of the autumn sun light up the foliage and seed-heads of wild-oats, *Chasmanthium latifolium,* growing beneath dogwood trees, *Cornus florida,* at the end of a west-facing path in the author's former Delaware garden.

Working with the Light in the Garden

To best capture the inherent translucency and luminous possibilities of ornamental grasses, it is important to develop an awareness of the direction, strength, and periods of sunlight in the garden. Even relatively shady gardens have points and moments when the sun's direct rays can work magic. It is equally rewarding to carefully consider the patterns of daily and seasonal activity in the garden. For example, think of the times of day an established or potential garden path will be used and the direction from which the sunlight will be coming. If planting a west-facing walk that will be used regularly at the end of the day, any grasses situated between the one walking the path and the setting sun will be naturally backlighted. Similar considerations are worthwhile when designing favorite sitting spaces, focal points, or views to the garden from inside the house.

The sun's backlighting enhances the already-gold autumn foliage and reddish brown spikelets of wild-oats, *Chasmanthium latifolium*, in mid-October.

Combinations for Contrasting Texture and Form

Combining the linear foliage, fine texture, and loose form of grasses with contrasting elements in the garden is both simple and satisfying. These items might include the broad leaves, flowers, seed-heads, or woody trunks of companion plants, the mass and clear outlines of hedges, stones, or architectural elements, and the strong forms of sculptural objects and garden furniture. Designs grounded in such juxtapositions generally have much longer periods of interest than those based on fleeting floral combinations.

In the author's garden, the fine foliage of grasses including blue wheatgrass, *Elymus magellanicus* (lower left), blue oat grass, *Helictotrichon sempervirens* (center), and *Miscanthus* 'Purpurascens' (upper right) provide interesting, multiseason contrast with broad-leaved companions, such as the biennial mullein, *Verbascum bombiciferum*, and lamb's-ears, *Stachys byzantina* 'Big Ears'.

At Great Dixter, East Sussex, England, Christopher Lloyd's combination of feather reed grass, *Calamagrostis ×acutiflora* 'Karl Foerster', and *Eryngium olivierum* retains its interest long after both plants have gone from flowers to seed.

In a German garden, the curiously attractive seed stalks of *Phlomis russeliana* provide late August contrast with the fine blue foliage of blue oat grass, *Helictotrichon sempervirens*. This combination will last into winter.

Giant coneflower, *Rudbeckia maxima*, produces its 5 in. (13 cm) wide flowers in late July, when *Miscanthus* 'Purpurascens' is also in bloom. These two continue to complement one another in the author's garden in late October. The bold bluish leaves and nearly black seed-heads of the coneflower contrast with the coppery autumn tones of the grass.

Bamboo muhly, *Muhlenbergia dumosa* (light green, center), provides fine-textured relief from the bold forms of cacti and other arid-region plants in late December at the University of California, Berkeley, Botanical Garden.

Opposite, top: Grasses can be used to provide a fixed, fine-textured background for contrasting, moveable objects. At Peckerwood Gardens near Waller, Texas, a container-grown specimen *Agave* is set against the soft texture of bamboo muhly, *Muhlenbergia dumosa*.

Opposite, bottom: Ornamental grasses have been interplanted to dramatic effect among conifers in the Gotelli Dwarf Conifer Collection at the U.S. National Arboretum, Washington, D.C. Grasses and conifers are similar in having much of their appeal based upon texture and form rather than on colorful flowers. Side-lighting of tall purple moor grass, *Molinia caerulea* subsp. *arundinacea* 'Karl Foerster', against a dark green background reveals its arching sculptural form, a sharp contrast to the strictly upright *Juniperus communis* 'Pencil Point'.

In full flower in early May, a fine groundcover sweep of variegated wood-rush, *Luzula sylvatica* 'Marginata', sets off the strong form of a venerable specimen redbud, *Cercis canadensis* 'Forest Pansy', at Springwood, the garden of Dick and Sally Lighty in eastern Pennsylvania.

The juxtaposition of massive boulders and waving plumes of feather reed grass, *Calamagrostis ×acutiflora* 'Karl Foerster', brings movement and the drama of diverse texture and form to a modest-sized interior courtyard at the University of Washington Center for Urban Horticulture, Seattle.

Spreading mounds of variegated Hakone grass, *Hakonechloa macra* 'Aureola', and fine tufts of Bowles' golden sedge, *Carex elata* 'Aurea', soften the ends of boldly elegant granite steps in the Israelit garden in Portland, Oregon, in late July. (Photo: Melinda Zoehrer)

Color Strategies

Most ornamental grasses are softly hued and readily harmonize with a wide array of flower and foliage colors of garden companions. The silvery tones of grass flowers are essentially neutral. They can add sparkle to a subtly colored border or provide a welcome respite in exceptionally bright compositions. The gently varied greens of grass foliage are almost universally color-compatible and can be employed to provide a harmonizing background for colorful flowering perennials. Grasses with cool blue or gray-blue leaves serve a similar purpose, or they may be used to reveal and enhance flower colors in a range of blues or in contrasting colors. Many of the bluish grasses retain their color through spring, summer, and autumn, offering opportunities for color combinations with a succession of flowering companions over the course of the gardening season. Though not colorful in the technical sense, the white-variegated foliage of grasses nevertheless provides some of the boldest possible contrast with colorful flowers. A few grasses with richly toned foliage of yellow and red easily rival the color impact of typical flowering perennials and may be treated as equal partners to flowers in color designs. This is also true of the many grasses that take on vivid autumn hues of gold, orange, red, and burgundy. Many superb designs result from the combination of grasses with colorful-leafed herbaceous plants, vines, trees, and shrubs. The muted late fall and winter tones of grasses provide ideal contrast with the brilliant autumn hues of deciduous woody plants, as well as the winter colors of bark and berries.

Subtly elegant silver tones of purple needle grass, *Nassella pulchra,* balance the super-saturated color of California poppies, *Eschscholzia californica,* in February at the Santa Barbara Botanic Garden, California.

The vivid blue foliage of blue wheatgrass, *Elymus magellanicus*, provides sharp color contrast with the flowers of *Stachys stricta* 'Dark Lilac' in Alan Bloom's garden in Bressingham, England, in mid-July.

A sophisticated color pairing of variegated Hakone grass, *Hakonechloa macra* 'Aureola', and buttercup ivy, *Hedera helix* 'Buttercup', brightens a mid-September border at Chanticleer, in Wayne, Pennsylvania.

In late October, the autumn red of a young sourwood tree, *Oxydendrum arboreum,* appears especially vivid against a background of *Miscanthus sinensis* 'Variegatus' in the author's former Delaware garden. Though these lower branches will not remain into the tree's maturity, they will nevertheless provide several years of display with the grass. Since most grasses are easy to plant and quickly reach mature size, they are ideal for relatively temporary plantings, such as this, filling spaces near young trees or between maturing shrubs.

During summer, pink-purple flowers are the dominant coloration of fountain grass, *Pennisetum alopecuroides*. By late October the flowers have faded and the gold tones of the foliage are the main attraction, complementing the autumn burgundies of flowering dogwoods, *Cornus florida,* and warming and softening neo-classical architecture at Winterthur Museum and Gardens, Delaware.

The airy, soft tan inflorescences of giant switch grass, *Panicum virgatum* 'Cloud Nine', and the rich reds and oranges of staghorn sumac, *Rhus typhina,* provide color and textural contrast in early November at Firefly Farm, the eastern Pennsylvania garden of Mary and Tom Shea. This combination of two locally native species at the periphery of the garden makes an elegant transition to the deciduous forest surrounding the historic farmstead.

Though muted, the light buff-colored foliage of giant miscanthus, *Miscanthus* 'Giganteus', is a more effective background for the bright red of winterberry holly, *Ilex verticillata,* than the gray tones of the beech woods beyond, in late November at Ashland Hollow, the Delaware garden of Mr. and Mrs. W. H. Frederick, Jr.

Sweeps and Masses

There is a near-universal appeal to a vast sweep of grasses in the landscape, rippling and rustling in the wind. Though the larger mass plantings are beyond the size limits of most residential gardens, they are worthy goals for including in public gardens, parks, preserves, and roadside rights of way. Meadow and prairie gardens can often be scaled to fit within residential boundaries, and with careful design and planning, even a modest drift of grasses can bring a contrived but beguiling wildness to the smallest urban garden. Many low-growing ornamental grasses also make fine groundcovers in gardens of any size.

A hillside community of broom-sedge, *Andropogon virginicus,* and little bluestem, *Schizachyrium scoparium,* adds its burnished copper tones to the late October landscape of Chester County, Pennsylvania. These locally native grasses are consciously maintained in keeping with the environmental management policy of Longwood Gardens for its outlying areas.

Elegant stone benches flank the entrance to the restored prairie on the Schuler estate in Lake Bluff, Illinois, gracefully underscoring the transition from the formal lawn nearest the house. Planted from seed with a mix of native flowering perennials and prairie grasses including big bluestem, *Andropogon gerardii,* and Indian grass, *Sorghastrum nutans,* this multi-acre prairie is burned annually.

This contemporary New Zealand dwelling is immersed in a restored native landscape mostly of red tussock grass, *Chionochloa rubra*. (Photo: Gordon Collier)

This kitchen-window view demonstrates how effective even a modest-sized sweep of grasses can be in introducing a delightful informality to an urban or suburban garden. Simple drifts of *Calamagrostis ×acutiflora* 'Karl Foerster' and *Sedum* 'Autumn Joy' overlap in mid-August in the Thomas-Kromer garden in eastern Pennsylvania.

A hillside sweep of switch grass, *Panicum virgatum,* provides multiseason interest at the historic Grove Park Inn in Asheville, North Carolina. In late July the grass is full sized and flowering.

By late February the tawny grass still stands tall.

Many lower-growing ornamental grasses are long-lived and well adapted for use in groundcovering sweeps and masses. Some, like the genus *Sesleria*, are also evergreen or semi-evergreen.

A cool-season grower, blue moor grass, *Sesleria caerulea*, has put on significant new growth and is in flower in early May in this groundcover planting at Longwood Gardens.

The blue-green foliage remains neat and attractive in late December, still furnishing a rich ground color to display the winter beauty of paperbark maple, *Acer griseum*. The cream-colored inflorescences in the background belong to tufted hair grass, *Deschampsia cespitosa*.

Grasses and Flowering Bulbs

Flowering bulbs are ideal partners to grasses in the spring garden. Although the new foliage of many grasses is quite attractive, relatively few species put on a floral display in the months of April and May. Conversely, early flowering bulbs are a floral delight in the spring garden, yet the foliage that follows their flowering is often a minor eyesore. Gardeners can have the best of both worlds by interplanting bulbs with grasses. The spring garden is brightened by colorful bulb flowers rising above new ornamental grass foliage, then the attractive growth of the grasses overtops and effectively masks the bulb foliage as it withers and dies after replenishing the bulbs' energy for the following season.

Colorful tulip flowers emerge from the attractive early May foliage of blue oat grass, *Helictotrichon sempervirens,* in this clever interplanting at the Scott Arboretum in Swarthmore, Pennsylvania.

Daffodils and narcissus of all sizes make excellent companions to grasses in the spring garden. At Longwood Gardens in early May, the light-lemon-colored flowers of the diminutive *Narcissus* 'Hawera' brighten a groundcover sweep of prairie dropseed, *Sporobolus heterolepis.* The emerging foliage of the grass will soon overtop and attractively mask the lingering, yellowing foliage of the narcissus as the bulbs go dormant. In late summer, the dropseed will produce its own floral display, and then in autumn its foliage will acquire rich tones of orange and umber.

Pools, Ponds, and Watersides

Ornamental grasses are often at their elegant best when grown at water's edge. The broad surface of water embodies the utmost in bold simplicity, revealing the fine-textured detail of ornamental grasses in a way few companion plantings can. The distinctive foliage of many aquatic plants also provides opportunities for unique textural compositions with grasses in the water garden.

Many sedges, rushes, and cat-tails are native to wet habitats and are obvious choices when designing waterside plantings. A surprising number of true grasses including *Miscanthus* species; cord grass, *Spartina pectinata*; and switch grass, *Panicum virgatum*, are also well adapted to growing near water's edge or even on periodically inundated soils. Many of these can be used to stabilize as well as to ornament sunny streambanks and pond edges.

Christopher Lloyd's artistry is evident in this blend of Bowles' golden sedge, *Carex elata* 'Aurea', *Nymphaea* waterlilies, and other semi-aquatics in a small pond at Great Dixter, East Sussex, England, in early July. Though this sedge grows satisfactorily in garden soils of average moisture, a pondside setting more closely resembles its native habitat preference.

Finely variegated *Miscanthus sinensis* 'Morning Light' makes a stunning focal point at the corner of an exquisite pool at Wave Hill, Bronx, New York, in mid-September. The still, dark surface of the water mirrors the cascading foliage of the grass along with billowy silhouettes of overarching trees.

Variegated manna grass, *Glyceria maxima* 'Variegata', is a running species that is sometimes too aggressive in mixed flower borders. This streambank planting at the Chicago Botanic Garden, Illinois, takes advantage of the plant's colonizing tendency and tolerance of wet soils, resulting in an attractive low-maintenance groundcover for what otherwise could be a difficult site. The vigor of the grass is well balanced with neighboring *Iris pseudacorus*. A narrow, buried edging and normal mowing keep the grass from invading the turf at the top edge of the bank.

Simply elegant, the vertical stems of common rush, *Juncus effusus,* dramatically contrast with the water's surface and the varied textures of aquatic and semi-aquatic companions in the Aquatic Display at Longwood Gardens in the end of August.

The cascading culms of tiger grass, *Thysanolaena maxima,* mimic water tumbling over vertical stone surfaces in the Roberto Burle Marx–designed Clemente Gomes garden, Fazenda Vargem Grande, near Areias, Brazil. Miniature papyrus, *Cyperus prolifer,* ventures into the shallow pool below.

Decorative Container Displays

Container growing introduces limitless other possibilities for enjoying ornamental grasses. With imagination, most grasses can be incorporated in creative designs in pots. Massive grasses, such as *Miscanthus* species; giant reed, *Arundo donax,* or pampas grass, *Cortaderia selloana,* require large tubs if they are intended to reach full size; however, these species often make attractive young specimens when grown in very modest containers. This is especially true of large variegated-leaf cultivars, which are beautiful even if they do not attain flowering size. The enduring foliage colors of grasses suggest myriad combinations with the variously hued clays and ceramic glazes to be found on antique and modern garden pots. Though grasses may be grown in separate containers, they lend well to combinations with flowering annuals, perennials, or colorful broad-leaved plants in the same pot. Cultivating grasses in containers also frees gardeners from limitations often imposed by stubborn soils, cold winters, or hot summers when growing plants in the

The powder-blue of lyme grass, *Leymus arenarius,* plays off the weathered copper tones of a venerable vessel amid a procession of colorful flowering companions in early July at The Coach House, Penelope Hobhouse's garden in southern England.

local earth. Soil for plants grown in pots can be modified to suit the most particular species. Tender grasses can be grown outdoors in warm seasons and held in cold frames or warm storage over winter, and alpine species can be moved to protection from summer heat and humidity. Containers also provide a safe way of enjoying running species, including bamboos, that can be difficult to manage in the garden. The delicate colors, textures, and translucency of grasses grown in pots are especially welcome in challenging settings, such as urban rooftop gardens. Many grasses with multiple-season interest are also sufficiently cold-hardy to be left outdoors in containers over winter.

Many bamboos are amenable to bonsai techniques. The restricted root space significantly diminishes the size of even large species, such as this black bamboo, *Phyllostachys nigra*, while retaining the beauty of the foliage and the color of the culms.

Wild-oats, *Chasmanthium latifolium*, shares a simple earthen-colored urn with eastern native species and cultivars, including white snakeroot, *Eupatorium rugosum* 'Chocolate', wild spikenard, *Aralia racemosa*, and *Coreopsis* 'Moonbeam'. This container carries a native theme from Longwood Gardens' Peirce's Woods garden to an entrance courtyard.

Suspended from slender wires, curiously narrow pots brimming with brightly variegated Hakone grass, *Hakonechloa macra* 'Aureola', brighten a shady pergola at Willowwood Arboretum in northern New Jersey in early September.

Larger grasses are easily grown in containers if provided with adequate moisture and sufficient space for root development. Many grasses, including those shown here, are sufficiently cold-hardy to remain outdoors in a container during winter.

The inflorescences and foliage of switch grass, *Panicum virgatum* 'Hänse Herms', take on burgundy tones at Longwood Gardens in late August, while nearby goldenrod, *Solidago sphaecelata* 'Golden Fleece', flowers and daylilies re-bloom.

By late October, *Panicum virgatum* 'Hänse Herms' has added deep gold to its colors, while narrow-leaved bluestar, *Amsonia hubrichtii,* glows bright yellow.

Cortaderia richardii in mid-July in Alan Bloom's garden in Bressingham, England.

CHAPTER 6

Growing and Maintaining Grasses

GRASSES are easy; they thrive in a great range of climatic and cultural conditions. Properly selected and used, grasses can contribute more beauty and interest with less maintenance than almost any other group of garden perennials. This chapter offers general approaches, techniques, and recommendations to help gardeners get the most from the grasses they grow. Further comments and recommendations specific to individual grasses appear in the encyclopedia entries in Chapter 7 of this book.

Selecting Grasses

When selecting grasses for a garden, aesthetic considerations are ultimately a matter of personal choice; however, there are practical and ecological points to consider that are independent of style and taste.

First, know the climate. Invariably, successful gardeners are familiar with the unique opportunities as well as the limitations of the local climate, and they choose plants accordingly. Horticultural techniques can do much to alter growing conditions, especially on a micro level; however, the larger cycles and extremes of climate must be considered if gardening is to be reasonably "low maintenance" and respectful of natural resources.

Second, be choosy. Look for species or cultivated varieties that are specially adapted to the garden's purposes. The huge number of ornamental grasses available today makes it possible to find cultivars uniquely fit to the design intent and cultural situations of any garden.

Third, consider provenance. All plants of a species are not identical; the genetic makeup of both individuals and communities within the species varies considerably and can significantly impact suitability for garden use. This variation is usually linked to the plants' specific origin or provenance. For example, the species *Sorghastrum nutans* occurs natively over much of central and eastern North America. There is a much higher incidence of glaucous-blue foliage among plants of central prairie-state provenance than among plants that evolved at the eastern extreme of the species' range, such as in Pennsylvania, where plants are routinely green-leafed. Such foliage color variation is readily apparent; other variation is not. Plants of different provenance may be superficially indistinguishable, yet may still possess genetic variation resulting in dramatically different non-visual characteristics. For example, due to subtle genetic differences, green-leafed plants of *S. nutans* from a warm provenance, such as Texas, may not be able to survive the sustained, below-freezing temperatures common to Pennsylvania.

Acquiring Grasses

Grasses may be purchased growing in soil in various-sized containers, as bare-rooted plants, and as seed. They are sold by retail nurseries, garden centers, and mail-order establishments as well as by wholesale firms catering to professionals only.

Commercial production of grasses is increasingly devoted to growing grasses in containers, a system offering production efficiencies and convenient handling for both producer and consumer. Whether bought from a local retail garden center or from a mail-order nursery, most container-grown grasses are best purchased in spring, before they attain much growth. These plants will readily establish in the garden and will usually out-grow larger plants bought later in season. Especially with deciduous grasses, spring buying often means acquiring plants long before they reach their peak attractiveness. Many gardeners who are accustomed to purchasing annuals in full bloom resist buying ornamental grasses until they, too, are in flower. Unfortunately, by this time grasses are often root-bound in containers that were meant for spring sale, not summer growing. Be confident that the spring purchase is the better value. Sometimes grasses are offered for sale in larger containers with sufficient space for root development over the course of the season, but this is the exception.

Wholesale production nurseries often grow grasses in container flats of "liner" or "plug"-sized plants. These small plants are transplanted to larger pots and grown on to normal retail size. Although liner and plug-sized grasses are much too small to be used by gardeners for typical plantings within established garden beds and borders, they establish very quickly if competition is minimal, and they can be a very cost-effective means for implementing large new sweeps or groundcover plantings. Liners and plugs of ornamental grasses are usually only available to wholesale buyers.

Whether container grown or field grown, grasses are often sold bare-rooted to reduce shipping weight expense, which might otherwise be prohibitive in large orders. Bare-rooted grasses are typically shipped in spring, when top growth is often dormant. The plants may appear lifeless when they arrive, but will rapidly establish if promptly planted, provided they have been kept from extreme heat or cold during shipment. The additional expense of express delivery services is often worthwhile when buying bare-rooted grasses. Bare-rooted grasses are an excellent means of establishing large mass plantings and groundcovers.

The growing popularity of ornamental grasses has led to a much wider choice of selections at retail garden centers; however, many of the newer and rarer cultivars and many regional native species are available only through specialty mail-order nurseries (see Nursery Sources at the back of this book). Most mail-order nurseries ship in spring, and some have additional fall shipping periods.

Seed is often the least expensive way to acquire ornamental grasses and is sometimes the only way to obtain certain species. Several nurseries offer seed by mail order. Collecting seed, legally and with appropriate permission, can be the best way to procure grasses from local provenance. For gardeners with a keen eye, starting grasses from seed affords the opportunity to watch for interesting variation and to make new selections. With cultivated varieties, it is important to re-

Plug-sized grasses, usually only available to wholesaler buyers, establish very quickly in the landscape if competition is minimal.

Most grasses are best purchased in spring, long before they are in full bloom.

member that a few retain their distinguishing characteristics when grown from seed, but most must be reproduced vegetatively if new plants are to accurately represent the named variety.

Growing Seasons and Optimum Times for Planting and Dividing

Although grasses from tropical climates are often capable of continuous, year-round growth, most ornamental grasses evolved in temperate or Mediterranean climates where they developed cycles of growth in response to different seasonal opportunities and limitations. For example, in cold-temperate climates winter cold may be the ultimate limitation to growth. In Mediterranean climates, growth is often checked by summer drought.

In a broad sense, grasses can be grouped as cool-season growers and warm-season growers. The periods of active growth are governed not only by temperature but also by light intensity and available moisture, factors that can be modified by gardening techniques. A basic familiarity with plant responses to cultural and climatic patterns will help the making of informed decisions about selecting grasses for a particular climate as well as choosing optimum times for planting, dividing, and propagating ornamental grasses.

Cool-season grasses grow well in temperatures from near freezing up to approximately 75°F (24°C). In a cold-temperate climate, this means they often have two periods of growth. A typical cool-season grass begins growth in late winter, develops significant foliage by early spring, and produces flowers anytime from late winter to early summer. This growth period coincides with a combination of moisture, warmth, and sunlight ideally suited to the metabolism and photosynthetic processes of this type of grass. As the summer progresses, temperature and sunlight intensity increase, often accompanied by a decrease in rainfall. These conditions are stressful to the metabolism of cool-season grasses. Unable to take advantage of the additional sunlight because of the excessive heat and lack of moisture, the net energy they capture through photosynthesis decreases. During this period, they usually go partly or fully dormant. Cool-season grasses resume growth when sunlight wanes, temperatures drop, and rainfall increases at summer's end. They continue growing until extreme winter temperatures force a complete cessation.

Cool-season grasses may be divided or transplanted from late winter into early spring, and again from late summer to mid-autumn. They should not be moved or divided as they approach or are in their summer dormant state, however partial it may be. The stress of summer can be relieved to some extent by planting cool-season growers in areas partially shaded in summer. Supplemental watering during summer droughts can also be helpful and may keep some species from going dormant. In cooler climates, many cool-season grasses are evergreen or semi-evergreen.

Not all cool-season grasses are alike in their physiological behavior. Striped tuber-oat grass, *Arrhenatherum elatius* subsp. *bulbosum* 'Variegatum', is an example of an extreme cool-season grower. It begins growth with the first warm days of winter or remains evergreen though mild winters. It blooms in spring and then goes completely dormant in the middle of a hot, dry summer. An effective design strategy is to situate other plants with summer interest to mask the dormant grass until it puts on a flush of fresh new growth entering autumn. Feather reed grass, *Calamagrostis* ×*acutiflora* 'Karl Foerster', is also a cool-season grower, but is much more tolerant of summer conditions. Although its growth will slow, it remains green and reasonably attractive in all but the worst summers. Other examples of cool-season grasses are blue oat grass, *Helictotrichon sempervirens;* most fescues, *Festuca* species; melic grasses, *Melica* species; and most *Stipa* and *Achnatherum* species.

Warm-season grasses like it hot. Although their metabolisms are less efficient than cool-season growers at lower temperatures, they are superbly adapted to temperatures of 80° to 95°F (24° to 27°C). Warm-season growers typically break winter dormancy late in spring and are very slow growing until summer arrives. They revel in the intense summer sun, growing steadily larger and gathering energy until they flower at summer's end. Their processes shut down with the onset of cold weather, and they remain dormant through winter. During this shut-down many warm-season grasses take on beautiful autumn colors.

Warm-season grasses are best divided or transplanted when they are in active growth but long before they begin blooming. Late spring into early summer is an ideal time. It can be risky to divide or transplant them in fall since much of the plants' stored energy has often just been spent on flower and seed production. In cold climates, fall divisions and transplants will make very little new growth before winter dormancy begins, and the plants will be forced to endure the stresses of freezing temperatures, and often excessive moisture, with depleted energy reserves. Fall transplanting works well only in mild climates. It is usually least successful in climates approaching the winter cold-hardiness of the grasses in question.

The various *Miscanthus* species; pampas grasses, *Cortaderia* species; giant reed, *Arundo donax;* and the fountain grasses, *Pennisetum* species are examples of warm-season growers, as are many North American natives, such as little bluestem, *Schizachyrium scoparium;* big bluestem, *Andropogon gerardii;* switch grass, *Panicum virgatum;* and Indian grass, *Sorghastrum nutans.*

Heat and Cold Hardiness

The hardiness zones indicated in Chapter 7 and elsewhere in this volume refer to the U.S. Department of Agriculture (USDA) Hardiness Zone map published in 1990 and reproduced at the back of this book. These zones are based on annual average minimum temperatures recorded in the United States and must be interpreted cautiously. Though such zones are certainly useful measures, they tend to reinforce the notion that hardiness is limited solely by plants' ability to survive cold. In many garden situations, other factors may be more life-threatening to plants.

When plants from distant parts of the world are grown outside their usual area of distribution, they are often subjected to climatic patterns that differ from their usual, even though the average low temperatures may be similar. For example, temperatures in Japan rise fairly steadily from winter through spring. Spring warming in eastern North America is usually interrupted by brief, late periods of freezing cold. Similarly, the eastern North American autumn is much more uneven in its cooling than is Japan's. Unaccustomed to this pattern, Japanese species in North American gardens will sometimes be adversely affected.

The winter hardiness of cool-season growers is often limited by high temperatures during summer days and nights. Cool-season species that are tolerant of extreme low temperatures in their native climate sometimes succumb during relatively mild winters in a foreign garden because they enter winter still weakened by excessive summer heat, sun, or drought. Conversely, the winter cold tolerance of warm-season species can be seriously reduced if summer temperatures and sunlight intensity are not high enough to adequately drive their metabolisms. This at least partly explains why, for example, the striped giant reed, *Arundo donax* 'Variegata', is winter hardy only in England's south, yet is completely reliable in the mid-Atlantic United States, which is much colder in winter but much hotter in summer.

Snowfall also dramatically affects winter survival of grasses. A steady cover of snow often results in soil temperatures remaining near freezing, while air temperatures drop to otherwise lethal lows. This important variable is not reflected in the hardiness zone map.

Frequently the hardiness zones listed in books and nursery catalogs are rather educated guesses than proven fact. There is still much research to be done on heat and cold tolerance of ornamental grasses. Some of the most important work in recent years has been conducted at the Minnesota Landscape Arboretum in Chanhassen, by University of Minnesota researchers led by Mary H. Meyer. During a six-year study, the performance of more than 150 cultivated varieties of ornamental grasses was observed and documented in this USDA zone 4a climate. Further research in diverse and extreme climates is needed.

Lastly, never underestimate the importance of microclimate. A garden is likely to include special niches that differ significantly from the regional climate. Sheltered corners, planting beds adjacent to warm walls of a dwelling, interior courtyards, or even roof gardens can afford the opportunity to enjoy grasses that might not normally be considered hardy in the area.

Sun and Shade

Generally, true grasses thrive in sunny situations, and sedges and wood-rushes tend to prefer shade; however, there are many exceptions. Individual preferences of various species and cultivars are included in the encyclopedia entries in Chapter 7.

Most sun-loving grasses perform adequately if provided three to five hours of direct sun each day. They are stronger and more upright in more sun, and weaker and somewhat lax in less. Large sun-loving grasses, such as *Miscanthus*, are more prone to falling over in shaded situations if soils are highly fertile.

Other than flowers, the peak attraction of many grasses is their autumn foliage color, which is usually most pronounced in high sun situations. Although a few variegated grasses, such as Hakone grass, *Hakonechloa*, require partial shade, bright sunlight brings out the best in most variegated grasses, sedges, and rushes.

Remember that the intensity of "full sun" differs dramatically in various parts of the world. Full sun in Cornwall, England, is still more like part shade in southern California. Full sun at high mountain elevations, which are often cloaked in clouds, may also equate to shade at valley bottom.

Soils

One of the reasons grasses are so popular is that they often thrive in what gardeners are wont to refer to as "bad" soils. While most grasses appreciate a well-drained, reasonably fertile loam, the many adaptable sorts, including *Miscanthus*, are undaunted by either poorly drained heavy clays or droughty infertile sands. As a group, grasses are also largely indifferent to normal variations in acidity and alkalinity, and many, especially the coastal species, are somewhat salt-tolerant.

Soil differences can, however, make a real difference in the performance of certain ornamental grasses. For example, some grasses, including the popular cultivars of blue fescue, *Festuca glauca*, require sharp drainage if they are to survive cold wet winters in good condition. Running grasses, such as blue Lyme grass, *Leymus arenarius*, may be manageable in dense clays but too aggressive in rich friable loam. Well-aerated soils high in organic matter are necessary for best growth of a few woodland sedges, including Fraser's sedge, *Cymophyllus fraserianus*.

Fertilization

I have gardened for more than two decades without having ever directly fertilized a grass. Except when grown on sterile sands, ornamental grasses generally do not benefit from supplemental fertilization. Adding concentrated chemical fertilizers to average soils can hurt performance. Excess fertility results in over-lush growth and is likely to cause plants to lose their shape and flop unmanageably. This is true especially in nutrient-efficient genera, such as *Miscanthus*. Staking large grasses to hold them upright is particularly tedious and is usually unnecessary if fertility and water are kept to reasonable levels. Grasses, such as broom-sedge, *Andropogon virginicus*, that are specially adapted to infertile soils may lose their competitive edge and be overgrown by other plants if nutrient levels are raised significantly. Running grasses that are easily managed in average soils can become aggressive nuisances in over-rich soils. Also, the super-green growth associated with high levels of fertility can seriously diminish the vibrancy of foliage variegation.

Moisture

Although standing with hose in hand seems to be a popular form of therapy, gardeners have better ways to relax in the garden. Drought tolerance is part of the natural appeal of ornamental grasses and should be appreciated. Other than the watering of new transplants, reasonably situated ornamental grasses can do much to free gardeners from the waste and tedium of watering.

Sometimes the challenge is how to deal with too much water in the garden. Grasses can often form part of the solution. Many species of ornamental grasses do well in over-moist or even partly inundated soils. This is particularly true of sedges, rushes, cat-tails, and certain restios.

Diseases and Pests

Grasses are still among the most pest-free and disease-free of all garden ornamentals; however, a few new problems have arrived along with the increased popularity of grasses. Not surprisingly, the two most recent, most troublesome pests affect the ubiquitous *Miscanthus*.

Miscanthus mealybug is a serious pest that fortunately appears to be restricted to the genus *Miscanthus*. The mealybug, *Miscanthicoccus miscanthi*, is an Asian native. It was first found in the United States in the late 1980s and is now in many northeastern states, south to Florida, and west to California. The mealybug is not capable of moving long distances unassisted; in fact, it probably cannot spread more than a few feet on its own. It has been dispersed unwittingly but entirely by the sale and exchange of infested plants. The presence of this insidious pest is not usually noticed until the population on an individual plant builds to high levels and superficial symptoms become readily apparent.

Up to 3/16 in. (4 mm) long, the mealybug lives in the tight space between the stem and the enclosing leaf sheath. Colonies are usually established first toward the base (crown) of the plant and spread upward as their numbers increase. The mealybugs are difficult to see until they reach mature adult size. The best way to confirm their presence is to pull a lower leaf sheath away from the stem of an infested plant. There, the white-powdery wax and syrupy honeydew that is produced by and obscures the individual mealybugs can be seen.

Miscanthus mealybugs live between the stem and the enclosing leaf sheath.

A general stunting of growth and an uncharacteristic twisting in the flower heads are usually the first superficial symptoms. The stem and sheath tissue often turn dark red in areas where the mealybugs are feeding, especially in late season. Severely infested plants are not killed, but are reduced to unsightly, misshapen masses with white powder covering the stems, especially in the lower portion. Affected plants often fail to flower at all, or the stalks of the inflorescences may be stunted, causing the flowers to open down among the foliage rather than gracefully above.

Topical sprays are ineffective at eradicating the miscanthus mealybug, since they do not adequately penetrate the protected crevices between sheath and stem. Research at Longwood Gardens also found the systemic insecticidal sprays Orthene®, Vydate®, and Merit® to be only marginally effective at treating plants growing in the ground. Burning plants to the ground in spring and even scorching the crowns with a propane torch also failed to kill mealybugs that overwinter deep in the crown, near the soil line. To date, no natural predators have been found to be effective control agents. One proven, legal means of eradication is to lift and divide plants into smaller pieces, and to soak or drench these with an organophosphate insecticide, such as Duraguard® or Dursban®. This approach may be practical if safety procedures are rigorously followed in a controlled commercial environment; however, it is definitely not recommended for the residential gardener. It is wisest to discard and incinerate infested plants, and to check new *Miscanthus* acquisitions carefully before adding them to the garden.

Miscanthus blight, newly described and identified by researchers at the USDA Agricultural Experiment Station in Maryland, is a foliar disease caused by *Stagonospora* and *Leptosphaeria* fungi. On mature plants, the blight is characterized by reddish brown spots or oval streaks on leaves and leaf sheaths. New leaf margins, tips, and older leaves become discolored and die. The disease can kill young seedlings and newly rooted cuttings. Fungicides, such as Banrot®, should provide effective control. See *Plant Disease*, the journal of the American Phytopathological Society, September 1996, for further details.

The stalks of inflorescences infected with miscanthus mealybug may be stunted, causing the flowers to open within the foliage rather than above.

The fungal disease miscanthus blight is characterized by reddish brown spots or oval streaks on leaves and leaf sheaths. (Photo: Nichole O'Neill)

Several grasses are susceptible to foliar rust diseases. Caused by fungi, rusts produce an orange or brownish discoloration on leaves. They are most likely to be a problem during warm, humid seasons, especially on cool-season grasses. Rusts can be avoided or minimized by planting susceptible grasses so that they have a maximum of air movement in warm periods, and by overall good garden culture that minimizes plant stress. Rusts can be chemically controlled with applications of wetable sulfur or fungicides, such as Zyban®.

Deer rarely bother grasses. In fact, they do not like large grasses with sharp-edged leaves, and these can be used effectively to screen and protect other more vulnerable garden plants and areas. Gophers and voles, however, can be serious pests, devouring grass roots and killing or mangling the plants. These animals can be particularly disruptive to large groundcover plantings. Though unsightly, wire mesh coverings may be reasonably used to protect smaller numbers of plants from gophers.

Rust diseases are characterized by an orange or brownish discoloration on the leaves of ornamental grasses.

Growth Habits: Runners and Clumpers

Though technically all grasses increase in width or spread to some degree by lateral shoots, for garden purposes it is common and practical to group grasses as either runners or clumpers.

Running grasses are those that spread rather rapidly by rhizomes, in which case they may also be called rhizomatous grasses, or by stolons, in which case they may be called stoloniferous. Most running ornamental grasses are rhizomatous. Stoloniferous growth is more common among turf grasses and weedy species, such as crab grasses, *Digitaria* species.

Appropriately utilized, running grasses can minimize maintenance. Their ability to knit together and cover large areas often makes them the best choice for groundcover use and soil stabilization. Running grasses are able to fill in gaps that may appear in a planting due to physical damage or disease, and many are so dense and strong in their growth that they keep weeds from establishing. In extremely difficult sites, such as urban traffic island, running grasses are often the most practical choice. Some running types, such as gold-edged cord grass, *Spartina pectinata* 'Aureomarginata', are tolerant of moist or wet soils and can be ideal for holding streambanks and margins of ponds or storm water retention basins.

Planted in the wrong situation, running grasses can cause serious problems in the garden. They can completely overpower less vigorous neighbors and turn once-diverse borders into absolute monocultures. Before planting a strongly running grass, carefully consider whether adjacent plantings and hardscapes are sturdy enough to contain its spread, and whether someone will have the time and energy for "editing" out its advances into unwanted areas.

The vigor of running species varies radically with climate and cultural conditions in the garden. For example, a warm-season spreader like giant reed, *Arundo donax*, may be unmanageable in a small garden in sunny Georgia, whereas the short, cool season of a Connecticut garden may slow it to the point that it behaves more like a clumping grass.

Clumping grasses essentially remain in place. They may slowly increase in girth, but new shoots will not appear at distances from the clump. Grasses that produce tight clumps may also be referred to as tufted, caespitose, or bunchgrasses. Though clump-forming grasses may take many years to reach mature size, the ultimate space they consume in the garden is more predictable, and for this reason they are often easier to design with than running types. Because they are not able to fill in large gaps between individual plants, however, they can sometimes require more long-term maintenance than running grasses when used as groundcovers, as happens with groundcover plantings of blue fescue, *Festuca glauca*.

A few grasses do not fit neatly into either the running or clumping categories. The growth habit of Hakone grass, *Hakonechloa macra*, has been variously described as caespitose or spreading. This grass increases by rhizomes and is capable of continuous spread if cultural conditions are ideal, yet its rate of increase is often so modest that, for most gardeners, it is a clump-former in the practical sense. Switch grass, *Panicum virgatum*, is another grass that is somewhere between strictly clump-forming and running. Its rhizomes occasionally stray noticeably from the clump, yet for most intents and purposes it is a clumping grass.

The running or clumping nature of grasses can vary between species belonging to the same genus. As examples, the genera *Miscanthus* and *Pennisetum* each include strictly clumping species and aggressively running species.

Planting and Mulching Techniques

Generally, planting grasses is just like planting other garden perennials. The root systems of container-grown plants should be loosened up before planting, and grasses should be thoroughly watered when planted and until they become established. Spring planting is suitable for most grasses, though cool-season growers often do well planted in autumn.

Grasses are sensitive to soil level, especially when young. Ideally, the crown of the grass should sit just slightly above the soil surface. Planting too low can rot grasses and planting too high can cause them to dry out and die.

Spacing of grasses has less to do with culture than design. Smaller grasses are relatively easy to transplant, so if the gardener's budget and energies allow, young plants can be spaced densely for quick effect and then re-arranged as they attain size. This approach is less practical with large grasses, which can require significant effort to move once established.

Grasses in native habitats are generally quite capable of establishing themselves in exposed soils; however, in the garden, mulch of all sorts can be an efficient method of controlling weeds and conserving soil moisture. Many species, such as the smaller fescues, *Festuca* species; the beard grasses, *Andropogon* species; and little bluestem, *Schizachyrium scoparium*, cannot tolerate having mulch pushed up around their crowns, a practice that often promotes rot and disease at the base of the plant. Mulching is most helpful to moisture-loving species, including many of the sedges and wood-rushes.

Young grass plants can be difficult to tell apart. Until one learns to recognize them reliably from their vegetative characters, it is wise to label plants or to sketch simple planting charts to record identities.

Weeding

Keeping ornamental grasses free of weeds can be uniquely perplexing since the weeds are often unwanted grasses that can be difficult to distinguish from young plants of ornamental species. This is especially true when grasses are small and when they are not in flower. It pays to be diligent about removing weedy grasses at least until newly planted ornamentals have achieved some size and distinction. When attempting to distinguish weed grasses based on vegetative characters, look for differences in their ligules, leaf color, width, and general roughness, smoothness or hairiness.

Even when ornamental grasses are mature, unwanted seedlings of other grasses sometimes germinate inside a clump. These should be pulled out by hand when they are noticed. It is easiest to do this when the soil is wet. If neglected for too long, weed seedlings can be impossible to remove unless the ornamental plant is lifted and divided.

Broad-leaf herbicides may be used around grasses; however, herbicides intended for weed grasses are often equally effective at eradicating ornamental species.

Invasiveness

The potential invasiveness of ornamental grasses is best approached from two perspectives: grasses that are invasive in the garden and those that can invade large ecosystems.

In the garden, grasses can occasionally become a nuisance due to aggressive running or by self-sowing. Although running species that have exceeded their welcome can require genuine effort to remove, they can usually be moved by mechanical means, with hand tools, such as spades and shovels. A few running species, once established, can be nearly impossible to remove without the use of strong herbicides. Examples are *Arundo plinii* and spreading fountain grass, *Pennisetum incomptum*. There are situations where such species may be appropriate, as in the contained spaces of traffic islands or parking lots, or in decorative containers in residential gardens, but it is important to remain aware of their invasive potential.

Although annual grasses have perhaps earned their reputation for self-sowing, perennial grasses, which are the sole subject of this book, are for the most part well behaved in the garden. There are a few simple ways to minimize maintenance necessary because of self-sown grasses.

Removing the inflorescences of grasses before seeds ripen is the surest way to eliminate self-sowing, but this method robs the winter garden of considerable beauty. If inflorescences are allowed to remain into winter, they should be cut back when they lose their visual appeal. This will at least reduce the number of seeds that reach the ground. When unwanted seedlings appear, they should be scratched out with the side of a trowel or small hoe before they have the chance to develop tenacious root systems.

Another way of avoiding grass seedlings is to select species and cultivars that are not capable of producing fertile seed in your region or climate. Details in the encyclopedia entries will help gardeners make these choices.

Grasses that self-sow to a minor extent can easily be managed with proper techniques. These seedlings of wild-oats, *Chasmanthium latifolium* should be scratched out when they are noticed.

The potential of ornamental grasses to become invasive in larger ecosystems is a serious, complicated issue involving many unknowns. The capacity for invasiveness in any given species can vary radically due to subtle genetic distinctions between populations and regional differences in soils, climates, and unrelated habitat disturbance. A few ornamental grasses have already become seriously invasive in certain parts of the world, yet these species are completely innocuous elsewhere. For example, giant reed, *Arundo donax*, has widely escaped and established itself in moist habitats in southern California; however, it rarely flowers and sets fertile seed in the northern states, and consequently poses little threat to native ecosystems there. Widely popular across the United States, *Miscanthus sinensis* is a serious invasive in moist bottomlands in the warm Southeast, yet it is completely benign in the many northern regions where seasons are too short for flowers or seeds to mature. Species need not be exotic to become problems. Of cosmopolitan distribution, common reed, *Phragmites australis*, is an opportunistic native species. Once balanced with many eastern North American plant communities, it has spread aggressively across vast areas since habitat disturbances, such as dredging, channeling, and waste discharge, have created conditions destructive to other once-native species but still tolerable to the reed.

Ethically responsible gardeners and horticultural professionals will seek ways to enjoy grasses and other introduced plants while protecting the remaining integrity of regional ecologies. Additional research to determine the relative fertility of existing ornamental grasses is much needed, and there is a wonderful potential for breeders and selectors to develop sterile cultivars for garden use.

Cutting Back and Burning

Most grasses contribute years of beauty to the garden with little maintenance other than being cut back once a year. As a rule, late winter or early spring is the best time to cut back grasses, when the first signs of new growth are apparent. Though gardening tradition commonly involves shearing everything to the ground as a means of "putting the garden neatly to bed" at the end of the growing season, this habit developed from a perception that the garden in winter had little to offer. Ornamental grasses are forcing a re-evaluation of this notion. Winter can truly be one of the peak seasons in gardens full of ornamental grasses and, for this reason alone, spring cutting is more rewarding. Grasses left standing though the cold season do much to keep the garden alive and dynamic. They continue to move with winter winds; they enhance the detail and beauty of frosts and snows; and they provide food and shelter for wildlife. From a purely practical standpoint, the stems and foliage from the past season often provide the crown of the grass with some protection from ice and cold.

Smaller grasses and a few larger grasses may be easily trimmed back with hand pruners. Always wear gloves (at least on the hand opposite the pruning hand) to protect from cuts. A few grasses, including *Miscanthus*, have sharp leaf margins that can cause cuts to unprotected hands and face. Manual hedge shears work well for trimming smaller grasses but are less precise than hand pruners. Electric hedge shears can make quick work of cutting back both large grasses and groundcover plantings of smaller species. An inexpensive bow saw can be a surprisingly efficient alternative to electric shears for cutting back large, thick-stemmed grasses. Power string trimmers and chain saws usually cause messy shattering and necessitate tedious clean-up.

Many evergreen grasses and sedges do not need to be cut back yearly and may grow attractively for several years with just minor grooming. One's fingers can be used to comb gently through the grasses and to pull out old or discolored foliage.

Though grasses in native habitats grow perfectly well without anyone to cut them back, they have often, over millennia, had the benefit of fire as a renewing agent. The efficacy of periodic firing of restored prairies and large meadow gardens is well proven; however, this is a potentially hazardous activity that is best undertaken only by institutions and individuals with considerable safety support.

Small-scale controlled burning of ornamental grasses in residential gardens can be practical if proper caution is exercised and local burning ordinances are observed. Many grasses, especially *Miscanthus*, burn with surprising intensity. When burning grasses, choose a calm day in late winter or early spring and keep a watering hose within reach. Ensure that children and pets are at a safe distance, and also check grasses for active bird nests and beneficial insect egg cases. Do not attempt to burn grasses if they are close to shrubs or trees, especially conifers.

A simple bow saw is useful for cutting back large, thick-stemmed grasses, such as *Miscanthus*..

In mid-March, horticulturist Harold Taylor uses electric hedge shears to trim a groundcover sweep of golden meadow-foxtail, *Alopecurus pratensis* 'Variegatus', at Longwood Gardens.

Dividing and Transplanting Techniques

Like many herbaceous perennials, older ornamental grasses may eventually begin to die at their centers and become unsightly and weak. Many can be easily renewed by division and transplanting. Grass plants made by division are best produced from the new outer growth, which is usually the strongest, healthiest material.

It is best to lift small and medium-sized grasses from the ground with a strong trowel or sharp spade and use a knife or narrow-edged trowel to divide them. Discard dead material from the center and thoroughly water divisions immediately following transplanting.

A sharp sturdy spade, not a shovel, is essential for dividing and managing the largest grasses. Mature specimens are often too big and heavy to be lifted in one piece and must be sectioned in the ground with a spade before they can be lifted. Unless one is working around buried electrical lines, the best type of spade is one constructed entirely of modern steel alloys, which are light but exceptionally strong. Some manufacturers offer spades with cushioning rubber foot pads at the top of the blade. This type of tool is comfortable to use when cutting into the roots of grasses and is strong enough to be used to lever heavy divisions out of the ground.

The centers of ornamental grasses may eventually die as plants age. This division through an old clump of ravenna grass, *Saccharum ravennae*, reveals dark brown dead growth.

The soil has been washed from this still-dormant young plant of *Miscanthus sinensis* 'Morning Light' to show the fibrous root system and the new culms developed at the margins of the clump. Grass plants made by division are best produced from the new outer growth, which is usually the strongest, healthiest material.

A knife or narrow-edged trowel is useful for dividing small and medium-sized grasses.

For dividing larger grasses, a steel spade is both light and exceptionally strong. The rubber foot pads at the top of the blade are for cushioning.

If its blade is kept sharpened, a quality spade is the ideal tool for dicing large grasses into manageable-sized pieces.

Propagating

To start perennial grasses from seed it is usually best to sow seeds in pots or flats in a cold frame or greenhouse, and then transplant young seedlings into the garden. Most may be sown in late winter or early spring and planted out after they reach a few inches in height and the danger of killing frosts is past. Larger meadow plantings may be direct-seeded, but require thorough, prior preparation of soil and additional effort to control weeds until desired grasses germinate and become established. Germination rates vary widely. Some grasses germinate in a few days, others take weeks or months, and certain species require periods of cold before they become capable of germination. Seed propagation of species is one way of ensuring a genetic diversity in the garden and in habitat restoration.

Many of the most ornamental grasses are selections that must be propagated vegetatively if they are to retain the special characteristics of the named variety. These are referred to as clonal cultivars. Nursery plant and seed catalogs only occasionally differentiate cultivars that must be maintained as clones from others that are suitable for seed propagation. If in doubt, it is best to assume that cultivars should be propagated by vegetative means. Seedlings of clonal cultivars may prove desirable and ornamental in new ways, but cannot honestly be represented as the original named variety.

Division is the preferred means of vegetative propagation for ornamental grasses and is usually best done when grasses are in active growth. Some grasses may also be rooted from stem cuttings or produced by tissue culturing.

To date, very few ornamental grasses have been patented or trademarked; however, these practices are likely to increase. Patented grasses may not legally be propagated for sale unless licensed by the patent holder. Trademarks (usually indicated by ™ or ®) do not exclude others from propagating plants, but restrict the commercial use of the trademark to the legal holder of the mark, or others licensed by the holder.

Cutting Grasses for Fresh and Dried Bouquets

The flowers and foliage of ornamental grasses make unusual, delightful additions to dried and fresh flower arrangements. The delicate, airy texture of their inflorescences is often the perfect foil for garden flowers and other bold-textured material. Cut grass inflorescences for fresh bouquets just before they fully open. They will open quickly in the arrangement, displaying their freshest colors, and subsequent shattering of small parts will be reduced. Leafy stalks of grasses, particularly of variegated cultivars, can dramatically brighten bouquets and last quite a while if kept supplied with water. Grasses may also be cut through autumn and winter to become beautifully enduring components of dried bouquets.

Mature plants of *Achnatherum calamagrostis* are dramatic in plantings at the Westpark, Munich, Germany, in late August.

CHAPTER 7

Encyclopedia of Grasses, Sedges, Rushes, Restios, Cat-tails, and Selected Bamboos

ENTRIES for individual genera and species are in alphabetical order by scientific name in bold italic type, followed immediately by the author name(s). In the case of genus entries, the description is preceded by the common and scientific names of the family to which the genus belongs, and by the common name(s) of the genus, if any. In the case of species entries, the description is preceded by synonyms of the species, if any, in brackets, and the common name(s) of the species, if any, in order of importance in popular usage. If a genus or species name appears to be missing from this alphabetical listing, it may be because the name has changed. To find the current name, look up the "missing" name in the Index of Botanical Names, where a cross-reference points to the correct entry. Cultivar names are in bold type enclosed by single quotation marks. Synonyms for cultivars, if any, follow the current name and are enclosed in parentheses. Translations of cultivar names originating outside the English language are also enclosed in parentheses, but unlike true synonyms, are neither capitalized (unless referring to a proper noun) nor enclosed in single quotation marks. For a full discussion of botanical names, see Chapter 3, "The Names of Grasses."

Achnatherum P. Beauvois.

Grass family, Poaceae.
Needle grass.

Densely tufted, clump-forming species from central and southern Europe, eastern Asia, and western North America, the majority split from the genus *Stipa*. The common name alludes to the numerous awns on the florets, a characteristic *Achnatherum* shares with *Stipa* and one that contributes to the feathery, luminescent qualities of the inflorescences. Most species are cool-season growers, freely flowering in spring or early summer, and often remaining attractive for months. They are most beautiful in areas with strong summer sun but cool nights and low humidity.

Achnatherum calamagrostis (Linnaeus) P. Beauvois.

[*Stipa calamagrostis* (Linnaeus) Wahlenberg].
Silver spike grass, silver spear grass.

Native to high-elevation clearings in central and southern Europe. One of the most graceful, free-flowering mid-sized ornamental grasses if provided plenty of sunlight, low humidity, and cool summer nights. Clump-forming and densely tufted, increasing slowly in girth. Produces a fountain of refined, medium-green foliage topped in June or July by full but equally fine-textured silver-green inflorescences. To 3 ft. (1 m) tall in bloom. The flowers turn beautifully tawny by August and remain attractive entirely through winter in milder climates. They make excellent cut material. The foliage turns mostly yellow in autumn, remaining slightly evergreen in mild climates and going fully dormant in colder regions. Unmanageably floppy in regions with warm summer nights and high humidity, or if grown in more than light shade. Grows best in well-drained soils with even moisture and low to average fertility. Showy enough for specimen use, also superb in drifts and sweeps. Propagate by seed or by division in spring. Zone 5.

'Lemperg'. Slightly more compact than the type. Propagate by division.

Achnatherum calamagrostis flowers are silver-green when they first open.

Achnatherum coronatum (Thurber) Barkworth.

[*Stipa coronata* Thurber].
Needle grass.

Native to dry, sunny, gravelly, rocky slopes and chaparral areas at elevations to 5000 ft. (1500 m) mostly in southern California. Flowers in spring, on upright culms

Achnatherum coronatum in early July at the University of California, Berkeley, Botanical Garden.

3–6 ft. (1–2 m) tall. Tufted, leaves mostly basal. Attractive and especially suited to sunny, dry sites. Propagate by seed. Zone 8.

Achnatherum extremiorientale (Hara) Keng.

[*Achnatherum pekinense* (Hance) Ohwi, *Stipa extremiorientalis* Hara, *Stipa sibirica* (Linnaeus) Lamarck].
Eastern feather grass.

This native of Japan, China, Korea, and Siberia is uncommon in cultivation but deserves further experimentation. In Japan it grows upright, to 5 ft. (1.5 m) tall at the edges of woods and grassy slopes in the mountains, flowering in mid to late summer. Vaguely resembles *Stipa gigantea;* however, the inflorescences are much more green, open, and airy, the leaves deeper green, to 5/8 in. (15 mm) wide. Best in fertile soils with regular moisture, in sun or part shade. Propagate by seed or division. Zone 7, possibly colder.

Achnatherum hymenoides (Roemer & Schultes) Barkworth.

[*Oryzopsis hymenoides* (Roemer & Schultes) Ricker].
Indian rice grass, sand grass, silky grass.

Once an important food grain for native peoples of the American Southwest. Native to northern Mexico and from California to British Columbia on well-drained or sandy soils in desert shrublands, sagebrush, and pinyon/juniper woodlands, this delicate, airy grass has suffered from severe habitat destruction due to cattle grazing. Fine textured, to 2 ft. (60 cm) tall, it is a cool-season grower, producing attractive, open flower panicles in early spring and going dormant for summer. Grows well in extremely dry situations. Will succumb to excess moisture. Propagate by seed. Zone 8.

Achnatherum speciosum (Trinius & Ruprecht) Barkworth.

[*Stipa speciosa* Trinius & Ruprecht].
Desert needle grass.

Native to desert communities from California to Colorado, south to Mexico and South America, this long-lived grass can get by on 5–10 in. (12–25 cm) annual rainfall. The extremely fine foliage forms a rounded basal tuft that turns from gray-green in spring and summer to rich tans

Achnatherum extremiorientale flowering in late July at André Viette's trial garden in Fishersville, Virginia.

Achnatherum speciosum in mid-June at the Santa Barbara Botanic Garden, California.

and light browns in winter. Narrow flower panicles appear in early spring and remain fluffy into summer. Makes a great textural foil for bold cacti and other desert succulents. Propagate by seed. Zone 8.

Achnatherum splendens (Trinius) Nevski.
[*Stipa splendens* Trinius].
Chee grass.

Native to steppes and semidesert sands, gravels, stony slopes, and alkaline areas in central Asia and Siberia, sometimes forming the basis of large vegetation groups known as chee grass associations. This stately grass can reach 8 ft. (2.4 m) tall in flower. A June to July bloomer, it produces open, feathery, purplish pink panicles held high on slender stalks above a large basal mound of slightly gray-green narrow foliage. The inflorescences fade to tan color but remain intact and attractive. A true cool-season grower that likes full sun but needs lower nighttime temperatures. As in its native habitat, it can thrive in alkaline or gravelly soils in the garden, an attribute sometimes particularly valuable in England. A magnificent specimen or focal point. Semi-evergreen in milder climates. Best propagated by seed. Zone 7.

Alopecurus Linnaeus.
Grass family, Poaceae.
Foxtail grass.

From the Greek *alopex* (fox) and *oura* (tail), referring to the soft, cylindrical flower panicles. Comprised of nearly 30 annual and perennial species native to north temperate regions and temperate South America. Most are meadow and pasture species of little ornamental value. Only the variegated form of the common foxtail grass, *Alopecurus pratensis*, is ornamentally significant.

Alopecurus pratensis Linnaeus.
Meadow foxtail, common foxtail grass.

This perennial meadow species is a Eurasian native that has naturalized over much of northern North America. It forms dense tufts to 3 ft. (1 m) tall in flower and spreads slowly by rhizomes. A cool-season grower, it is nearly evergreen in mild temperate climates. The typical form of the species has solid-green leaves and is rarely grown ornamentally.

'Variegatus' ('Aureovariegatus', 'Aureus'). Golden meadow foxtail, variegated foxtail grass, gold-variegated foxtail grass. Among the most colorful yellow-leaved grasses. Shorter-growing than the species, with a flowering height of only 2 ft. (60 cm). The narrow leaves vary from bright green with vivid yellow longitudinal stripes to nearly solid yellow, producing an overall golden effect, especially when back-lit or side-lit. Yellow color is most intense when plants are grown in full sun, although half-shaded

Achnatherum speciosum adds rich tans and browns to the early February landscape at the University of California, Berkeley, Botanical Garden.

Achnatherum splendens at flowering peak in mid-July in Beth Chatto's garden in Colchester, England.

plantings are still a pleasing chartreuse. Nearly evergreen in mild temperate climates. Flowers in late April or May are of minimal ornamental value. Often best to cut plants back to about 5 in. (12 cm) when flowering begins. This helps retain foliage color in summer, when this cool-season grower tends to go lax and semi-dormant, especially in warm, humid climates. If uncut, the flowers and foliage become unsightly by July or August. Colorful, new growth resumes with the subsiding of summer's heat, and plants remain attractive until temperatures drop to freezing. A reliable performer of easy culture, tolerant of a wide range of soil types and moisture conditions. Effective as a color accent or in large groundcover sweeps. Propagate by division in spring or fall; the variegation does not come true from seed. Zone 4.

Ammophila Host.

Grass family, Poaceae.
Beach grass, dune grass.

From the Greek *ammos* (sand) and *philos* (loving), referring to the preferred habitat. Two species of coarse, strongly rhizomatous warm-season grasses, one native to coastal Europe and northern Africa, the other to eastern coastal North America. Not truly ornamentals, but critical to the stabilization of coastal dunes. New shoots produced from the rhizomes allow these grasses to survive burial by shifting dune sands, but they do not withstand foot-traffic. Both are salt-tolerant. Selected forms are usually propagated by division, and planted 1 ft. (30 cm) deep.

Alopecurus pratensis 'Variegatus' is colorfully back-lit in mid-May at Longwood Gardens.

Ammophila arenaria (Linnaeus) Link.

European beach grass, European dune grass.

Native to coastal Europe and northern Africa. The species epithet means "of the sand." This adaptable, aggressively running species has been widely employed for erosion control in dunes and other sandy soils, and has unfortunately displaced native dune grasses, especially on the West Coast of North America. Although also introduced to the East Coast, it has not proved as adapted as the North American beach grass and has not persisted. Zone 5.

Ammophila breviligulata Fernald.

American beach grass, American dune grass.

Native to eastern coastal North America and essential to the character of eastern sandy beaches and dunes. It has proved better-adapted in its native region than the introduced European beach grass. Cultivars based on provenance are available for different regions. Plant divisions anytime from mid-October to mid-April, except when ground is frozen. Do not plant in summer. Zone 5.

'Cape'. A superior selection from Cape Cod, Massachusetts. Performs best from Maine, south through the mid-Atlantic states.

'Hatteras'. Performs better than 'Cape' in southern areas.

Ampelodesmos Link.

Grass family, Poaceae.
Mauritania vine reed.

Comprised of a single species native to the coastal Mediterranean.

Ampelodesmos mauritanicus (Poiret) T. Durand & Schinz.

Mauritania vine reed.

The botanical and common names refer to early use of the leaves of this plant to tie together grapevines. Strictly clump-forming. Tender but majestically imposing, forming a huge fine-textured mound of evergreen foliage from which strikingly upright, mostly one-sided panicles arise in spring or summer. To 9 ft. (2.7 m) tall in flower. Remains attractive through winter. A superb focal point for sunny spot. Propagate by seed or by division in spring. Zone 8.

Andropogon Linnaeus.
Grass family, Poaceae.
Beard grass.

From the Greek *aner* (man) and *pogon* (beard), referring to the silky hairs on the flower spikelets of some species. Comprised of more than 100 species of annual and perennial grasses native from tropical regions to temperate North America. The important ornamental species are all clump-forming, warm-season North American natives. Most flower in late summer and enliven autumn and winter landscapes with rich, long-lasting orange, red, and copper colors. All are deciduous and are best cut back in late winter or early spring. Propagate by seed or by division in spring.

Andropogon gerardii Vitman.
Big bluestem, turkey foot.

Occurs on moist and dry soils, in prairies and open woods, from central Mexico throughout much of the United States and into Canada. Neil Diboll of Wisconsin's Prairie Nursery rightly refers to this regal species as the "monarch of the prairie grasses." The tallest North American member of the genus, it grows 5–8 ft. (1.5–2.4 m) tall. Upright and strictly clump-forming, leaves to 3/8 in. (9 mm) wide, green or blue-green in summer, reliably turning rich orange and copper-red in autumn, sometimes with deep burgundy tints. Terminal inflorescences appear in late August or early September, opening red and turning darker with age, three-parted and vaguely resembling an upside-down turkey foot. They are interesting but not showy. The main appeal of this grass is its lush summer foliage and fall and winter color. In the garden, the size and upright stature can be quite dramatic. Ideal for deciduous screening, naturalizing, meadow gardens, and prairie restorations. May grow lax and floppy if shaded. Adapted to a wide range of soil and moisture conditions. Propagate by seed or by division in spring. A sturdy, long-lived grass. Zone 3.

Andropogon glomeratus (Walter) BSP.
[*Andropogon virginicus* var. *abbreviatus* (Hackel) Fernald].
Bushy beard grass.

Inhabits low, moist ground, marshes, and swamps in the eastern coastal United States. Typically 2–4 ft. (60–120 cm) tall. Foliage to 3/8 in. (9 mm) wide, green in summer, turning copper-orange in autumn. Flowers in September, enclosed in densely clustered bushy bracts at the top of the stems. Flowering stems very attractive on the plant and in cut or dried arrangements. Differs from other *Andropogon* species in this book in its preference for moist or nearly wet sites. Grows in garden soils of aver-

Ampelodesmos mauritanicus is still magnificent in February at the University of California, Berkeley, Botanical Garden.

Andropogon gerardii beginning to flower in mid-August in southern Germany.

Andropogon gerardii contributes rich copper tones to a Chicago prairie restoration in late October, along with frost asters.

age moisture, but not drought tolerant. Full sun to very light shade. Sturdy and upright, retaining its fall color long through winter. Propagate by seed or by division in spring. Zone 5.

Andropogon glomeratus var. _scabriglumis_ C. S. Campbell.
Southwestern bushy beard grass.

Native to moist open areas and seeps from California to New Mexico. Taller than the eastern variety of bushy beard grass, to 5 ft. (1.5 m) in height. Zone 7.

Andropogon gyrans Ashe.
[*Andropogon elliottii* Chapman].
Elliott's broom-sedge, Elliott's beard grass.

Found on dry or moist fields and open woods in the eastern states, often with broom-sedge, *Andropogon virginicus*, from which it differs in having the inflorescences clustered at the upper portion of the stem, surrounded by broad, showy sheaths. Green in summer, the culms and sheaths turn vivid orange in late autumn and winter, and are quite striking. Stands through repeated snows. Strictly clump-forming, 2–3 ft. (60–90 cm) tall. Best in groups, sweeps, or meadow gardens in full sun or very light shade. Drought tolerant. Grows on poor soils. Cut stems suitable

Andropogon glomeratus growing native in coastal New Jersey in mid-October.

Andropogon glomeratus var. *scabriglumis* in late February at the Santa Barbara Botanic Garden, California.

for dry arrangements. Does not tolerate heavy mulch at base. Propagate by seed or by division in spring. Zone 5.

Andropogon ternarius Michaux.
Split-beard broom-sedge.

Native from southern Delaware, often on sandy soils along the coastal plain to Florida and Texas, but also on clay soils from Georgia to Missouri. Similar enough to *Andropogon virginicus* to be mistaken for it until the flowers appear, held out from the stems on conspicuous slender stalks. Inflorescences very silvery when dry, especially attractive back-lit. Summer foliage often glaucous blue-green, turning shades of purple-bronze, copper, and red in fall. A beautiful, under-appreciated grass. Worth growing for cut flowers alone, especially dried. Full sun. Drought tolerant. Does not tolerate heavy mulch at base. Propagate by seed or by division in spring. Zone 6.

Detail of *Andropogon ternarius* naturally back-lit in late October.

Andropogon gyrans in early January in the managed meadow garden at Longwood Gardens.

Andropogon ternarius in late November in the author's garden.

Andropogon virginicus Linnaeus. Broom-sedge, beard grass.

Ranges over much of North America on open ground, old fields, and sterile hills, on dense or sandy soils. Upright, strictly clump-forming, to 4 ft. (1.2 m) tall in flower. Stems and leaves green in summer, suffused dark red-purple when flowers first appear in September, turning bright orange in late fall, the color persisting through winter and into the following spring. Inflorescences attractively silver when back-lit. Rarely noticed in summer, this grass is primarily responsible (along with little bluestem, *Schizachyrium scoparium*) for the tawny-orange winter color of many old fields and pastures. Stunning in vast sweeps. Not for the formal garden, but a fine addition to meadow gardens, natural areas, highway medians, and embankments. Requires full sun and is longest lived on relatively infertile soils. Extremely drought tolerant. Does not tolerate heavy mulch at base. Propagate by seed or by division in spring. Zone 3.

Andropogon virginicus in late October on Longwood Gardens peripheral grounds.

Detail of *Andropogon virginicus* naturally back-lit in late November.

Andropogon virginicus in sweeps along a Georgia highway embankment in late January.

Anemanthele Veldkamp.
Grass family, Poaceae.
New Zealand wind grass.
Native to New Zealand. Split from *Stipa*.

Anemanthele lessoniana (Steudel) Veldkamp.
[*Stipa arundinacea* (Hooker f.) Bentham, *Oryzopsis lessoniana* (Steudel) Veldkamp].
New Zealand wind grass, pheasant's-tail grass.

This New Zealand endemic occurs at the edges of small streams at elevations to 1500 ft. (640 m). Rarely grown outside its home country and England, it deserves wider attention. Forms a dense tussock of arching, fine-textured, semi-evergreen foliage that is medium green in summer, with various gold and orange tints appearing in autumn and winter. In early summer, slight, feathery inflorescences arch outward just above the leaves, to 3 ft. (1 m). Flower and foliage colors best in full sun, but tolerate partial shade. Propagate by seed or by division in spring.

'Autumn Tints'. Leaves flushed deep red-orange in late summer.

'Gold Hue'. Leaves flushed gold in late summer.

Aristida Linnaeus.
Grass family, Poaceae.
Three-awn.

Comprised of more than 300 species of bunchgrasses native to warmer, usually arid parts of the world. A few species are noxious weeds.

Anemanthele lessoniana in flower in early July at Great Dixter, East Sussex, England.

Aristida purpurea Nuttall.
Purple three-awn.

Native to dry areas across the North American plains and into northern Mexico. Very variable and often segregated into numerous botanical varieties. Foliage green or sometimes glaucous-blue. Erect-growing, to $2^1/2$ ft. (80 cm) tall. Flowering stems strongly purple-tinted in late summer and fall. A beautiful component of dry grasslands, especially when the conspicuous long awns catch the autumn light. Smaller groupings can enhance arid-region gardens, but self-sowing can be a nuisance. Full sun. Does not tolerate moist conditions. Propagate easily by seed. Zone 6.

Arrhenatherum P. Beauvois.
Grass family, Poaceae.
Oat grass.

From the Greek *arren* (male) and *ather* (awn), referring to the bristled staminate (male) flowers. Comprised of six perennial species in Europe, Africa, and Asia, only one of which is grown ornamentally.

Aristida purpurea in January in southern California.

Arrhenatherum elatius* subsp. *bulbosum (Willdenow) Schübel & Martens.
[*Arrhenatherum bulbosum* (Willdenow) C. Presl].
Tuber oat grass, false-oat.

Native to Europe. Produces conspicuous bulbous storage organs at the base of the stems, which root readily to produce new plants. Green-leaved plants are rarely cultivated for ornament and can be invasive; however, the variegated cultivar is well behaved and is among the brightest whites of all the grasses.

'Variegatum'. Striped tuber oat grass. Clear white longitudinal stripes dominate dark green leaves, so that the plant appears nearly all-white from a few feet away. This cool-season grower is stunning in climates with dry summers and cool nights, where it produces a neat mound of spreading foliage to 1 ft. (30 cm) tall, remaining attractive into winter. In humid, hot areas where night temperatures remain high, it is often afflicted with foliar rust diseases by midsummer, becoming very unattractive and often going completely dormant. Partial shade minimizes summer stress and does not affect intensity of variegation. New foliage appears in fall, and the plants are again beautiful going into winter. Mildly attractive flowers produced on upright stems in summer only in cooler climates. Needs frequent division, best in spring or fall, to remain vigorous and attractive. An excellent subject for display in pots. Zone 4.

Arrhenatherum elatius subsp. *bulbosum* 'Variegatum' in late May with *Brunnera macrophylla* 'Langtrees'.

Arundo Linnaeus.
Grass family, Poaceae.

From the Latin *arundo* (reed). Comprised of three species, all strongly rhizomatous, warm-season growers native mostly to damp places and riverbanks from the Mediterranean to eastern Asia.

Arundo donax Linnaeus.
Giant reed.

Long a source of reeds for wind instruments, this Mediterranean native grows larger and taller than any other grass hardy in cool temperate regions, excepting the bamboos. Even in regions like the northeastern United States where it dies to the ground each winter, it can attain 14 ft. (4.2 m) tall in a single season. It may reach 18 ft. (5.5 m) tall in warm regions where it remains evergreen. Stems upright, leaves coarse, gray-green, to 3 in. (7.5 cm) wide.

Arundo donax flowering in late October at Longwood Gardens.

Strongly spreading by thick rhizomes (see Figure 2-3). Foot-tall inflorescences top the culms at summer's end, opening with a pink cast and drying to silver. Full and fluffy, the inflorescences are dramatic in the landscape and in dried arrangements. Requires a long warm season for flower production, but worth growing in other areas for the bold stems and leaves. E. A. Bowles called it "the king of grasses for foliage effect." Leaves brown with freezing temperatures, becoming tattered by winter winds, at which time the plants are best cut to the ground. Striking as a specimen or screen planting. Young plants are ideal container specimens. Full sun promotes growth and flowering, but the sturdy stems remain upright even in somewhat shady garden spots. Not particular as to soils or fertility. Drought tolerant, yet also tolerates periodic standing water. Sets fertile seed only in warm climates, such as southern California, and there it has become a serious invader of moist native habitats. Old, established specimens require considerable effort to divide, transplant, or remove due to sheer weight and size. Fortunately, the rhizomes are relatively soft, and a sharp spade easily cuts through them. Propagates easily by rooting rhizome pieces. Best divided in spring. Zone 6. Figure 2-3.

'Macrophylla'. Leaves broader and more glaucous than those of the species. Many plants commonly grown in the United States fit this description, but are sold without name.

'Variegata' ('Versicolor'). Striped giant reed. Leaves and stems dramatically striped cream-white. Variegation is brightest white in cool springs, becomes cream-yellow with warmth, and may fade to yellow-green by end of a hot summer. Shorter-growing and more tender than the species. Flowers infrequently. Stunning when grown in a pot. Zone 6.

Arundo formosana Hackel.

Taiwan grass.

Native to Taiwan, where it is usually found on cliffs with somewhat pendent stems, and China. Introduced to the United States from China. Smaller in all parts than *Arundo donax*, growing to 8 ft. (2.4 m) tall with leaves 1/2 in. (12 mm) wide. Bamboolike in appearance, with side-branching of the culms in late season. Inflorescences loose and airy, opening pink, turning buff. Strongly rhizomatous. Has not set viable seed in Indiana trials. Invasive potential unknown. Zone 5.

'Golden Fountain'. Culms and leaves mostly yellow, longitudinally striped green. Shorter-growing. Selected by Crystal Palace Perennials of Illinois.

'Green Fountain'. More rounded than the type. Propagate by cuttings. Plants introduced from China by Jim Waddick.

Arundo plinii Turra.

[*Arundo pliniana* Turra].

A Mediterranean native similar to but smaller in all its parts than *Arundo donax*, more resembling *Phragmites communis*. Attractive, flowering in late summer, but has proved a tenacious runner in trials at Longwood Gardens, and can only be recommended for planting where it will be

A full-sized specimen of *Arundo donax* 'Variegata' in late June in northern Florida.

The exquisite detail of *Arundo donax* 'Variegata' in central Japan in late October.

well contained. Zone 6. An unnamed bluish green form with sharp narrow leaves is often offered commercially. It may represent a semi-permanent juvenile type of growth. It is equally aggressive.

Austrostipa S. W. L. Jacobs & J. Everett.
Grass family, Poaceae.
Australian feather grass.

A genus segregated from *Stipa* and comprised entirely of Australian natives. See *Telopea* 6(5): 579–595 (1996).

Austrostipa elegantissima (Labillardière) S. W. L. Jacobs & J. Everett.
[*Stipa elegantissima* Labillardière].
Australian feather grass, feather spear grass.

Native to temperate Australia. Clump-forming, to 3 ft. (1 m) tall. The airy flower panicles are produced from spring through fall in response to rains. The inflorescences accumulate over the season, drying to silver. Foliage is evergreen in mild climates, but plants look best if cut to the ground each winter. Propagate by seed. Zone 8.

Austrostipa ramosissima (Trinius) S. W. L. Jacobs & J. Everett.
[*Stipa ramosissima* (Trinius) Trinius].
Pillar of smoke, Australian plume grass, stout bamboo grass.

Grows to 8 ft. (2.4 m) tall in moist, well-drained gullies near the edges of forests or woods in its native Australia, flowering most of the year in response to rains. The name pillar of smoke is apt. Upright and clump-forming, this grass blooms nearly continuously in cultivation, producing a dense, towering mass of fine-textured inflorescences. Propagate readily by seed. Zone 8, possibly colder.

Arundo plinii in research trials at Longwood Gardens in early November.

Austrostipa elegantissima in late July at the University of British Columbia Botanical Garden in Vancouver.

Austrostipa ramosissima in mid-December in Berkeley, California.

Bothriochloa Kuntze.
Grass family, Poaceae.

From the Greek *bothrion* (shallow pit) and *chloe* (grass), referring to the pits in the lower glumes of some species. Approximately 28 species of wide distribution in warm temperate to tropical regions. Very closely related to and sometimes included in *Andropogon*. Most species, including the four following, are warm-season growers, deciduous in cold climates.

Bothriochloa barbinodis (Lagasca) Herter.
[*Andropogon barbinodis* Lagasca].
Cane bluestem.

Native on dry slopes and gravelly places in Oklahoma, New Mexico, Texas, and California, south into Mexico. Strictly clump-forming, upright, to 3 ft. (1 m) tall. Blooms anytime from May to October. Inflorescences held above foliage on slender stalks, slender and silver at first, more feathery and translucent at maturity and after drying. Stems lax after flowering. Very drought tolerant. An attractive addition to meadow gardens and naturalistic designs in dry regions. Propagate by seed. Zone 7.

Bothriochloa barbinodis in early flowering stage in July at the Santa Barbara Botanic Garden, California.

Bothriochloa caucasica (Trinius) C. Hubbard.
[*Andropogon caucasicus* Trinius].
Purple beard grass, Caucasian bluestem.

Native to stony slopes, screes, open woods, and riverside gravels in the Russian Caucasus, into Iran and the Himalayas. Clump-forming, but of sprawling habit, especially after flowers are produced in mid to late summer. Otherwise attractive for its terminal purple-pink inflorescences and often blue-green foliage. To 3 ft. (1 m) tall. Propagate by seed or by division in spring. Zone 5.

Bothriochloa ischaemum (Linnaeus) Keng.
[*Andropogon ischaemum* Linnaeus].
Yellow bluestem.

Native to dry places in southern Europe. Similar to *Bothriochloa caucasica* in many respects but finer-textured, branches of the inflorescence fewer. To 2½ ft. (80 cm) tall. Foliage conspicuously blue-green. Summer blooming. Propagate by seed or by division in spring. Zone 5.

Bothriochloa saccharoides (Swartz) Rydberg.
[*Andropogon saccharoides* Swartz].
Silver beard grass, silver bluestem.

Native to prairies, plains, and dry, open places over much of the central and southwestern United States.

Bothriochloa ischaemum flowering in mid-August at the Royal Botanic Gardens, Kew, England.

Clump-forming, of upright stature 3–4 ft. (90–120 cm) tall. Named for the small but conspicuous silver inflorescences, held on slender stalks branching from the stems. Blooms spring into fall. Leaves medium green. Similar in overall appearance to *Andropogon ternarius* and, though not as showy, better adapted to hot drier regions. Foliage turns orange and red in autumn, remaining colorful into winter. Zone 5.

Bouteloua Lagasca.

Grass family, Poaceae.
Grama, grama grass.

Named for Spanish botanist brothers Claudio and Esteban Boutelou. Approximately 28 annual and perennial species native to dry open grasslands in the Americas, from Canada to Argentina. Two are the predominant species of the North American short-grass prairie. Also called the Great Plains, this region is drier than the tall-grass prairie. Both species are clump-forming, warm-season growers with considerable cold-hardiness. They are quite distinct in flowering appearance.

Bouteloua curtipendula (Michaux) Torrey.

Side-oats grama.

Native to North America from Ontario to California, and south to Argentina. The common name refers to the oatlike spikelets, which are held mostly to one side of the inflorescences (see Figure 2-8). The numerous inflorescences arch above the basal mound of gray-green foliage, to a height of 3 ft. (1 m), and are purplish when they first appear in June or July. Continually produced through most of the summer, they bleach to straw color as they

Detail of one-sided inflorescences of *Bouteloua curtipendula* in early August at Longwood Gardens.

A mass planting of *Bouteloua curtipendula* in the North American section of the Berlin-Dahlem Botanic Garden in Germany.

age. Autumn foliage colors include bronze-purple, orange, and red. Requires full sun, but tolerates a range of soils and prolonged drought. Cut back in late autumn. A subtle ornamental, most effective in mass plantings or groupings, especially against contrasting background. A fine addition to a meadow garden but overwhelmed by other grasses in moist settings. Propagates readily by seed or by division in spring. Zone 4. Figure 2-8.

Bouteloua gracilis (HBK) Griffiths.
[*Bouteloua oligostachya* Torrey ex A. Gray].
Blue grama, mosquito grass.

Found mostly on dry plains from Wisconsin to Manitoba, south to southern California and Texas. Usually only 8–15 in. (20–38 cm) tall in full flower, this diminutive grass produces its curious inflorescences in June through September, suspended horizontally like tiny brushes from the tip of each flowering stem. They are strongly red-tinted at first, bleaching to straw color. Best in a sunny garden spot near a path or on top of a ledge, or in a decorative container, where its detail can be appreciated. Can also be planted densely and mowed to 2 in. (5 cm) to provide a water-conserving lawn or groundcover in dry areas. Propagate by seed. Self-sows but is easily managed. Zone 3.

Bouteloua gracilis in mid-September at Kurt Bluemel's nursery in Maryland.

Briza Linnaeus.
Grass family, Poaceae.
Quaking grass.

Comprised of 20 annual and perennial species native to grasslands in temperate Eurasia and South America, and widely introduced elsewhere for their ornamental flower spikelets. *Briza media* and *B. subaristata* are ornamental perennials. Two annual species are also grown: *B. maxima* Linnaeus, greater quaking grass, a Mediterranean native with larger spikelets; and *B. minor* Linnaeus, lesser quaking grass, a Eurasian native with smaller spikelets.

Briza media Linnaeus.
Common quaking grass, rattle grass, pearl grass, shivering grass, trembling grass, cow quakes, didder, totter, dillies, doddering dickies.

A plethora of vernacular names speaks of the broad ability of this grass to entertain and amuse. This Eurasian native is common nearly throughout the British Isles on a variety of soils from light to heavy, dry to damp, and acid to calcareous. A cool-season grower. Diffusely branched

Briza media flower detail in June, showing color tints.

inflorescences appear in May and are tipped with pendent spikelets resembling puffy oats. To $2^1/2$ ft. (80 cm) tall, these are conspicuously attractive in the landscape, rattling and rustling delightfully in spring and summer breezes. They also make superb cut flowers. At first green with tints of red-purple, they bleach to light straw color by midsummer. Cutting them at various stages preserves colors. Clump-forming, producing a dense tuft of soft, deep green, fine-textured foliage that is semi-evergreen even in cold climates. No appreciable fall color. Reliable and easy to grow in full sun or even partial shade. Tolerant of poorly drained, heavy soils and somewhat drought tolerant. Appearance is often improved by removing remaining inflorescences in late summer, which by then are in disarray. Shearing foliage lightly at this time encourages a new flush of autumn growth that remains attractive into winter. Durable and long-lived. Sweeps and masses planted for flower effect also double as groundcovers. Zone 4.

Briza media in early July at Longwood Gardens.

Briza subaristata Lamarck.
[*Briza rotundata* (HBK) Steudel].

An attractive perennial native to hillsides and canyons, bluffs, and openings in forests in mountains around the Mexican Central Plateau. Flowers May to January, on gently nodding stalks to 3 ft. (1 m) tall. Little known as an ornamental, deserves further experiment. Zone 8, possibly colder.

Bromus Linnaeus.
Grass family, Poaceae.
Brome, chess.

From the Greek *bromos* (oat). Approximately 100 species mostly native to north temperate regions.

Bromus inermis Leysser.
Smooth brome.

Perennial with creeping rhizomes. Native to Europe, Siberia, Mongolia, and Manchuria. Naturalized in the western United States where it is often used as a hay and

Briza subaristata in mid-August at the University of California, Berkeley, Botanical Garden.

pasture grass. Of ornamental importance for the following variegated cultivar.

'Skinner's Gold'. Skinner's gold brome. Leaves mostly green-margined with broad, light yellow longitudinal variegation. Flower stalks also yellow-colored, giving a light yellow overall appearance to the plant. To 3 ft. (1 m) tall in flower in midsummer. Propagate by division in spring. Zone 7.

Bromus inermis 'Skinner's Gold' in mid-July in Alan Bloom's garden in Bressingham, England.

Buchloe Engelmann.

Grass family, Poaceae.
Buffalo grass.

Name shortened from *Bubalochloe* (buffalo grass). Comprised of a single perennial species native to the North American Great Plains, as far north as Montana and south into Mexico. Ornamental in that it is a water-conserving, fuel-conserving alternate to typical lawn grasses.

Buchloe dactyloides (Nuttall) Engelmann.

Buffalo grass.

This strongly stoloniferous warm-season grower is rapidly gaining favor as an alternative lawn grass. Naturally drought tolerant and only 4–8 in. (10–20 cm) tall at maturity, new selections have the potential to reduce

A groundcover turf of *Buchloe dactyloides* in mid-November after a full season of foot-traffic at the National Wildflower Research Center in Austin, Texas.

or eliminate watering, fertilizing, and mowing. Deciduous, growing blue-green through warmer seasons and turning golden-brown in winter dormancy. Returns to green earlier in spring than St. Augustine grass or Bermuda grass, and its texture is much finer, more welcoming to bare feet. Withstands considerable foot traffic. Among a minority of dioecious grasses, having male and female flowers on separate plants (see Figure 2-4). May be grown from seed, which produces a mix of male and female plants; however, selections for lawn use are often vegetatively propagated female clones that provide a more uniform appearance. Female plants are also pollen-free. Does best in sun on heavy soils. Does not tolerate constant moisture. Of proven performance in the southwestern United States and showing promise for other areas, including the Northeast. Cultivars are being developed for best performance in various regions. **'Prairie'** and **'609'** grow to 8 in. (20 cm) tall if unmowed. **'Cody'** and **'Tatanka'** are even shorter. Zone 4. Figure 2-4.

Calamagrostis Adanson.
Grass family, Poaceae.
Reed grass.

From the Greek *kalamos* (reed) and *agrostis* (a kind of grass). Comprised of 250 perennial species mostly native to moist areas, including wet woodlands, alpine meadows, beaches, and coastal marshes in north temperate regions. Plants can be promiscuous, and this genus is; occasionally indiscriminate in its sexual unions, producing many taxonomically confounding natural hybrids. Though the Eurasian species are most often seen in gardens, the many beautiful western North American natives deserve to be better known.

Calamagrostis ×acutiflora (Schrader) De Candolle.
Feather reed grass.

This hybrid of *Calamagrostis epigejos* and *C. arundinacea* occurs naturally but infrequently in Europe, and rarely produces viable seed. It and both parent species are upright, cool-season growers. For years plants representing this cross were known as *C. epigejos* 'Hortorum'. The renowned German nurseryman Karl Foerster recognized the hybrid nature and called the plants *C. ×acutiflora* 'Stricta'. Though in use for a few years, the Latinized cultivar name 'Stricta' is not acceptable under nomenclatural rules. 'Karl Foerster' has since been substituted and is the name by which most of the world knows this plant. Side-by-side trials in Longwood Gardens have proved plants sold as 'Stricta' and 'Karl Foerster' to be identical. In the future, if other clonal selections are made with similar hybrid origin, they cannot be called 'Stricta'.

'Karl Foerster' ('Stricta'). Karl Foerster's feather reed grass is understandably one of the most popular ornamental grasses worldwide. It is beautiful, versatile, and nearly care-free. The deep green, lustrous foliage of this cool-season grower is effective by early spring and lasts into winter. Clump-forming and strictly upright, it produces vertical inflorescences to 6 ft. (2 m) tall that are loosely feathered and subtly purplish when they first appear in early summer. By late summer they become narrow vertical plumes of a delicate buff color, remaining upright and attractive through most of winter. Suitable for fresh or dry arrangements. This limber grass is one of the best for introducing motion to the garden; it moves gracefully with even a barely perceptible breeze. Always regains its upright posture even after heavy rains and never needs staking. Stunning as a specimen or vertical accent. An excellent screen due to fast growth, reliability, and multi-season duration. Sterility recommends it for large-scale residential or commercial use without fear of compromising adjacent natural areas. No appreciable fall foliage color. Tolerates a wide range of conditions in full sun or up to half shade. Grows best on well-drained fertile soils with adequate moisture, but tolerates heavy clays. May suffer from disfiguring foliar rust diseases in wet summers, especially if air circulation is poor. Cut back to about 5 in. (12 cm) by early March. Divide or transplant in spring or fall. Plants in containers make attractive specimens and survive most winters without protection. Zone 4.

Calamagrostis ×acutiflora 'Karl Foerster' is open and feathery when first flowering in mid-June in eastern Pennsylvania.

Inflorescences of *Calamagrostis* ×*acutiflora* 'Karl Foerster' constrict to narrow plumes by midsummer.

'Overdam'. Variegated feather reed grass. Similar to 'Karl Foerster' except the foliage is longitudinally cream-white striped, and plants and flowers are less robust. Variegation is most pronounced in climates with low humidity and cool summer nights. Suffers in hot, humid weather. Zone 5.

Calamagrostis arundinacea (Linnaeus) Roth.
Feather reed grass.

Native from Europe to Asia Minor. Unimportant as an ornamental except as one of the parents involved in *Calamagrostis* ×*acutiflora*. Inflorescences not as full and attractive as the hybrid. Runs strongly by rhizomes and self-sows. Zone 5.

Calamagrostis brachytricha Steudel.
[*Calamagrostis arundinacea* var. *brachytricha* (Steudel) Hackel].
Korean feather reed grass.

This species varies considerably across its native range in eastern Asia, where it most frequently occurs in moist woodlands and at the edges of woods. The material in cultivation was originally introduced to Western gardens in 1966 by Dick Lighty of Pennsylvania, who collected

Calamagrostis ×*acutiflora* 'Overdam' in mid-July in Alan Bloom's garden in Bressingham, England.

seed of plants growing wild in Korea. More of a warm-season grower, flowering in September. The inflorescences begin with a strong purple-red tint, fading to silver-gray, remaining open and feathery even when dry, unlike *Calamagrostis* ×*acutiflora* 'Karl Foerster'. Flowers last into winter, suitable for fresh or dry arrangements. Clump-forming, upright-arching in overall form, to 4 ft. (1.2 m) tall in flower. Sometimes attractively lax in growth. Foliage slightly coarse in appearance, with leaves to 1/2 in. (12 mm) wide, glossy green. Fall foliage an undistinguished yellow. Easily grown on a range of soils in partial shade or in full sun if provided with sufficient moisture. Self-sows in moist shady situations to a minor extent but is easily managed. Cut back by late winter. Propagate by seed or by division in spring. Effective as a specimen, in groups or masses. An excellent container subject. Zone 4.

Calamagrostis canadensis (Michaux) P. Beauvois. Bluejoint.

Native to marshes, wet places, open woods, and meadows across much of northern North America. Of minor ornamental importance. Not as fluffy in flower as the Eurasian species and not as well behaved as the clump-forming western U.S. species. Runs strongly by rhizomes and self-sows prolifically. Foliage sometimes burgundy-tinted in autumn. Zone 3.

Calamagrostis brachytricha is tinted red-purple when first flowering in mid-September at Brookside Gardens in Wheaton, Maryland.

A sweep of *Calamagrostis brachytricha* is strong and upright in full sun in late September at the Chicago Botanic Garden, Illinois.

Calamagrostis epigejos (Linnaeus) Roth.
Feather reed grass, wood small-reed, bush grass.

A Eurasian native. In the British Isles it forms thick clumps in wet woodland, scrub, and fens, often growing on heavy soils in England. One of the parents of *Calamagrostis ×acutiflora*, but attractively fuller-flowered and more relaxed in habit. A mildly invasive spreader that self-sows, yet a planting at Longwood Gardens has been maintained for nearly a decade with modest effort, using a spade to remove errant growth every few years and scratching out unwanted seedlings. Zone 5.

Calamagrostis foliosa Kearney.
Mendocino reed grass, leafy reed grass.

A highly ornamental species native to coastal bluffs, cliffs, scrub, and forest in northern California. Tufted and clump-forming, to 2 ft. (60 cm) tall. Blooms May to August, producing arching sprays of feathery flowers above the blue-green foliage. Ideal for sloping sites, forming a floral cascade. In California, prefers light shade, moderate moisture, and good drainage. Foliage semi-evergreen. Propagate by seed or division. Zone 8, possibly colder.

Calamagrostis epigejos in early August at Longwood Gardens.

Calamagrostis nutkaensis (C. Presl) Steudel.
Pacific reed grass.

Native along the Pacific coast in moist soil or wet forested hills from Alaska to central California. Tufted and clump-forming to 3–5 ft. (1–1.5 m) tall. Foliage rather coarse, semi-evergreen in mild climates. Feathery inflorescences open purplish in spring, drying to straw color. Does well in full sun if soil is moist. Somewhat salt-tolerant. A cool-season grower, it may suffer from foliar rusts in over-wet or humid midsummer periods. Propagate by seed or division. Zone 7.

Calamagrostis ophitidus (J. Howell) Nygren.
Serpentine reed grass.

Occurs on serpentine soils in northern California. Tufted and strictly clump-forming to 3 ft. (1 m) tall. Upright in form, resembling *Calamagrostis ×acutiflora* 'Karl Foerster' but more delicate and better adapted to infertile soils in a warm climate. Propagate by seed. Zone 8.

Carex Linnaeus.
Sedge family, Cyperaceae.
Sedge.

In the broad sense, the word *sedge* refers to any of the nearly 3600 species that make up the sedge family, but in the more usual, narrower sense, the word refers to any of nearly 1000 species comprising the huge genus *Carex*. Most ornamental sedge species originate from moist or wet habitats in temperate regions around the world and are often adapted to similar situations in the garden. Otherwise, they are so diverse in color, form, size, growth, and use that it is difficult to speak generally about them.

Calamagrostis foliosa in mid-August in Roger Raiche's garden in Berkeley, California.

Calamagrostis nutkaensis flowering in mid-June at the Santa Barbara Botanic Garden, California.

Flowers are often of minor ornamental importance, but foliage colors match or exceed the diversity found in grasses, including myriad greens, blues, yellows, browns, and oranges as well as bold variegations. Evergreen or deciduous, some sedges form small fountains of fine foliage; others are broad-leaved and quite upright. Many are dense clump-formers; others are strong runners. In the garden they can be specimens, accents, groundcovers, lawns, or container specimens. Most can be propagated by division in late spring. Deciduous types should be cut back annually in spring. Evergreens or semi-evergreens are best cut back occasional years in late spring to remove old or winter-desiccated foliage. The brown-leaved New Zealand species are susceptible to root mealybugs in excessively hot climates.

One certain generalization is that sedges are too little known and too little used in the garden. Some of the best known sedges, such as the true *Carex morrowii* 'Variegata', are among the least exciting, even if durable. Many excellent new ornamentals have been introduced, includ-

Calamagrostis nutkaensis is dramatic in the February landscape at the University of California, Berkeley, Botanical Garden.

Calamagrostis ophitidus in mid-August at the University of California, Berkeley, Botanical Garden.

ing such beautifully refined selections as *C. morrowii* var. *temnolepis* 'Silk Tassel', *C. dolichostachya* 'Kaga Nishiki', and many colorfully unique species from New Zealand. Other established varieties, such as Bowles' intensely yellow *C. elata* 'Aurea', are finding new niches in the water-gardening renaissance. California's John Greenlee and others are experimenting with evergreen, drought-tolerant sedges as lawn substitutes.

Carex albula Allan.
Blonde sedge, frosted curls sedge, frosty curls sedge.

One of the best and most distinctive New Zealand natives, producing cascading fountains of the finest-textured foliage. So light green it appears silver from a short distance. Best planted on slopes, in pots, or other places where its foliage can trail. Flowers insignificant. Prefers sun to part shade. Tolerates various soils and drought. Often confused with *Carex comans*, or sold as a cultivar, variously named 'Frosted Curls' or 'Frosty Curls', but these are common names. This is a distinct species that is uniform when grown from seed. Self-sows to a pleasant extent in milder climates. Zone 7, possibly colder.

Carex baccans Nees ex Wright.
Crimson-seeded sedge.

Native to India, Sri Lanka, and China. An unusual sedge, valued primarily for the bright red color of the inflorescences as seeds ripen. A coarse-textured plant, with medium-green leaves 1/2 in. (12 mm) wide, flowering stems to 3 ft. (1 m) tall. Flowers green in summer, turning red by late autumn and remaining colorful during winter in mild climates. Partial shade, fertile soil, with plenty of moisture. Good near streamsides. Propagate by seed or by division in spring. Zone 8.

Carex baltzellii Chapman ex Dewey.
Baltzell's sedge.

Native to Alabama, Florida, Georgia, and Mississippi. New to cultivation and little-known. Foliage 1/4 in. (6 mm) wide, very glaucous-blue. Does well in the heat of the southeastern United States. Zone 8?

Carex bergrenii Petrie.

A diminutive New Zealand native, barely 4 in. (10 cm) tall, with densely tufted foliage, usually copper or bronze-toned. Slowly rhizomatous. Needs moisture. Color is most pronounced in sun. Zone 6.

Carex albula in early August.

Carex baccans in early February at the University of California, Berkeley, Botanical Garden.

Carex buchananii Berggren.
Leatherleaf sedge.

One of the best known and most popular New Zealanders. Tufted and erect in growth, especially when young. The narrow foliage is copper-bronze-colored, to 2 ft. (60 cm) tall, and best in full sun. The bronze-leaved New Zealand sedges can be stunning if contrasted with silvers or with flower colors. Viewed against bare soil or mulch, they look dead. Needs good drainage for hardiness in colder zones. Propagate by seed or by division in spring. Zone 7.

Carex caryophyllea Latourrette.
Spring sedge.

Native to Europe. In England, occurs in calcareous grasslands and on acid mountain soils. Leaves dark green, recurving, to 12 in. (30 cm). Ornamentally important only for the following cultivar.

'The Beatles'. May be a hybrid, but is believed by many to belong in this species. Makes a deep green mop of narrow foliage 6 in. (15 cm) tall, spreading slowly. A useful low groundcover, evergreen in milder climates. Requires moisture. Zone 5.

Carex comans Berggren.
New Zealand hairy sedge.

This New Zealander was one of the earliest to reach Western gardens. It is quite distinct from *Carex buchananii* in form, with pendent, flowing foliage. Typically bronze-colored, best in full sun with good drainage. Many New Zealand sedges exhibit leaf color variations from green to bronze, and this has caused much confusion. Many green-leaved plants offered commercially as *C. comans* var. *stricta* and most offered as 'Frosted Curls' or 'Frosty Curls' are *C. albula*. Zone 7.

'Bronze'. Foliage deeply bronze-colored all year. Zone 7.

Carex conica Boott.
Hime kan suge.

Suge is the Japanese name for sedge. Common in open woods on hillsides and low mountains in Japan, also native to southern Korea. Densely tufted, forming a neat mound of narrow, glossy green foliage. Leaves 3/16 in. (4 mm) wide. Known ornamentally for the following variegated cultivar.

'Snowline' ('Marginata', 'Variegata'). Leaves deep green with conspicuous white edges. Long-lived but slow to increase in size, which has led to the belief that there are different-sized cultivars. Eventually, with good soil and adequate moisture, this plant can grow to 15 in. (38 cm)

Carex buchananii with violets in late May at the Brooklyn Botanic Garden, New York.

Carex comans in mid-July at Foggy Bottom, Adrian Bloom's garden in Bressingham, England.

Carex conica 'Snowline' in mid-July in Alan Bloom's garden in Bressingham, England.

tall by 24 in. (60 cm) wide. Best in light shade in climates with intense summer sun. Evergreen in mild climates. In colder climates, cut foliage back if winter-damaged just before new growth begins in spring. Zone 5.

Carex crinita Lamarck.

Fringed sedge.

Native to wet woods and swales in eastern North America. Similar in appearance to the European native *Carex pendula* but much more cold-hardy. A large species, to 4 ft. (1.2 m) tall to the top of the arching inflorescences, which are produced in early summer and last into late autumn. Architecturally interesting. Pliant-stemmed, moves gracefully with woodland breezes. Largest in a moist or wet shady site, but can be grown on soils of average moisture in part sun. Propagate by seed or by division in spring. Zone 5.

Carex crinita flowering in mid-June in its native habitat in northern Delaware.

Comparison of variegated sedges. From top: *Carex conica* 'Snowline', *C. elata* 'Aurea', *C. dolichostachya* 'Kaga Nishiki', *C. morrowii* var. *temnolepis* 'Silk Tassel', *C. morrowii* 'Ice Dance', and the bottom two are *C. oshimensis* 'Evergold', showing older foliage with cream-yellow median variegation, and fresh new foliage with the median still mostly cream-white.

Carex digitata Linnaeus.

Fingered sedge.

A Eurasian native, preferring chalk or limestone soils, which perhaps contribute to its proven cold-hardiness in alkaline northern Minnesota. Small, to 10 in. (25 cm) tall, leaves dark green, to $^{3}/_{16}$ in. (4 mm) wide. Semi-evergreen in milder zones. A reliable tufted groundcover. Zone 4.

Carex dolichostachya Hayata.

Miyama kan suge.

Native to Japanese mountain woodlands. Important ornamentally for the following variegated cultivar.

'Kaga Nishiki' (Gold Fountains is a commercial trade name). Kaga brocade sedge. A superb selection from Kenji Watanabe of Gotemba Nursery in Japan, introduced to the United States by Barry Yinger. In Japanese, *Kaga* is the old name for the Ishikawa Prefecture and *nishiki* means "brocade," an apt description for the lacy beauty of this finely gold-variegated sedge. Leaves to $^{3}/_{16}$ in. (4 mm) wide, medium green in center and gold at the edges, forming a symmetrical fountainlike mound, eventually to 2 ft. (60 cm) in diameter. Long-lived and durable. Suited for accent or groundcover sweeps. Evergreen into zone 6. Light shade or full sun with adequate moisture. Prefers fertile organic soils. Reasonably drought tolerant. Propagate by division in spring. Zone 5.

A young plant of *Carex dolichostachya* 'Kaga Nishiki' in late August.

Carex eburnia Boott.

Native from Newfoundland to British Columbia, south to Virginia, Missouri, Nebraska, and Texas mountains, in dry sand or especially on limestone bluffs. Very fine, almost needlelike foliage, in neat symmetrical clumps to 12 in. (30 cm) wide, soft green in color. Slowly rhizomatous. Introduced to cultivation by Plant Delights Nursery from an Ohio population found by Tony Resnicek. Does well in cold areas or in the heat of the southeastern United States, in sun or shade. Zone 3.

Carex elata Allioni.

[*Carex stricta* Goodenough, non Lamarck].

Tufted sedge, European tussock-sedge.

Native to swamps, mires, fens, edges of lakes, and riverbanks in northern and eastern Europe. Forms dense tussocks, sometimes in extensive stands. Analogous in form and preferred habitat to the North American *Carex stricta*. The green-leaved species is not often cultivated, but the variegated forms are perhaps the most brightly colored of all sedges.

'Aurea' ('Bowles Golden'). Bowles' golden sedge. British author Graham Stuart Thomas quotes E. A. Bowles de-

Carex elata 'Aurea' in shallow water at Longwood Gardens, in early June.

scription of this as "a very beautiful sedge, with golden-striped leaves, another of my finds in the Norfolk Broads." This graceful plant grows upright to 2½ ft. (80 cm) tall. The leaves are to 5/16 in. (8 mm) wide, mostly yellow with faint, random longitudinal green stripes. Yellow color is most intense in full sun. Foliage looks good through the growing season on plants at waterside or even shallowly submerged. Burns if too dry, losing much appeal by late summer. Shady siting is necessary in drier soils, in which case leaves are rich lime-yellow in color. Does not do well in hot climates. Vertical inflorescences in early May are subtly attractive, soon disappearing amid developing foliage. Propagate by division in spring. Zone 5.

'Knightshayes'. Similar to 'Aurea' but leaves yellow.

Carex firma Host.

Native to central Europe. Leaves blue-green, tufted, less than 4 in. (10 cm) tall. Useful in rock gardens. Zone 7.

'Variegata'. Leaves striped cream-yellow. Zone 7.

Carex flacca Schreber.

[*Carex glauca* Scopoli].

Glaucous sedge, carnation grass.

Native to calcareous grasslands, sand dunes, and estuary marshes in Europe. Also native to northern Africa and naturalized in eastern North America. A very variable species growing 6–24 in. (15–60 cm) tall, with leaves to 3/16 in. (4 mm) wide, sometimes green above and glaucous-blue below, sometimes glaucous-blue on both sides, resulting in an attractive bluish overall appearance. The foliage is similar in color to that of carnation leaves, hence the common name. Many different forms are in cultivation, some intensely blue and short-growing, others greener or taller. Dry conditions limit height. Flowers, appearing in late spring on culms to 12 in. (30 cm) tall, are relatively insignificant, although there is a noticeable purple-black color to the male and female spikes. Strongly rhizomatous, this species spreads slowly but steadily to form dense, fine-textured masses and is very useful as a groundcover in full sun to light shade. Very drought tolerant. Adaptable to a wide range of soils, including alkaline types, and can also withstand some salinity. Most plants sold in the United States as *Carex nigra* are actually *C. flacca*. The individual flowers of *C. flacca* have three stigmas; flowers of *C. nigra* have two stigmas. Zone 4.

'Bias'. Leaves variegated on one side.

Carex flacca in late May.

Carex flaccosperma Dewey.

[*Carex glaucodea* Tuckerman].

Native to rich, often calcareous woods and bottomlands in eastern North America, forming loose tussocks of green to glaucous blue-green leaves, 5/8 in. (15 mm) wide. The basal leaves last through winter, so this sedge is essentially evergreen. Relatively insignificant flowers appear in early spring. Fairly drought tolerant. Not particular about soil. Propagate by seed or by division in spring. Zone 5.

Carex flaccosperma var. *glaucodea* (Tuckerman) Kukenthal.

Bluer than the typical species and a subtly attractive addition to shady or partly shady gardens.

Carex flaccosperma var. *glaucodea* in late September.

Carex flagellifera Colenso.

A New Zealand native very similar to *Carex buchananii* but less vertical, even when young, and scarcely distinguishable from bronze plants of *C. comans*. Zone 7.

Carex grayi Carey.

Gray's sedge, mace sedge, morning star sedge.

Named for eminent American botanist Asa Gray (1810–1888). A clump-forming native of eastern North American meadows and alluvial woodlands. To 3 ft. (1 m) tall, leafy, medium-green. Flowering in May, producing conspicuous and attractive light green seed-heads, shaped like maces, 3/4–1 1/2 in. (2–4 cm) diameter at maturity. Shade to part sun. Needs moisture. Propagate by seed or by division in spring.

'Morning Star'. A selection with seed-heads 1 in. (25 mm) wide.

Carex flagellifera.

Carex grayi in early June at Springwood, the eastern Pennsylvania garden of Dick and Sally Lighty.

Carex hachijoensis Akiyama.

Hachijo kan suge.

Native to Hachijo Island off Japan's main island, Honshu. Not as cold-hardy as the similar but more densely tufted *Carex oshimensis*, and probably not in cultivation in Western gardens. The variegated cultivar 'Evergold' belongs to *C. oshimensis*.

Carex lupulina Muhlenberg ex Willdenow.

Hop sedge.

Native to wet woods and swamps, from Nova Scotia to Minnesota, south to Florida and Texas. Deciduous, clump-forming, with upright stems to 30 in. (75 cm) tall and medium green leaves to 1/2 in. (12 mm) wide. Flowers abundantly in late spring to early summer. The dramatic female spikes are to 1 1/4 in. (32 mm) long and hop-like in appearance. Larger-flowered but lesser known than

Carex lupulina in moist woodlands in northern Delaware in mid-June.

Gray's sedge, *Carex grayi,* this species is worth trying in moist or wet woodland gardens. Adapted to periodic standing water. Sunny dry sites cause yellowing of growth. Propagates readily by seed or division. Zone 4.

Carex montana Linnaeus.

Mountain sedge.

Native from eastern Europe to central Asia. A narrow-leaved rhizomatous species useful as a groundcover, usually growing less than 2 ft. (60 cm) tall. Evergreen or semi-evergreen even in colder climates. Tolerates alkaline soils. Propagate by division in spring or by seed. Zone 4.

Carex morrowii Boott.

[*Carex fortunei* hort].

Kan suge.

Native to woods in low mountains of central and southern Japan. The Japanese have been interested in variegated plants for centuries. The leaves of this species are typically solid green, but variegated forms were introduced to Western horticulture by the mid-1800s. Among gardeners and the nursery industry this species often serves as a "catch-all" name for Japanese sedges, resulting in much confusion. In cultivation, it is correctly represented by two distinct varieties. The typical variety has thick, leathery leaves to 1/2 in. (12 mm) wide and is somewhat coarse-textured. Generally clump-forming or slowly rhizomatous, evergreen except in the coldest climates. Very long lived plants of easy culture on a wide range of soils. The rhizomatous forms are especially suited for groundcover use. Zone 5.

Carex montana in mid-July in Alan Bloom's garden in Bressingham, England.

'Gilt'. Distinct cream-white leaf margins. Introduced from Japan and named by Hans Simon of Germany. Slowly rhizomatous.

'Gold Band'. Slightly wider, cream-yellow variegated leaf margins than typical for plants sold as 'Variegata'.

'Ice Dance'. Strong cream-white marginal variegation. Rhizomatous and carpet-forming. Knits together but not invasive. Introduced from Japan by Barry Yinger.

'Variegata'. Not a clonal cultivar, but a name suitable for any of the numerous, otherwise unnamed selections of the species having white leaf margins in common. The variegated margins may be distinct or barely conspicuous.

Carex morrowii var. *temnolepis* (Franchet) Ohwi.

[*Carex temnolepis* Franchet].

Hosoba kan suge.

Native to mountain woods on Japan's main Island, Honshu. Having threadlike leaves just over 1/8 in. (3 mm) wide, this botanical variety is so different from the typi-

Carex morrowii 'Gilt' in early July at Longwood Gardens.

cal that it is difficult for casual observers to believe it represents the same species. In fact, nineteenth-century botanist Adrien Franchet originally thought it to be a distinct species. Represented in Western gardens by the following variegated selection.

'Silk Tassel'. Leaves only 1/8 in. (3 mm) wide, dark green at margins and clear white at center, forming an exquisite fountain of shimmering, fine-textured foliage. Eventually to 1 ft. (30 cm) tall by 2 ft. (60 cm) wide. Grow in sun with moisture or in shade. Introduced and named by Barry Yinger, from a 1976 trip to Japan. Zone 5.

Carex muskingumensis Schweinfurth.
Palm sedge.

Native to low woods and wet meadows in north-central North America. Creeping by rhizomes. Numerous narrow, tapered leaves radiate from lax stems growing to 2 ft. (60 cm) tall. Capable of forming large groundcover masses. Flowering in early June, neither adding nor detracting significantly from appearance. Grow in full sun and moist soil, or in shade. Propagate by division in spring. Typical leaves colored a solid medium-green. Zone 4.

A young plant of *Carex morrowii* 'Ice Dance' showing the rhizomatous habit that is ideal for groundcover use.

Carex morrowii var. *temnolepis* 'Silk Tassel' in late June in Don Jacobs' Eco Gardens in Georgia.

An example of *Carex morrowii* 'Variegata' with good marginal variegation.

Carex muskingumensis in early October in Pauline Volmer's garden, Baltimore, Maryland.

'Oehme'. Leaves evenly green in spring. Narrow yellow margins become increasingly evident as the season progresses. A sport from Wolfgang Oehme's garden, named by Tony Avent of Plant Delights Nursery. Zone 4.

'Silberstreif'. Leaves green and white variegated, slightly smaller-growing. Introduced in Germany by Eckhard Schimana.

'Wachtposten' (sentry tower). Typical of the species, perhaps slightly more erect-stemmed.

Carex nigra (Linnaeus) Reichard.
Black-flowering sedge.

This extremely variable species is native to bogs, marshes, and streamsides in Europe and to eastern coastal North America. Grows 1–2½ ft. (30–80 cm) tall, spreading by rhizomes or (particularly in American native forms) forming dense tussocks. Leaves often glaucous-blue, to 3/16 in. (4 mm) wide. Flowers in late spring, the female flowers blackish, interesting but not showy. Most plants sold by this name in the United States are correctly *Carex*

Carex muskingumensis 'Oehme' has yellow-margined leaves. (Photo: Tony Avent.)

A young plant of *Carex nigra* 'Variegata' at Longwood Gardens, early June.

Carex muskingumensis 'Wachtposten' at Longwood Gardens in late October.

Carex nudata flowering in March in a glasshouse garden at Longwood Gardens.

flacca. The individual flowers of *C. flacca* have three stigmas; flowers of *C. nigra* have two stigmas. Zone 5.

'Variegata'. Leaves glaucous-green with thin marginal light yellow variegation. To 12 in. (30 cm) tall, spreading. Small blackish flowers in late spring; stigmas two. Full sun or light shade. Zone 5.

Carex nudata W. Boott.

California black-flowering sedge.

Native along wet sandy or rocky streambeds, below the high-water mark, in northern California. Densely tufted, forming raised tussocks reminiscent of the eastern North American *Carex stricta*. Flowers truly black when opening in late winter or early spring, conspicuous, and ornamental, held on arching stems above the foliage, to 2 ft. (60 cm) tall. Best in sun with moisture. An interesting container specimen for colder climates. Propagate by seed or by division in spring. Zone 7.

Carex ornithopoda Willdenow.

Bird's-foot sedge.

Native to Europe. Tufted narrow green leaves, low growing. The variegated selection is most frequently grown. Zone 7.

Carex oshimensis 'Evergold' in late July at the University of British Columbia Botanical Garden in Vancouver.

'Variegata'. Leaves striped white. Diminutive, to 8 in. (20 cm) tall, slow-growing, well suited to rock gardens. Sometimes confused in the nursery trade with young plants of *Carex oshimensis* 'Evergold'.

Carex oshimensis Nakai.

Oshima kan suge.

Native and common in dry woods and rocky slopes throughout Honshu Island, Japan. Represented in cultivation mostly by the following cultivar.

'Evergold' (also sold as 'Aureo-variegata', 'Everbrite', 'Old Gold', and 'Variegata'). One of the most ornamental and widely grown variegated sedges. Densely tufted, forming a thick, spilling tussock of fine-textured foliage to 16 in. (40 cm) tall. Leaves glossy to 5/16 in. (8 mm) wide, dark green at the margins, with a broad median stripe that is cream-white on emerging foliage, maturing to cream-yellow. Flowers, produced in early spring, are ornamentally insignificant. This cultivar is often listed as belonging to *Carex hachijoensis*, a species that is similar but less tufted, slightly wider-leaved, later-flowering, and less hardy. Performs well in a broad range of cultural conditions but suffers in extreme heat. A truly beautiful sedge, useful as accent, in groups, groundcover masses, or as a container subject. Zone 6.

Carex pallescens Linnaeus.

Pale sedge.

Native to Europe, Asia, and North America, usually in open woods and at the edges of woods. Shortly rhizomatous, with narrow leaves to 2 ft. (60 cm) tall. Represented in gardens by the following introduction. Zone 5.

'Wood's Edge'. Creamy marginal variegation. Zone 6?

Carex oshimensis 'Evergold' at Longwood Gardens in June.

A sedge lawn of *Carex pansa* in early February, planted by John Greenlee in Malibu, California.

Carex pendula ornaments a courtyard at Little Thakeham, Storrington, England, in early July. The courtyard was designed by Sir Edwin Lutyens (1869–1944).

Carex pansa Bailey.
California meadow sedge.

Native to coastal sands in California and Washington. John Greenlee of California has pioneered the use of this species as an alternative to typical turf grass lawns. Rich green foliage is somewhat tousled, to 6 in. (15 cm) tall if unmowed. Spreads sufficiently by rhizomes to form a solid carpet, but not invasive. Summer dormant unless watered in warmer, drier regions. Full sun to medium shade. Best established by planting plugs. Zone 8.

Carex pendula Hudson.
Great drooping sedge, pendulous sedge, weeping sedge.

A wide-ranging species, native to Europe, Asia, and northern Africa. Clump-forming, with gracefully arching stems to 6 ft. (2 m) tall, from which hang delicate, cylindrical male and female flower spikes. It self-sows freely and is the quintessential, accidental tourist in British gardens. Although most texts suggest relegating it to the wilder parts of the garden, it is sometimes the perfect, architectural counterpoint to a stone wall or spare courtyard of a stately home, where it will be content to grow between cracks in the pavers. Zone 8.

Carex pendula 'Moonraker'. (Photo: Dan Heims/Terra Nova.)

'Moonraker'. A strikingly cream-yellow variegated cultivar pulled out of a hedgerow in Wiltshire, England, by a farmer's tractor. The variegation is most pronounced in the early, cooler part of the growing season. Propagates slowly by division. Zone 8.

Carex pensylvanica Lamarck.

Pennsylvania sedge.

Native to thickets and woods in eastern North America. Individual plants of this apparently delicate little sedge are so slight they are easy to overlook; however, this resilient species is proving adapted to use as a lawn alternative, planted thickly in dry sunny or shady sites. It is capable of producing a soft, uniform cover of green even in dry, sandy wooded settings. Semi-evergreen even in moderately cold climates. Has proved useful as a mowable groundcover in lightly shaded parking lot islands at the Chicago Botanic Garden. Slender green leaves grow to 8 in. (20 cm) tall or can be mowed as low as 2 in. (5 cm). May flowers are insignificant. Propagate by seed or by division in spring. Zone 4.

'Hilltop'. A low-growing selection from Maryland.

Carex pensylvanica in early May in its native habitat in eastern Pennsylvania.

Carex petriei Cheesman.

Dwarf brown New Zealand sedge.

Native to New Zealand. Grows only 8 in. (20 cm) tall, leaves copper-brown to bronze, often curling at tips. Vertical and upright in form, looks like a small *Carex buchananii.* Prefers moisture and sharp drainage. Good for rock gardens. Propagates easily from seed, which produces numerous leaf color variations. Zone 7.

Carex phyllocephala T. Koyama.

Tenjiku suge.

An unusual Chinese native, originally introduced to Japan for medicinal purposes. Leaves nearly in whorls, clustered toward the top of the 2-ft. (60-cm) tall canelike stems. The green-leaved plant is interesting, but not showy. Sometimes surviving zone 6 winters, it is more cold-hardy than the spectacular variegated sport, which originated in Japan. Best in fertile organic soil with adequate moisture. Propagate by seed or division. Self-sows manageably. Zone 7.

'Sparkler'. Fuiri Tenjiku suge. *Fuiri* means "variegated" in Japanese. This stunningly variegated selection was both introduced from Japan and named by Barry Yinger. The leaves are dark green in center with broad, conspicuous white to cream-white margins, creating an overall white effect. Makes an excellent summer container specimen in zones too cold for permanent planting in-ground. Grows well in part shade, or in full sun with plenty of moisture. Zone 8.

Carex phyllocephala 'Sparkler' in mid-March, overwintered under glass at Longwood Gardens.

Carex pilulifera Linnaeus.
Pill sedge.

A diminutive Eurasian native. Requires acid conditions. Represented in gardens by the following variegated cultivar.

'Tinney's Princess'. Leaves dark green at the edges, with a broad central cream-white stripe, densely tufted, less than 12 in. (30 cm) tall. Found and introduced by Gerald Mundy, from a plant on his estate near Salisbury, England. Zone 7.

Carex plantaginea Lamarck.
Plantain-leafed sedge, broad-leafed sedge.

Native to rich moist woods in eastern North America. Clump-forming. Leaves unusually broad, to 1 1/8 in. (3 cm) wide, shiny green, with prominent parallel veins. The basal leaves overwinter, so the plant is effectively evergreen. A delightful bold-textured companion to ferns and woodland wildflowers in native habitats and in the garden. Requires regular moisture and part shade for best growth. Propagate by seed or by division in spring. Zone 5.

Carex praegracilis W. Boott.
Western meadow sedge.

A rhizomatous California native, often occurring on alkaline soils. Low growing and adapted to use as a lawn

Carex plantaginea in early May at Springwood, the eastern Pennsylvania garden of Dick and Sally Lighty.

Carex pilulifera 'Tinney's Princess' in mid-July in Alan Bloom's garden in Bressingham, England.

Carex riparia 'Variegata' in mid-July in England.

alternative in western states. Tolerates sun or shade. Reasonably drought tolerant. Grows on heavy soils and bears some foot traffic. Zone 8.

'Laguna Mountain'. A dark green, compact selection from the Laguna Mountain area in San Diego County, California. Zone 8.

Carex riparia Curtis.

Greater pond sedge.

Widespread throughout the Northern Hemisphere, often forming large stands around ponds, by slow-moving rivers, and by other wet places. Spreads aggressively by rhizomes. Typically green-leaved, stems to 4 ft. (1.2 m) tall.

'Variegata'. Variegated pond sedge. Long arching leaves are boldly striped white. Occasional all-white leaves are produced in spring. Full sun, moist or wet. Can be an invasive runner. Zone 6.

Carex siderosticha Hance.

Creeping broad-leafed sedge, tagane so.

Native to mountain woods in Japan, also Korea, Manchuria, and China. Slowly creeping by rhizomes, forming a dense mass of bold-textured foliage. Leaves $1^1/4$ in. (32 mm) wide, solid green, to 8 in. (20 cm) tall. Prefers part shade, moisture, fertile soil. The typical green-leaved form is undeservedly uncommon. This is a long-lived, durable sedge for woodland gardens. Besides the white striped cultivar below, there are yet-unnamed yellow-striped and mottled selections existing. Zone 5.

'Variegata'. Striped broad-leafed sedge. Leaves green with clear white stripes, especially toward the margins. One of the most strikingly ornamental hardy sedges. Provided moisture and partial shade, it is beautiful from the time the new spring foliage emerges until autumn. The new leaves are sometimes attractively pink-tinted during cool springs. Fully deciduous in winter. To 8 in. (20 cm) tall. Spreads slowly by rhizomes. Propagate easily by division in spring. Superb for accent or in groundcover patches to brighten a woodland garden. Zone 6.

Carex solandri Boott.

New Zealand forest sedge.

Native to woodlands in New Zealand. Distinct from most cultivated New Zealand sedges in having green leaves. Grows 1–2 ft. (30–60 cm) tall. Fine textured, makes a good groundcover in well-drained, shaded garden areas. Zone 8.

Newly emerging foliage of *Carex siderosticha* 'Variegata' in late April at Longwood Gardens.

Carex siderosticha 'Variegata' in June at Springwood, the eastern Pennsylvania garden of Dick and Sally Lighty.

Carex spissa Bail.
San Diego sedge.

Native along watercourses in southern California. Striking gray-blue leaves to 5 ft. (1.5 m) tall distinguish this sedge from all others. Spreads slowly by rhizomes, forming large clumps but never invasive. Quite beautiful when planted at water's edge. Dark black-brown inflorescences to 18 in. (45 cm) in spring. Foliage is evergreen, but is best cut back occasional years to remove accumulations of dead or discolored leaves. Does well in southeastern United States if grown in water or moist soil, but self-sows. Cut back after flowering to avoid unwanted seedlings. Propagate by seed or division. Zone 7.

Carex stricta Lamarck.
Tussock sedge.

Native to wet swales, marshes, and creeksides in northeastern North America. Similar in form and preferred habitat to the European *Carex elata*. Develops dense tussocks raised above water's surface, each with an accumulation of old leaves surrounding the base. Spreads by underground rhizomes to form new tussocks, sometimes creating large stands. Rich green and fine-textured, beautiful

Carex stricta flowers in early May in its native habitat in eastern Pennsylvania.

Carex spissa in mid-December in Berkeley, California.

Carex testacea in Alan Bloom's garden in Bressingham, England, mid-July.

in contrast to skunk cabbage (*Symplocarpus foetidus*), cinnamon fern (*Osmunda cinnamomea*), and other eastern natives of wet woods and the edges of woods. Can be grown away from water if soil is moist. Zone 4.

Carex testacea Solander ex Boott.
Orange New Zealand sedge.

A common native on New Zealand's North and South Islands. Clump-forming, making a fine-textured mound of foliage to 15 in. (38 cm) tall, copper-brown in summer with distinct orange tints in winter. Appreciates moisture, good drainage. Self-sows pleasantly. One of the cold-hardier New Zealanders. Zone 6.

Carex tumulicola Mackenzie.
Berkeley sedge, foot-hill sedge.

Native on dry soil, from Washington south through Oregon and in coastal California south to Monterey. Creeping by rhizomes, foliage deep green, to 18 in. (45 cm) tall, fully evergreen in milder climates. When planted densely, creates a lush groundcover. Can be mowed periodically to create a more turflike effect. Drought tolerant, water-conserving. Propagate by seed or by division in spring. Zone 7.

Chasmanthium Link.
Grass family, Poaceae.
Wild-oats, wood-oats.

Comprised of six species native to eastern North America and northern Mexico. One species is of ornamental importance and is closely related to and was once included in *Uniola*.

Chasmanthium latifolium (Michaux) Yates.
[*Uniola latifolia* Michaux].
Wild-oats, wood-oats.

Native to wooded slopes, moist thickets, and creek bottoms in southeastern North America from Texas north to Pennsylvania and New Jersey. Once included in the genus *Uniola*, sea-oats, which it resembles, although it has nothing to do with the sea. It is an inland species, and any appellation referring to the sea is a misnomer. A clump-forming, warm-season grower to 4 ft. (1.2 m) tall in rich moist soil. Very upright in sun, attractively lax-stemmed in shade. In intensely sunny regions, needs moisture for good green foliage color in sun. Grows well even in very dry shade. In England it requires full sun. Especially valued for the dangling oatlike spikelets, held on slender nodding stems above the foliage (see Figure 2-1). Begins flowering in midsummer. Spikelets light green at first, becoming red-bronze in autumn and finally light salmon-buff, remaining attractive through winter, especially encased in ice or dusted with snow. Worth growing just for

Carex tumulicola in Malibu, California, in early February.

fresh cut or dried arrangements. Leaves to 3/4 in. (2 cm) wide and to 8 in. (20 cm) long, medium green in summer, turning a vibrant gold in autumn. Of easy culture on a wide range of soils. Self-sows readily in moist gardens, but seedlings are easily scratched out when young. Cut back in spring before new growth begins. A versatile grass for formal accent, groups, sweeps, groundcovering, naturalizing, or container display. Propagate by seed or by division in spring. Zone 5. Figure 2-1.

Chionochloa Zotov.

Grass family, Poaceae.

Snow grass, tussock grass.

Comprised of approximately 20 species native to New Zealand and Australia, mostly in alpine and subalpine zones, all clumping and forming dense tussocks. Some valued for flowers, many for foliage texture. Closely related to *Danthonia* and *Cortaderia.* Propagate by seed or division.

Chasmanthium latifolium in early October sun at Longwood Gardens.

Chasmanthium latifolium in part shade in early August in Pauline Volmer's garden, Baltimore, Maryland.

Chionochloa flavicans in mid-June at the Huntington Botanical Gardens, San Marino, California.

Chionochloa conspicua (Forster f.) Zotov.
Plumed tussock grass, hunangamoho.

Endemic to New Zealand, found throughout in lowland and subalpine forests and clearings, especially near streams. Produces huge feathery inflorescences to 7 ft. (2.1 m) tall, reminiscent of pampas grass, *Cortaderia* species, but more open and airy. Summer blooming. Useful for cut or dried flowers. Zone 8.

Chionochloa flavescens (Hooker f.) Zotov.
[*Danthonia flavescens* Hooker f.].
Broad-leafed snow tussock.

Native to low alpine regions in New Zealand. Densely tufted, to 6 ft. (2 m) tall in flower. Blooms spring to summer. Useful for cut or dried flowers. Leaves green with red-brown tints. Zone 8.

Chionochloa flavicans Zotov.
Green-leaved tussock grass.

Native to high elevations in New Zealand. Similar to *Chionochloa flavescens* but leaves green. Needs strong sun for flowering, but best in regions with cool nights. Summer blooming. Useful for cut or dried flowers. Zone 8.

Chionochloa rubra Zotov.
Red tussock grass.

Widespread and sometimes occurring in great drifts in lowland and low-alpine areas in the volcanic mountains of New Zealand. Common on the mineral belts of the South Island and on poorly drained peaty valley floors or rolling slopes mostly below the tree line. Not especially showy in flower, but attractive for the strong red-copper foliage. Shorter than *Chionochloa flavicans* when in flower. Zone 8.

Chionochloa rubra in early October in its native habitat east of Te Anau on New Zealand's South Island.

Chondropetalum Rottboell.
Restio family, Restionaceae.

Comprised of approximately 15 rushlike, dioecious species native to the South African Cape region, forming tussocks to 6 ft. (2 m) tall. They are part of the fynbos plant community, which is characterized by natural burning, and are generally found on well-drained soils low in fertility. Sometimes used for roof thatching. Cool-season growers, most active in spring and autumn, but having an evergreen presence. Many are quite beautiful but little known in cultivation. Research at the National Botanical Garden, Kirstenbosch, in Cape Town, South Africa, has found that smoke treatment of seeds often dramatically increases germination rates. This makes it possible to propagate various restios more readily, so they may become more common in gardens in mediterranean and warm temperate regions.

Chondropetalum tectorum (Linnaeus f.) Rafinesque.

Occurs in marshes and seeps from Clanwilliam to Port Elizabeth, South Africa. Forms an erect tussock to 4 ft. (1.2) tall, very slowly rhizomatous. Stems rich dark green, unbranched and bare of recognizable leaves, giving the appearance of a huge common rush, *Juncus effusus*, but more relaxed, the stems radiating in an arc and touching

Chondropetalum tectorum in mid-September at the National Botanical Garden, Kirstenbosch, Cape Town, South Africa.

the ground. Male and female flowers on separate plants, similar in appearance, dark brown, narrowly clustered at the tips of stems. A beautifully sculptural plant, stunning when moving in the wind or catching sunstreams. Propagate by seed. Difficult to divide as the roots do not like to be disturbed. Resents high fertility. Best planted in spring or autumn in mediterranean climates. An excellent seasonal container subject in areas beyond its winter cold-hardiness. Zone 8.

Cortaderia Stapf.

Grass family, Poaceae.

Pampas grass, toe toe, tussock grass.

From *cortadera,* the Argentinian word for this grass, which has the same root as the Spanish *cortar* (to cut), referring to the leaves of *Cortaderia selloana,* which are sharp-edged and can cause lacerations. Comprised of approximately 24 species of large, tussock-forming grasses, mostly native to South America but also to New Zealand and New Guinea, usually in open habitats. Closely related to *Chionochloa.* Though best known for the Argentine pampas grass, *Cortaderia selloana,* and its cultivated varieties, this genus includes other species of ornamental merit in mild climates, especially the New Zealand native, *C. richardii.* It also includes *C. jubata,* which is invasive in California.

These species are appreciated ornamentally for their grand size and huge flower plumes. Flowers bisexual or unisexual, the plants sometimes dioecious. Female plants produce the most impressive plumes. If intended for cut-flower use, it is best to cut the inflorescences just before they are fully open. They will continue to expand to full size on drying and subsequent shattering will be reduced.

In mild regions, cortaderias are undemanding and long-lived if provided a sunny site, fertile soil, and adequate moisture. Though the basal tussocks are essentially evergreen, over years they can accumulate considerable old, dead foliage. In England, old tussocks are reported to be a favorite hiding place for hibernating hedgehogs. The tussocks are best cut back occasionally, with gloved hands and pruners or power shears. In native habitats, pampas and tussock grasses are naturally burned back, but in the garden, burning can be dangerous to both plant and gardener due to the volume of flammable material and the potential for uncontrolled burning.

Although a few of the smaller-sized and more recent selections are cold-hardy in zone 6, most *Cortaderia* species require more warmth. Plants promoted in colder zones as "hardy pampas grass" are sometimes, in fact, *Saccharum ravennae,* which is best called ravenna grass. All *Cortaderia* species are best propagated from division in spring. The New Zealand species reproduce well from seed, but pampas grass seedlings are very variable and often inferior to the clonal selections available.

Cortaderia fulvida (Buchanan) Zotov.

Kakaho, tussock grass.

Native to New Zealand, especially on the North Island, from sea level to subalpine regions, occurring in open places, along streamsides, and at the margins of forests. Inflorescences tawny, to 6½ ft. (2 m) tall. Does well in waterside situations in the garden. Though sometimes grown ornamentally in England, it is similar but inferior to *Cortaderia richardii,* which is larger, with clearer white inflorescences. Zone 8.

Cortaderia jubata (Lemoine) Stapf.

Purple pampas grass.

Native to the mountains of Ecuador, Peru, and Chile. Earlier blooming than *Cortaderia selloana,* but not nearly as ornamental. Inflorescences rosy lavender when first opening, eventually drying to dull grayish tan, though ap-

Cortaderia jubata in coastal California in early September.

pearing silver when sunlit. To 9 ft. (2.7 m) tall in flower. Very drought tolerant. This species has escaped from cultivation and become widely naturalized in north coastal California, seriously threatening and displacing native plant communities. All known plants of this species are female and produce copious quantities of fertile seeds through apomixis, which contributes to their spread. Zone 8.

Cortaderia richardii (Endlicher) Zotov.

Toe toe, tussock grass, plumed tussock.

Native to moist, open places in New Zealand. Although the plumes are not as large and full, this species truly rivals the majesty of pampas grass, *Cortaderia selloana*. It grows to 10 ft. (3 m) tall in bloom, with the inflorescences often gently nodding on top of a multitude of stalks ascending at different angles from the center of the clump. Plumes near-white or with a slight, attractive brassy tint, often slightly one-sided. Blooms mid to late summer. A magnificent grass for streamside or pondside. Needs moisture, not as drought tolerant or as cold-hardy as the Argentine species. Zone 8.

Cortaderia selloana (Schultes & Schultes f.) Ascherson & Gräbner.

[*Cortaderia argentea* (Nees) Stapf].

Pampas grass.

Native to Brazil, Argentina, and Chile. The quintessential ornamental grass of the Victorian era. Though ostrich feathers and pampas grass plumes were in their heyday more than a century ago, *Cortaderia selloana* is certainly among the most dramatic of all ornamental grasses for flower effect. Outstanding for fresh or dried floral bouquets, the huge feathery plumes are still widely available as cut flowers. Mature plants can top 10 ft. (3 m) in height, with nearly equal spread. The flower stalks are held erect, produced in late summer and early autumn, and remain attractive into winter. The foliage is evergreen in mild climates, green or often strikingly gray-green. In its native habitat, the pampas grasslands of South America, this warm-season grower is accustomed to moist winters and hot, dry summers. Little wonder it is so well adapted to gardens in the southeastern United States, where it has become a beautiful cliché. Requires full sun but tolerates varying soils, and established plants are extremely

Cortaderia richardii in mid-July in Alan Bloom's garden in Bressingham, England.

Cortaderia richardii detail of plumes in mid-July.

drought tolerant. Propagate, divide, or transplant only in late spring or early summer. More compact cultivars, such as 'Pumila' or 'Patagonia', fit in modest-sized gardens, but the classic large types are best in gardens with truly grand scale. The foliage of the variegated cultivars is so striking that these are worth growing in containers in cold areas, or they may be planted in the ground each season and dug and overwintered in a cold frame or other sheltered place. Such treatment dramatically reduces the plant's size, though it often results in a lack of flowering. Zone 8.

'Albolineata' ('Silver Stripe'). White-striped pampas grass. A long-established selection with leaves longitudinally white-striped. Valued primarily for the variegated foliage, which is most distinct later in season. Plumes white, modest-sized. Zone 8.

'Andes Silver'. Plumes silver, 7 ft. (2.1 m) tall. More cold-hardy than the species. Introduced by Kurt Bluemel. Zone 6.

Cortaderia selloana in mid-June in the Mitchell Park Conservatory in Milwaukee, Wisconsin.

Cortaderia selloana 'Aureolineata' foliage detail.

Cortaderia selloana 'Aureolineata' in mid-August at the Royal Horticultural Society Wisley Garden, Surrey, England.

'Aureolineata' ('Gold Band'). Golden-variegated pampas grass. Leaves with dramatic longitudinal yellow stripes mostly near the margins, but some blades nearly all-yellow. Valued primarily for the foliage, which is most intensely colored later in season. Plumes white, modest-sized. An excellent container subject. Zone 8.

'Bertini'. Compact-growing, to only 3 ft. (1 m) tall in flower. Plumes white.

'Monstrosa'. A huge green-leaved selection with immense white plumes.

'Monvin'. Yellow-striped leaves. Introduced and patented by Monrovia Nursery of California, and marketed under the name Sun Stripe™.

'Patagonia'. Plumes silver, to 6 ft. (2 m). Leaves bluish gray-green. More cold-hardy than the species. Introduced by Kurt Bluemel. Zone 6.

'Pink Feather'. Plumes large, with pink blush. Zone 8.

'Pumila'. Compact pampas grass. Plumes medium-sized, white, 4–6 ft. (1.2–2 m) tall, appearing in late summer. Leaves gray-green. Although not as grand as the larger forms of the species, this cultivar is still quite showy and is much more cold-hardy. In fact, it is among the most cold-hardy of the true pampas grasses. An excellent choice for gardens of moderate size. Always hardy in zone 7, usually hardy in zone 6.

'Rendatleri'. Plumes large, purplish pink, to 9 ft. (2.7 m) tall. Zone 8.

'Rosea'. Plumes mostly silver-white with a pink blush, to 8 ft. (2.4 m) tall. Zone 8.

'Silver Comet'. White-striped pampas grass. An improvement over 'Albolineata' with more pronounced white variegation. Valued primarily for the foliage. Plumes white, medium-sized. To 8 ft. (2.4 m) tall in flower. Zone 8.

Young plant of *Cortaderia selloana* 'Patagonia' at Longwood Gardens in early August.

Cortaderia selloana 'Pumila' in early October in Kurt Bluemel's garden, Fallston, Maryland.

Cortaderia selloana 'Silver Comet' at Alan Bloom's garden in Bressingham, England.

'Sunningdale Silver'. Widely acclaimed as the best of the larger types for the grandeur and quality of its silvery plumes. Can grow to more than 10 ft. (3 m) tall. Zone 8.

'White Feather'. Plumes large, white. Zone 8.

Cortaderia toetoe Zotov.

Toe toe.

Native to low, open, moist areas in New Zealand, growing to 10 ft. (3 m) tall in flower. The species was first published in 1963. Its description is similar enough to *Cortaderia richardii* that the two may be confused in cultivation. Adding to the confusion, the common name toe toe is sometimes used generally when referring to New Zealand *Cortaderia* species.

Cortaderia selloana 'Silver Comet' flowering in late August at Longwood Gardens.

Ctenium aromaticum in late June in North Carolina.

Ctenium Panzer.

Grass family, Poaceae.

From the Greek *ktenos* (comb), referring to the comblike inflorescences. Comprised of approximately 20 species native to tropical and subtropical America and Africa.

Ctenium aromaticum (Walter) Wood.

Toothache grass, lemon grass, orange grass.

Native to savannahs, bogs, and wet pine barrens from Louisiana to Florida and north on the coastal plain to Virginia. Leaves mostly basal, the slender flowering stems to 4 ft. (1.2 m) tall, each ending in a comblike, slightly curved inflorescence to 6 in. (15 cm) long. All parts of the plants are aromatic, having a citruslike fragrance when crushed. Also found by some people to have analgesic properties useful in treating toothaches. A curious and delicately graceful grass suited to informal garden areas or native habitat restorations. Blooms mid to late summer, the inflorescences lasting into winter. Needs full sun, moisture. Propagate by seed or by division in spring. Zone 8.

Cymbopogon Sprengel.

Grass family, Poaceae.

Comprised of approximately 50 clump-forming, mostly perennial species native to tropical and subtropical Africa, Asia, and Australia. Most are strongly aromatic, including citronella, *Cymbopogon nardus*. Oils from these grasses are used for cooking, perfumes, herbal remedies, and insect repellents.

Cymbopogon citratus at Longwood Gardens in late August.

Cymbopogon citratus (De Candolle ex Nees) Stapf.

Lemon grass.

Native to southern India and Ceylon. The oil from this species is strongly lemon-scented, and the leaves are widely used for flavoring in Southeast Asian cuisine. The plant is also quite handsome. Though too tender to survive winter in most temperate regions, it can be held over the cold season in a greenhouse or sunny window and planted out for the summer and autumn, in the ground or in a decorative pot. It is delightful to savor the scent of a crushed leaf while strolling the garden on a summer evening. Clump-forming and upright, growing 2–3 ft. (60–90 cm) tall over the course of a summer, with light green leaves to 1 in. (25 mm) wide. Needs full sun, moisture. Not particular about soils. Zone 9.

Cymophyllus Mackenzie.

Sedge family, Cyperaceae.

From the Greek *cyma* (wave) and *phyllon* (leaf), referring to the minutely undulate margins of the leaves. Comprised of a single eastern North American species. A long debate has raged whether this plant belongs in the genus *Carex*.

Cymophyllus fraserianus (Ker-Gawler) Kartesz & Gandhi.

[*Carex fraseri* Andrews, *Carex fraseriana* Ker-Gawler, *Cymophyllus fraseri* (Andrews) Mackenzie ex Britton].

Fraser's sedge.

Named for its discoverer, John Fraser (1750–1811). This stunning North American native is rare in the wild and rarer in cultivation. Found locally in rich, sloping, upland

Cymophyllus fraserianus flower detail in early May.

woods and streambanks in eastern Tennessee and northwestern South Carolina, north in Virginia and West Virginia, and in extreme south-central Pennsylvania. Clump-forming, with broad, flat basal leaves. Blooms May to June. The flowers are bright white, held above the foliage on stems to 15 in. (38 cm) tall. Male flowers have conspicuous threadlike anthers and are clustered at the top of each inflorescence, just above the females. New leaves develop after flowering, eventually growing to 20 in. (50 cm) long by 3/4 in. (2 cm) wide, deep green and glossy, persisting through winter. A truly ornamental sedge, worth growing for foliage or for flowers. Requires partial shade, well-drained soil with plenty of organic matter, and steady moisture for best growth. Does well on shaded slopes. Tolerates dense deciduous shade. A handsome addition to the woodland garden. Propagate by division or seed. Zone 7.

Cymophyllus fraserianus flowering in its native habitat in the Smoky Mountains of North Carolina in early May.

Cyperus Linnaeus.
Sedge family, Cyperaceae.
Galingale, umbrella plant, umbrella sedge.

The second-largest genus in the sedge family, next to *Carex,* comprised of approximately 600 species, mostly perennial, native to wet habitats mainly in the tropics and subtropics. Diverse in size and appearance, including the famous Egyptian paper reed or classical papyrus, *Cyperus papyrus,* and the infamous yellow nutsedge, *C. esculentus,* a pernicious weed in temperate gardens. Chufa, *C. esculentus* var. *sativus,* is grown for its edible tubers, which have a sweet nutty flavor after roasting. Many of the mostly ornamental species are tropicals requiring winter protection in a greenhouse, with minimum temperatures of 50°F (10°C). Often called umbrella plants because of the leaf-like bracts that spiral outward and downward from the top of the stem, like the ribs of umbrellas. Some species have well-developed basal leaves; others have leaves reduced to bracts that closely sheathe the stems. All prefer constantly moist soils, and many are semi-aquatic, preferring to grow in shallow water. They make excellent year-round conservatory specimens, at the edge of a pool or pond under glass. They can also be grown in a pot with the base standing in a tray of water and can be set out during warm seasons as marginals in water gardens. Their texture provides fine contrast with the broad, bold leaves of waterlilies and other aquatics and semi-aquatics. Most are best in full sun. Several excellent variegated selections are available. The ornamental species are mostly clump-forming, but some are runners. Propagate by division in spring, by seed, or by upper stem cuttings rooted in water. The names of *Cyperus* species have undergone considerable change, and there is much confusion and uncertainty regarding the labeling of plants in cultivation.

Cyperus albostriatus Schrader.
[*Cyperus diffusus* hort., non Vahl, *Cyperus elegans* hort., non Linnaeus].
Broad-leaved umbrella plant, broad-leaved umbrella sedge.

Native to southern Africa. Distinct from the other umbrella sedges in having well-developed basal leaves and bracts of the inflorescence leafy and broad, to 6 in. (15 cm) long and 1 in. (25 mm) wide, with prominent longitudinal veins. The leaves are typically dark green. Needs moist soil but does not like to be deeply submersed in water. Tolerates shade better than most and is well adapted to cultivation as a house plant. Zone 9.

'Variegatus'. This name is used for at least two different variegated selections. One has dark green leaves with bright white stripes. Another has leaves nearly evenly greenish white. Both are highly ornamental, and both benefit from partial shade in hot, sunny climates. Zone 9.

Cyperus albostriatus in late February, grown under glass at Longwood Gardens.

Variegated selection of *Cyperus albostriatus* in late May, grown in moist soil under glass at the New York Botanical Garden.

Variegated selection of *Cyperus albostriatus* in Roger Raiche's garden in Berkeley, California, in mid-August.

Cyperus alternifolius Linnaeus.

Umbrella plant, umbrella sedge, umbrella-palm.

Native to Madagascar. The most commonly cultivated, long a favorite for use as a house plant or in water gardens around the world. Basal leaves are lacking. The slender leafless stems grow to 3 ft. (1 m) tall, each topped by an umbrella-like spiral of to 25 dark green bracts. The bracts are flat and narrowly leaflike, to 5/8 in. (15 mm) wide and 4–12 in. (10–30 cm) long. This species is not clearly distinguishable from *Cyperus involucratus*, and many believe the two to be the same. Although the name *C. alternifolius* is long established in horticultural circles, the name *C. involucratus* is gaining favor, in which case the following cultivars are listed under it. Zone 9.

'Gracilis'. Compact and smaller in all parts, to 18 in. (45 cm) tall.

'Variegatus'. Leaves, bracts, and stems striped or entirely cream-white. Somewhat unstable, occasionally reverting to green.

Cyperus alternifolius 'Variegatus' in the conservatory at the New York Botanical Garden in late May.

Cyperus eragrostis Lamarck.

[*Cyperus vegetus* Willdenow].

Pale galingale.

Native of tropical America, introduced to England for ornamental purposes and naturalized there in some areas.

Cyperus alternifolius in early June at the Jardin de Aclimatacion de La Orotava, Tenirife, Canary Islands.

Pale green, to 24 in. (60 cm), with leaves as tall as the stem. Flowering in late summer. Inflorescence bracts relatively few. Not as showy as the umbrella-sedges, but valued for its greater cold-hardiness. Grows in garden soils of steady, average moisture. Zone 8.

Cyperus giganteus Rottboell ex Kunth.

Giant papyrus.

Native to Paraguay, Uruguay, and Colombia, north to Honduras and the Great Antilles, also possibly native to extreme southeastern Texas. Despite the name, this species is not necessarily larger than *Cyperus papyrus,* and is similar in many respects. It differs in having fewer inflorescence rays, but the rays are branched and form secondary umbels. Plants labeled *C. papyrus* 'Mexico' may be a form of *C. giganteus.* Zone 9.

Cyperus haspan Linnaeus.

Not in cultivation; plants labeled as such generally belong to *Cyperus prolifer.* The true *C. haspan* is not ornamental, but a rather slight plant with only two narrow upward-pointing inflorescence bracts. The umbels are loose and open, with up to 10 unequal rays, not globelike. It is native in North America to swamps and shallow water, mostly along the coast from Virginia to Florida and Texas, and widely distributed in tropical and subtropical regions of both hemispheres.

Cyperus eragrostis outdoors in England in mid-July.

Cyperus involucratus Rottboell.

[*Cyperus flabelliformis* Rottboell].

Umbrella plant, umbrella sedge, umbrella-palm.

Native to Africa. Nearly identical to *Cyperus alternifolius* (which see) but sometimes slightly taller with a few more bracts in the inflorescence. Zone 9.

Cyperus longus Linnaeus.

Galingale.

Native to coastal marshes and pondsides in England, also Europe, Asia, and North Africa. Slender and upright to 3 ft. (1 m) tall, lacking the umbel or umbrella-like inflorescences common to other species. Bracts of the inflorescence few, slender, erect or ascending. Valued ornamentally for the fine-textured, almost grassy effect, and cold-hardiness. Runs strongly. Zone 7.

Cyperus papyrus Linnaeus.

Papyrus, Egyptian paper reed.

Native to Africa. Egyptians used this species, which once grew along the river Nile, to make the paperlike papyrus they wrote upon. The stems were cut vertically into thin strips and laid parallel to each other, then another layer was laid at right angles. The resulting mat was pressed together and dried in the sun. This species is also believed to be the bulrush referred to in the Bible. It is a majestic

Cyperus involucratus in late May, grown under glass at the Brooklyn Botanic Garden, New York.

Cyperus papyrus in early June at the Jardin de Aclimatacion de La Orotava, Tenirife, Canary Islands.

plant, capable of growing 15 ft. (4.5 m) tall, though ornamental specimens are usually much shorter. Basal leaves are lacking. The stout, leafless stems are topped by inflorescences forming huge umbels 1 ft. (30 cm) wide or more, looking vaguely like giant onion flowers. The numerous rays of the inflorescence are threadlike, each ending in clusters of flower spikelets. The inflorescences are produced through the summer and are particularly beautiful when side-lit or back-lit by the sun. Spreads by stout rhizomes, but can easily be maintained as a clump. Zone 9.

Cyperus prolifer Lamarck.

[*Cyperus isocladus* Kunth, *Cyperus prolifer* var. *isocladus* (Kunth) Kukenthal]. Miniature papyrus, dwarf papyrus.

Native to edges of swamps and streams in eastern and southern Africa, Madagascar, and the Mascarene Islands. Very much resembles *Cyperus papyrus* in miniature. Stems slender, to 3 ft. (1 m) tall. The inflorescence an umbel, usually $2\frac{1}{2}$–4 in. (6–10 cm) in diameter. Plants in cultivation frequently produce sterile umbels,

Cyperus prolifer in late February, grown under glass at Longwood Gardens.

lacking spikelets at the ends of the rays. The rays radiate stiffly from the center, looking slightly like exploding green fireworks. Basal leaves lacking, the leaves reduced to sheaths. Runs by rhizomes but easily managed as a clump. Prefers constantly moist or wet soils. Grows well in shallow water. Zone 9.

Dactylis Linnaeus.

Grass family, Poaceae.

From the Greek *daktylos* (finger), referring to the finger-like branches of the inflorescence. Comprised of a single variable species, native to moist and dry sunny habitats, including meadows and open woodlands, in temperate Eurasia.

Dactylis glomerata Linnaeus.

Orchard grass (North America), cocksfoot (England).

Native in England and widely introduced and naturalized in North America, this slightly coarse species is a familiar presence in sunny fields, roadsides, and disturbed sites. It has been widely used for grazing and haymaking. Tufted and clump-forming, green-leaved, to 4 ft. (1.2 m) tall. Self-sows. Only the following variegated selection is grown for ornament.

'Variegata'. Variegated orchard grass, variegated cocksfoot. Leaves conspicuously striped white, giving an overall light green or white appearance. This cool-season grower can be an effective accent or small groundcover. It is best in spring and autumn, and in milder climates the foliage is semi-evergreen. In midsummer heat it often looks ragged and is best cut back to allow a flush of new, clean growth for autumn. Less vigorous than the species, this variegated cultivar rarely tops 2 ft. (60 cm) and does not flower heavily. It may self-sow, and seedlings are often green-leaved and more vigorous, and should be removed. Of easy culture in a range of soils in sun or light shade, average moisture. Propagate by division in spring or fall. Zone 5.

Dactylis glomerata 'Variegata' in northern Germany in mid-August.

Deschampsia P. Beauvois.

Grass family, Poaceae.

Hair grass, tussock grass.

Named for French naturalist Louis Deschamps (1765–1842). Comprised of approximately 40 mostly perennial species of circumboreal distribution, mostly native to meadows, moorlands, upland grasslands, and open woods.

Deschampsia cespitosa (Linnaeus) P. Beauvois.

[*Aira cespitosa* Linnaeus].

Tufted hair grass, tussock grass.

The specific epithet is often spelled *caespitosa*. A superb ornamental, valued for its neat, dark green foliage and for the cloudlike quality of its inflorescences, which form billowing masses of the finest, hairlike texture. This variable species has a wide native distribution in temperate zones, including Europe, Asia, and North America. A cool-season grower, it prefers moist habitats, such as shores, mead-

Deschampsia cespitosa in late August at the Hamburg Botanical Garden in Germany.

ows, bogs, and damp woodlands, often on heavy soils. Toward the southern extremes of its range, it is found mostly at higher, cooler elevations. Variability in foliage and flowers has led taxonomists to formulate many botanical varieties and subspecies; however, these intergrade and there is wide disagreement as to their distinction. Most selections currently in cultivation as ornamentals are derived from plants of European provenance. These perform very well in many North American regions but are not really suited to the hotter zones, especially if conditions are dry. Selections developed from plants native to warmer regions might offer improved performance. Strictly clump-forming and tufted, with a basal tuft of narrow, dark green leaves, 1–2 ft. (30–60 cm) tall, evergreen except in the coldest zones. Flower panicles produced in late June or July, emerging in various shades of green to gold, drying to light golden-straw color and lasting through winter unless broken down by snows. To 4 ft. (1.2 m) tall in bloom under ideal conditions. Long-lived and of easy culture in sun or shade, though flowering is much heavier in sun. Useful as accent, but especially beautiful in mass, forming huge sweeping clouds of flowers that change color over the course of the seasons. Superb when contrasted against a dark background or bold-leaved companion plantings. Beautiful when dew-covered in autumn mornings. Propagates readily by seed, although the following cultivars are produced by division

Deschampsia cespitosa 'Goldschleier' at Longwood Gardens in early July.

Deschampsia cespitosa 'Goldtau' in mid-July at Alan Bloom's garden in Bressingham, England.

in spring or fall. The flower color differences between cultivars are subtle and are most noticeable in mass plantings. Self-sows but easily managed. Zone 4.

'Bronzeschleier' (bronze veil). Has bronze-green inflorescences. One of the best-flowering cultivars for the U.S. Pacific Northwest. Zone 4.

'Fairy's Joke'. A viviparous oddity, producing tiny young plants in place of seeds. The inflorescences are weighted down by these plantlets, sometimes rooting at point of soil contact. Such plants are considered by some to merit recognition as *Deschampsia cespitosa* var. *vivipara*. Zone 4.

'Goldgehänge' (golden pendant). Inflorescences open golden-yellow, branches somewhat pendulous. Zone 4.

'Goldschleier' (gold veil). Inflorescences open golden-yellow. Zone 4.

'Goldstaub' (gold dust). Inflorescences open golden-yellow. Zone 4.

'Goldtau' (gold dew). Inflorescences open yellow-green. Zone 4.

'Northern Lights'. A dramatic variegated selection found in a seed flat by Harlan Hamernik's Bluebird Nursery of Clarkston, Nebraska, and named by Steve Schmidt of Oregon. Leaves with cream-white longitudinal stripes, sometimes suffused pink in cool seasons, to 10 in. (25 cm) maximum height. Has not been observed to flower. Zone 4.

'Schottland' (Scotland). Scottish tufted hair grass. As the German cultivar name implies, this selection is of Scottish origin. Leaves dark green, with light green inflorescences. Zone 4.

'Tardiflora'. Slightly later blooming, flowers in late summer. Zone 4.

'Tauträger' (dew carrier). Inflorescences more slender than the type. Zone 4.

Deschampsia flexuosa (Linnaeus) Trinius.

[*Aira flexuosa* Linnaeus].

Crinkled hair grass, wavy hair grass, common hair grass (North America).

Native to North America and Eurasia, mostly in drier habitats in sun or in open woodlands. Densely tufted, similar to *Deschampsia cespitosa* but smaller in all its parts, usually less than 2 ft. (60 cm) tall. The inflorescences are billowy but not always as dense. The spikelets vary in color from bronze to pale greenish yellow. Of easy culture on a variety of soils in part sun or shade. One of the few grasses that grows well in dry woodland settings. A cool-

Deschampsia cespitosa 'Schottland' at Longwood Gardens in early August.

season grower, flowering in midsummer. Propagate the species by seed, the cultivars by division in spring or fall. Self-sows manageably. Zone 4.

'Aurea' ('Tatra Gold'). Has yellow-green foliage, especially in early season, and comes true from seed. Flower spikelets soft bronze. Zone 4.

'Mückenschwarm' (fly swarm). Has a profusion of small, very dark spikelets. Zone 4.

Dichanthelium (Hitchcock & Chase) Gould.
Grass family, Poaceae.

Originally named as a subgenus of *Panicum,* to which it is closely related, but now recognized as a distinct genus. Comprised of more than 100 species widely distributed in tropical and temperate zones. Only the following species is grown ornamentally.

Dichanthelium clandestinum (Linnaeus) Gould.
[*Panicum clandestinum* Linnaeus].
Deer-tongue grass, deer-tongue panic grass.

Native on moist open ground over much of the eastern United States. The common name refers to the shape of the leaves, which are relatively wide, to 1 1/4 in. (32 mm), and short, to 7 in. (18 cm) long. Forms dense clumps to 30 in. (75 cm) tall, but can also spread aggressively by rhizomes, creating large masses. Summer foliage color is a bright green, turning yellow-brown with the coming of autumn frosts. Subtly attractive as it adds its tawny masses to the whites, purples, and yellows of asters and goldenrods in fall meadows. Can also be extremely invasive by seed or by rhizomes, especially on loose soils in a small garden, and may require control even in large meadow situations. Flowers ornamentally insignificant. Of easy culture in sun or part shade. Propagate by seed or division. Zone 4.

Dulichium Persoon.
Sedge family, Cyperaceae.
Three-way sedge.

Comprised of one species, native to wet habitats across North America. It is also known in the fossil records of Europe and eastern Asia.

Dichanthelium clandestinum at Longwood Gardens in early October.

Deschampsia flexuosa billowing over boulders in the Blue Ridge mountains of Virginia in late July.

Deschampsia flexuosa 'Aurea' at Mt. Cuba Center, Greenville, Delaware, in early May.

Dulichium arundinaceum (Linnaeus) Britton. Three-way sedge.

Native to swamps and margins of pools and streams, often in standing water, from Newfoundland to British Columbia, south to Florida, Texas, and California. The bright green leaves are arranged in three distinct ranks that are evident when viewing the plant from above, hence the common name. The stems are upright, 2–3 ft. (60–90 cm) tall, with narrow leaves, giving a somewhat bamboolike appearance. Flowers midsummer, ornamentally insignificant. Runs strongly by rhizomes, the dense colonies forming bright green ribbons venturing into shallow water. Beautifully characteristic of many eastern North American wetlands. Of easy culture in sun or part shade if provided constantly moist or wet soil. A fine addition to water gardens, providing contrast with bold-textured waterlilies and other broad-leaved plants. Propagate by seed or by division in spring. Zone 6.

Elegia Linnaeus.
Restio family, Restionaceae.

Approximately 30 dioecious species native to the Cape region of South Africa. Part of the fynbos plant community, which is characterized by natural burning, they are generally found on well-drained soils low in fertility. Variable in appearance, some species rushlike, others bearing a striking resemblance to horse-tails, *Equisetum*. Cool-season growers, most active in spring after winter rains. Many are quite beautiful but little known in cultivation. Research at the National Botanical Garden, Kirstenbosch, in Cape Town, South Africa, has found that smoke treatment of seeds often dramatically increases germination rates, making it possible to propagate various restios readily enough that they will become more common in gardens in mediterranean and warm temperate regions.

Elegia capensis (Burman f.) Schelpe.

Usually occurs along streamsides and low mountain seeps from Clanwilliam to Port Elizabeth, South Africa. Clump-forming, to nearly 7 ft. (2.1 m) tall, bearing an uncanny resemblance to a giant horsetail, with dense whorls of threadlike branches spaced along the vertical stems.

Dulichium arundinaceum in the New Jersey pine barrens in late June.

Elegia capensis detail at the National Botanical Garden, Kirstenbosch, Cape Town, South Africa, early September.

Brown male and female flowers on separate plants, at the tops of stems. Conspicuous papery leaf bracts, held closely to the stems, are a striking ornamental feature of this species. Propagate by seed. Difficult to divide as the roots do not like to be disturbed. Likes full sun and moisture. Resents high fertility. Best planted in spring or autumn in mediterranean climates. An excellent seasonal container subject in areas beyond its winter cold-hardiness. Zone 8.

Elegia juncea Linnaeus.

Native to moist and dry open places in South Africa from Tulbagh to Peninsula and in the Swartberg Mountains. Densely tufted. Stems simple, rushlike, to 30 in. (75 cm), topped by bright cinnamon-sheathed inflorescences. Propagate by seed. Zone 8.

Eleocharis R. Brown.
Sedge family, Cyperaceae.
Spike-rush.

From the Greek *helos* (marsh) and *charis* (grace). Approximately 150 species of worldwide distribution in wet soil or shallow water, many creeping by rhizomes to form dense mats. The leaves are reduced to bladeless sheaths, the stems slender and unbranched, each topped by a terminal spikelet. The unobtrusive simplicity of these plants is often overlooked, yet they can be a graceful, fine-textured presence in wet habits and in water gardens. Many look alike and can be difficult to tell apart. The two following species are different and distinct.

Eleocharis acicularis (Linnaeus) Roemer & Schultes.
Slender spike-rush, needle spike-rush, hair grass.

The species epithet means "needle-shaped," referring to the very slender stems and spikelets. Native to low ground and damp shores, often in standing water, in North America from Greenland to Alaska, south to Florida and Mexico, and in Eurasia. Tufted and creeping by rhizomes to form dense mats. Stems fine and almost hairlike, to 1 ft. (30 cm) tall, upright or lax. A graceful addition to marginal areas in water gardens, also sometimes grown in indoor aquaria. Of easy culture in sun and moist soil or shallow water. Does best in slightly acid conditions. Propagate by division in spring or by seed. Zone 5.

Eleocharis dulcis (Burman f.) Trinius ex Henschel.
Chinese water-chestnut, mai-tai.

Though simple and attractive, this widespread native of Asia and western Africa is more often grown for the edible tubers than for ornament. Jointed cylindrical green stems are to $^{3}/_{16}$ in. (4 mm) in diameter, to 4 ft. (1.2 m) tall. The terminal spikelet to 2 in. (5 cm) long, sometimes absent. Spreads by elongated stolons that terminate in

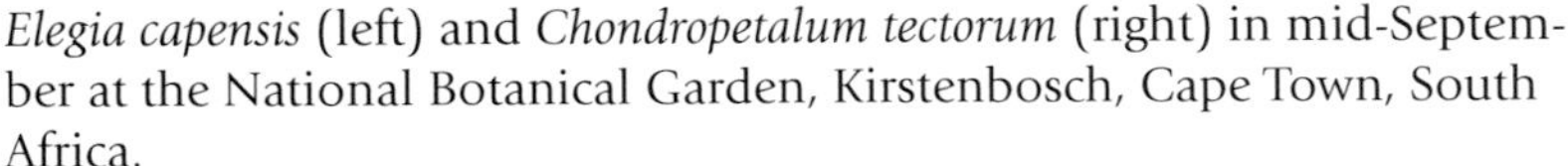

Elegia capensis (left) and *Chondropetalum tectorum* (right) in mid-September at the National Botanical Garden, Kirstenbosch, Cape Town, South Africa.

Elegia capensis detail of papery leaf bracts.

rounded tubers to 1 1/2 in. (4 cm) in diameter. Eaten fresh or cooked, the tubers are the familiar white crunchy vegetable common in Chinese foods. Of easy culture in full sun and shallow water. Propagate by offsets from tubers. Zone 9.

Eleocharis acicularis in shallow water along the New England coast, early August.

Elymus Linnaeus.
Grass family, Poaceae.
Wild rye, wheatgrass.

Nearly 150 perennial species, clump-forming or spreading by rhizomes, native throughout temperate latitudes of the Northern and Southern Hemispheres, in a variety of habitats, including meadows, prairies, woodlands, steppes, and dunes. This genus is contiguous with *Leymus*, and separation of the two is contentious, based on ambiguous criteria, such as whether spikelets are single or paired, and on characteristic arrangements of nerves on the glumes. Nevertheless, most current treatments transfer a few *Elymus* species familiar and important to gardeners, such as the blue lyme grasses, *E. arenarius* and *E. racemosus*, to the genus *Leymus*, a practice followed in this book. The species below are of minor ornamental significance except for *E. magellanicus*, which is unrivaled among grasses for the intense blue color of its foliage.

Elegia juncea in mid-September in its native habitat in the Cape region of South Africa.

Elymus canadensis Linnaeus.
Canada wild rye.

Native along riverbanks, prairies, open ground, and often dry sandy soil over much of the United States and Canada. Clump-forming, 3–6 ft. (1–2 m) tall, flowering in mid to late summer. The inflorescences are reminiscent of cultivated rye, nodding gently and remaining attractive long into winter. The foliage is coarse-textured, usually green but sometimes glaucous blue-green, although the blue color is never as strong as that of its relatives *Leymus arenarius* or *L. racemosus.* A fast-growing but somewhat short-lived prairie grass sometimes included in seed mixes to serve as a nurse crop for slower-growing prairie grasses and forbs. Of easy culture in sun on almost any soil, moist or dry. Propagates easily from seed or may be divided in spring. Self-sows, which is desirable in meadows or prairie restorations but may be a nuisance in small gardens. Zone 3.

Elymus glaucus Buckley.
Blue wild rye.

Native to moist or dry open thickets across northern North America. Clump-forming and densely tufted, leaves usually glaucous blue-green. Of minor ornamental value, this species is not often cultivated; however, the name *Elymus glaucus* hort. is often used in error in nursery catalogs and garden books to refer to *Leymus arenarius,* a running species with strongly glaucous foliage. Zone 5.

Elymus magellanicus (Desvaux) Á. Löve.
[*Agropyron magellanicum* Desvaux, *Agropyron pubiflorum* (Steudel) Parodi].
Magellan wheatgrass, blue wheatgrass.

Native to higher elevations in South America. This tufted clump-former has the most intense blue foliage of all the grasses. Its color is so strong that other grasses traditionally considered bluish, such as *Helictotrichon semper-*

Elymus canadensis flowering in late June at Longwood Gardens.

Elymus canadensis in late October in Wisconsin.

virens and *Festuca glauca*, appear dull in comparison. Foliage is semi-evergreen in mild climates. Unfortunately, this cool-season grower really resents humid summers with high night temperatures. In southern England it is prone to severe foliar rust disease. Still, the dramatic color is worth some coddling. Sharply drained soil is a necessity, especially in areas with wet winters. Light shade helps to relieve summer sulks in hot climates. Does well in coastal areas. Makes a superb container subject. Propagate by seed or by division in spring. Zone 6.

'Blue Tango'. Introduced by Kurt Bluemel. Collected in South America.

Elymus virginicus Linnaeus.

Virginia wild rye.

A very variable clump-forming species native to rich thickets, alluvial soils, shores, and sometimes alkaline areas over much of eastern North America. Of minor ornamental importance. Similar to *Elymus canadensis* but more coarse and usually green-leaved, occasionally slightly glaucous, the inflorescences with less-pronounced awns. Flowers midsummer. Propagate easily by seed. Zone 3.

Elymus magellanicus in late May in the author's garden.

Eragrostis Wolf.

Grass family, Poaceae.

Love grass.

From the Greek *eros* (love) and *agrostis* (grass). Approximately 350 annual perennial species of cosmopolitan distribution, many in tropical and subtropical zones.

Eragrostis curvula (Schrader) Nees.

Weeping love grass, African love grass.

This grass is cold-hardy far beyond what might be expected, since it is native to southern Africa. Strictly clump-forming and densely tufted, it forms a neat mound of very fine-textured foliage, overtopped in mid to late summer by arching, lavender-gray flower panicles, to 3 ft. (1 m) tall. Foliage is evergreen in mild climates, dying to the ground in cold zones. Leaves green in summer, often acquiring yellow-bronze tints in autumn. A subtle but graceful ornamental, this grass is useful as an accent or groundcover grouping and was widely planted for grassland stabilization and for erosion control on roadside embankments and other rights-of-way across the southern United States, where it has escaped and since become naturalized. Self-sows manageably. Propagate by seed or by division in spring. Zone 7.

Eragrostis spectabilis (Pursh) Steudel.

Purple love grass, tumble grass.

Native on sandy soil in full sun from Maine to Minnesota, south to Florida, Arizona, and Mexico. In late August through September, this grass produces volumes of fine-textured flower panicles that appear like reddish purple clouds hovering just above ground level (see Figure 2-7). The foliage is somewhat coarse and messy in appear-

Eragrostis curvula in Wiehenstephan, Germany, in late August.

ance, with dull green, mostly basal leaves to 3/8 in. (9 mm) wide. Fortunately, this is almost completely hidden once the plant comes into bloom. Overall height is under 2 ft. (60 cm). The inflorescence color fades to soft brown by October, and the plant is fully dormant in winter. Requires full sun but is drought tolerant and does not mind sandy, infertile, or poorly drained soils. Tends to be short-lived. Self-sows readily on disturbed soils in or out of the garden. Cut back soon after flowering to avoid seeding or let seed-heads remain if naturalizing in meadow gardens. Drifts or sweeps can be a beautiful addition to the late-summer landscape. In smaller gardens, the panicles show up well against gray or silver-leaved groundcovers. Occurs naturally in association with *Eupatorium hyssopifolium*, and this combination can be quite attractive in the garden. Propagates easily by seed. Zone 5. Figure 2-7.

Eragrostis spectabilis in eastern Pennsylvania in late August.

Eragrostis spectabilis blooming with tickseed sunflowers in a moist northern Delaware meadow in mid-September.

Eragrostis trichodes (Nuttall) A. Wood.
Sand love grass.

Native to sandy barrens and open sandy woodlands from Illinois to Colorado and Texas. Much taller than *Eragrostis spectabilis*, with upright, leafy flowering stems often reaching 4 ft. (1.2 m) in height. Inflorescences in July and early August, reddish pink tinted, but not as strongly colored as those of *E. spectabilis*. Easily grown in sun on any well-drained soil. Drought tolerant. Self-sows manageably. Propagate by seed or by division in spring. Zone 5.

'Bend'. Lax-stemmed, arching under the weight of its flowers and gently leaning on neighbors in late season, usually with pleasing results. Introduced and named by Dick Lighty of Pennsylvania. Zone 5.

Eriophorum Linnaeus.
Sedge family, Cyperaceae.
Cotton grass.

From the Greek *erion* (wool) and *phoros* (bearing), referring to the woolly flower heads. Approximately 20 species native throughout north temperate and arctic zones,

Eragrostis trichodes 'Bend' beginning to bloom in mid-July in North Carolina.

all perennials, most occurring in acid swamps and sphagnum bogs, often at higher elevations. They are distinct among sedges in having numerous fine bristles extending beyond the flower spikelets to form dense tufts resembling balls of cotton. The color of the bristles varies from tawny and dull to nearly pure white. A high mountain bog filled with thousands of cotton grasses is a spectacular sight in late autumn, as deciduous trees and shrubs add their color to the landscape. Cotton grasses are superb cut flowers but should never be picked from wild populations. Some species are clump-forming, others run by rhizomes. All require full sun, cool summer conditions, plenty of moisture, and acid conditions for best growth. Propagate by seed or by division in spring.

Eriophorum angustifolium Honckeny.

Cotton grass, common cotton grass.

Native to bogs from Greenland across North America to Alaska, south to New York, Michigan, Iowa, and Washington, common throughout the British Isles, also native to Europe and Asia. To $2^{1}/_{2}$ ft. (80 cm) tall, creeping extensively by rhizomes. Bristles white. Zone 3.

Eriophorum gracile Koch.

Slender cotton grass.

Native to swamps and bogs from Newfoundland to British Columbia, south to Pennsylvania, Indiana, Colorado, and northern California, also Eurasia. Usually under 2 ft. (60 cm) tall, spreading by rhizomes. Bristles white. Zone 4.

Eriophorum latifolium Hoppe.

Broad-leaved cotton grass.

Native in wet places scattered throughout the British Isles, less common than *Eriophorum angustifolium*. Also native in Eurasia. Tufted and clump-forming, to 28 in. (70 cm) tall. Bristles white. Zone 4.

Eriophorum vaginatum Linnaeus.

[*Eriophorum spissum* Fernald].

Hare's tail cotton grass, tussock cotton grass.

Native in moorland bogs and other damp, peaty places in the British Isles, also in Europe and across northern North America. Clump-forming and densely tufted, forming broad tussocks. Bristles white. Zone 4.

Eriophorum virginicum Linnaeus.

Virginia cotton grass, tawny cotton grass,

Abundantly native in swamps, bogs, and wet meadows, only in North America, from Newfoundland and Quebec to Manitoba and Minnesota, south through the New Jersey pine barrens to Florida and Kentucky. Tufted and clump-forming, to 3 ft. (1 m) tall. Bristles white or tawny. Tolerates warm, humid summers better than species restricted to cool climates. Zone 4.

Eriophorum virginicum growing native at Cranberry Glades in the mountains of West Virginia, mid-October.

Fargesia Franchet.
Grass family, Poaceae.
Chinese mountain bamboo.

In the 1880s French missionary and naturalist Paul Guillaume Farges found an unusual clump-forming bamboo in Sichuan, China, and sent material to Parisian botanist Adrien Franchet, who named the plant *Fargesia spathacea*. The genus is now comprised of as many as 40 species native to the mountains of central China.

The two species below are included in this book because of their refined beauty, because they are the most cold-hardy clump-forming bamboos widely in cultivation, and because their modest size makes them as easy to manage as a large grass. The two are superficially similar, except that one tends to be more upright in form and its culms are often darker-colored. Both produce many closely spaced culms to 1/2 in. (12 mm) in diameter and grow 9–14 ft. (2.7–4.2 m) tall. They form dense clumps, increasing only 2–3 in. (5–7.5 cm) in diameter each year, never sending out the distant runners that make many bamboos unwelcome in gardens. Their leaves are to 5/8 in. (15 mm) wide by 4 in. (10 cm) long, medium to light green. The overall texture of the plant is quite fine. Both are evergreen and reliably cold-hardy at least to -20°F (-29°C). They drop a portion of their leaves each year, in late fall, and during this period the plants are a rich mix of green and gold.

Both, but especially fountain bamboo, *Fargesia nitida*, produce late-season canes that do not develop leaves or branches until the following spring. In winter, it is easy to mistake these for dead canes, but they should never be cut, since they are important to the plants' growth. Both grow best in moist, fertile soils in sun or part shade, with protection from strong winds, especially in winter. Plants exposed to desiccating winds tend to roll their leaves, sometimes dramatically. Extreme summer temperatures or dry spells also cause leaves to roll, but they unfurl when temperatures drop or with more moisture. Propagation is by division in midspring, and is easy and reliable as long as plants are not allowed to dry out at any time. Divisions can be easily cut from the perimeters of established clumps with a sharp spade. New transplants must be kept especially moist until established.

Both species are versatile garden plants, particularly useful as specimens or screens, and make excellent container subjects if kept moist. The one caveat is that *Fargesia* is among bamboo genera that often die after flowering and seed set. The various species have internal "clocks," and all plants of a particular species tend to flower together—not precisely at once, but over a period of a few years or a few decades. Umbrella and fountain bamboos flower approximately once every century, and they are in that period at the time of this writing. Umbrella bamboo began flowering first, and although many established specimens died after flowering, there is already a new generation of seedling plants available to gardeners. Seeds have

Fargesia murielae at the Palmengarten, Frankfurt, Germany, mid-August.

Fargesia murielae flowering at Longwood Gardens, mid-April 1997.

a relatively short viability and should be sown soon after maturing. With the advent of flowering comes the chance to select seedlings for variations in size, habit, stem color, and other attributes that expand the versatility of these bamboos in garden designs.

The botanical names of these bamboos have undergone considerable change during the 1900s. This is largely because taxonomists have had to work without the flowering characteristics usually of critical importance to plant classification. The flowering of these bamboos is likely to lead to further name shifts.

Fargesia murielae (Gamble) Yi.

[*Arundinaria murielae* Gamble, *Arundinaria spathacea* (Franchet) D. McClintock, *Fargesia spathacea* Franchet, *Sinarundinaria murielae* (Gamble) Nakai, *Thamnocalamus spathaceus* (Franchet) Söderstrom].

Umbrella bamboo.

First collected in China in 1907 by Ernest Wilson, who sent plants to Arnold Arboretum, Jamaica Plain, Massachusetts, which sent plants to the Royal Botanic Gardens, Kew, England. The species epithet honors Wilson's daughter, Muriel. Culms are typically green, and overall form is widespreading, with stems lax and arching especially on older specimens. Flowering began in the late 1970s in northern Europe and is still in progress. Cultivars have already been selected from the new seedling generation, including **'Mary'**, **'Simba'**, **'Thyme'**, and **'Zampa'**. Zone 4.

Fargesia nitida (Mitford) Keng f. & Yi.

[*Arundinaria nitida* Mitford, *Sinarundinaria nitida* (Mitford) Nakai].

Fountain bamboo.

The species epithet, *nitida*, means "shining" or "polished," referring to the culms, which are often dark mahogany-colored to near-black and glossy. Culms may also be covered with a waxy bloom, giving a purplish appearance, and the leaves are often slightly glaucous gray-green. More upright in form than umbrella bamboo; however, older specimens are still quite relaxed and graceful. Russian zoologist Berezovski collected seed of this species during an expedition to China in 1884–1886. He sent seed to the Botanic Garden in St. Petersburg, which sent seed to the Veitch nursery in England, and plants were eventually established at the Royal Botanic Gardens, Kew, England. The clonal cultivars below date from this seed generation. Flowering of *Fargesia nitida* has begun at the time

Fargesia nitida is still green in early November in the author's garden, amid the fall color of deciduous shrubs and herbaceous plants entering dormancy.

of this writing, but there are no seedlings yet in cultivation. Zone 4.

'Anceps'. Leaves small. Rapid-growing, quick to increase, and therefore especially easy to propagate. Better heat tolerance but perhaps slightly less cold-hardy than some.

'Chennevières'. Leaves slightly narrower than the type. Compact growing.

'Eisenach'. Leaves smaller and darker than the type.

'Ems River'. Culms develop and retain a strong purple-black color. Compact growing.

'McClure'. Large growing.

'Nymphenburg'. Leaves exceptionally narrow, overall texture very fine.

Festuca Linnaeus.

Grass family, Poaceae.
Fescue.

From the Latin *festuca* (stalk, stem). Approximately 300 tufted or rhizomatous perennial species of cosmopolitan distribution, but mainly in temperate zones. Fescues are often important, fine-textured constituents of lawns; however, most ornamental garden species are tufted clump-formers valued for various shades of blue-green or glaucous-blue foliage. They vary in size from rock-garden miniatures less than 1 ft. (30 cm) to medium-sized grasses topping 3 ft. (1 m). Most prefer full sun and sharply drained soils. They are cool-season growers, often suffering during hot, humid summer periods. Propagate the species by seed, the cultivars by division only. Individual clumps tend to be relatively short-lived, dying out in the center as they age. Plants are best renewed by division every few years. Many benefit from being cut back yearly in late winter or early spring. There has been much confusion over which species the common blue fescue cultivars represent, with various texts ascribing them to *Festuca cinerea*, *F. glauca*, or *F. ovina*. They are treated here under *F. glauca*, in accord with increasing taxonomic consensus.

Festuca amethystina Linnaeus.

Large blue fescue.

Native to central Europe. Tufted and clump-forming, to 2 ft. (60 cm) tall in flower. Leaves rolled and thread-like, the foliage texture extremely fine, color varying from blue-green to intensely glaucous gray-blue. The June flowers are attractive, held well above the foliage on slender stalks. Of similar garden use to the common blue fescue, *Festuca glauca*, but slightly larger. Zone 4.

'Aprilgrün' (Aprilgreen). Leaves green. Flower stems lack the amethyst color of 'Superba'.

'Bronzeglanz'. Lightly tinted bronze.

'Klose'. Leaves olive-colored, shorter than typical. Named for German nurseryman Heinz Klose.

'Superba'. Foliage intensely blue-silver, to 1 ft. (30 cm) long, rivaling the best of the *Festuca glauca* cultivars. Flowers in June to 2 ft. (60 cm) tall. Remarkable and outstand-

Fargesia nitida in Pauline Volmer's garden, Baltimore, Maryland, in late April.

Fargesia nitida 'Ems River' detail shows dark culms, early May.

ing for the slender amethyst-colored stalks supporting the inflorescences. The color can be vivid for about three weeks in June.

Festuca californica Vasey.
California fescue.

Native to dry open ground, chaparral, thickets, and open forests to approximately 5000 ft. (1500 m) in elevation in Oregon and in California west of the Sierra Nevada, occasionally on serpentine soils. Often found on north-facing slopes. A truly beautiful mid-sized grass, with slightly flat, blue-green or glaucous blue-gray leaves in a loose mound 2–3 ft. (60–90 cm) tall, topped by airy flower panicles anytime from April through June. A cool-season grower, fully evergreen in milder climates. Long-lived and durable. Effective as a specimen or massed for groundcover. At the University of California, Berkeley, Botanical Garden, a hillside sweep of this grass mingled with the burgundy stems of native *Arctostaphylos* species makes a stunning combination. Easily grown on a variety of soils. Fairly drought tolerant but looks best with moisture. Use fingers or a stiff rake to comb out occasional accumulations of old foliage. Propagate by division in spring or fall, or by seed. Zone 7.

'Mayacmas Blue'. Foliage gray-blue.

'Salmon Creek'. Foliage blue-gray.

'Serpentine Blue'. Foliage intensely grayish blue, a strong bloomer. Introduced by the University of California, Berkeley, Botanical Garden from a plant growing on a serpentine seep in Marin County, California.

Festuca amethystina 'Superba'.

Festuca filiformis Pourret.
[*Festuca ovina* subsp. *tenuifolia* (Sibthorp) Dumortier, *Festuca tenuifolia* Sibthorp].
Hair fescue, fine-leafed sheep's fescue.

Native to the British Isles on acid, sandy soils, and to western and central Europe. Strictly clump-forming,

Festuca californica in mid-December at the University of California, Berkeley, Botanical Garden.

Festuca filiformis at Longwood Gardens, late June.

densely tufted, leaves green and very fine-textured. Foliage a neat mound, to 6 in. (15 cm), flowers in late June, to 12 in. (30 cm), relatively insignificant. Subtly attractive, a useful contrast to the blue-leaved fescues. Prefers full sun or light shade, sharp drainage. Cool-season grower. Propagate by seed or division. Zone 4.

Festuca gautieri (Hackel) K. Richter.
Bearskin fescue.

Native to France and Spain. Strictly clump-forming, foliage densely tufted, to 5 in. (12 cm). Leaves green, stiff, and needlelike, especially in the following compact selection, which is most frequently cultivated. Often sold as *Festuca scoparia*. Zone 4.

'Pic Carlit'. Miniature, to 3 in. (7.5 cm) tall. A good rock garden subject. Zone 4.

Festuca glauca Villars, non Lamarck.
[*Festuca ovina* var. *glauca* (Lamarck) Hackel, *Festuca cinerea* Villars, *Festuca cinerea* var. *glauca* (Villars) Stohr].
Blue fescue, common blue fescue, garden fescue, gray fescue.

Native to southern France. Strictly clump-forming, foliage densely tufted, forming neat mounds 6–10 in. (15–25 cm) tall, topped by upright flower panicles in June. Inflorescences at first colored like the foliage, soon bleaching to light tan. Plants often look best if flowers are sheared off upon drying. Common blue fescue makes a superb color accent and grows well in containers. A cool-season grower, it often sulks during hot, humid summers. Though it is frequently employed in groundcover masses and can be quite stunning in this manner, its short-lived nature guarantees that a fair amount of maintenance is necessary to keep plantings looking neat and uniform. Individual plants tend to die out at center after two to four years, especially if stressed by summer heat or waterlogged soils in winter. In any case, annual shearing in late winter often contributes to longer life and neater appearance. A plethora of foliage color forms has been selected and named. In careful designs, it may be desirable to specify a precise hue; a blue-silver plant versus a silver-blue plant, for example. Unfortunately, cultivars are frequently mislabeled in commerce, clonal cultivars are adulterated by seed-propagation, and leftover stock of all names is sometimes lumped as generic "blue fescue." It often pays to inspect plants before purchase. Below are some of the more distinct, widely grown selections. Most are reliably hardy to Zone 4.

'Azurit'. Leaves blue-silver.

'Blaufink' (blue finch). Leaves silver-blue.

'Blaufuchs' (blue fox). Leaves silver-blue.

'Blauglut' (blue glow). Leaves silver-blue.

'Blausilber' (blue silver). Leaves blue-silver. One of the best primarily silver-leaved selections.

'Daeumling' ('Tom Thumb'). Compact, foliage less than 6 in. (15 cm).

'Elijah Blue'. If in doubt, choose this one. Leaves strongly silver-blue. One of the more durable and longer-lived selections. Discovered and named by Lois Woodhill of The Plantage Nursery, Cutchogue, Long Island, New York.

'Frühlingsblau' (spring blue). Leaves silver-blue.

'Meerblau' (sea blue). Leaves rich sea-blue, with some green hues, too. Distinct and attractive.

'Seeigel' (sea urchin). Leaves blue-green.

'Silberreiher' (silver egret). Leaves blue-silver.

'Solling'. Leaves silver-gray.

Festuca glauca with *Carlina acaulis* at the Berggarten in Germany, late August.

Festuca glauca 'Blaufink' at Longwood Gardens, early June.

Festuca glauca 'Blausilber' at Longwood Gardens, late June.

Festuca glauca 'Meerblau' in mid-July in Alan Bloom's garden in Bressingham, England.

Festuca glauca 'Elijah Blue' at Longwood Gardens, late September.

Festuca idahoensis Elmer.

Idaho fescue, blue bunchgrass.

Despite the common name, this species is native to open woods and rocky slopes from British Columbia to Alberta, south to central California and Colorado. A cool-season grower, clump-forming, densely tufted and longer-lived than *Festuca glauca*. Trial plants at Longwood Gardens have persisted without center dieback for nearly a decade without division, and have appeared more tolerant of wet winter soils. Foliage blue-green to silver-blue, to 14 in. (35 cm) tall. Propagate by division or seed. Zone 5.

Festuca mairei St. Yves.

Atlas fescue.

Native to the Atlas Mountains of Morocco, at elevations to 7500 ft. (2300 m). Well known to German grass pioneer Karl Foerster, this unique and useful mid-sized grass is handsome and still generally under-appreciated. It makes a neat mound of flat, gray-green foliage 2–2½ ft. (60–80 cm) tall, topped by very slender flower panicles in June. A cool-season grower, but more tolerant of hot summers than many fescues. Slow-growing but durable and long-lived. Fully evergreen in milder climates. Use fingers or a stiff rake to comb out occasional accumulations of old foliage. Prefers full sun. Propagate by division in spring or by seed. Zone 5.

Festuca idahoensis in mid-July at Longwood Gardens.

Festuca mairei in Berlin, Germany, late August.

Festuca ovina Linnaeus.
Sheep's fescue.

Widespread in temperate zones, but not important to ornamental gardens. The common blue garden fescues belong to *Festuca glauca*.

Festuca rubra Linnaeus.
Creeping red fescue.

A widespread native throughout Europe and North America. Runs strongly by rhizomes and is best known for the many selections that have been developed for use as mown turf grasses. These green-leaved varieties generally require generous moisture for good growth, and many are escaped and naturalized. Bluish-leaved selections from native California populations have proved fairly drought tolerant and show promise as ornamental groundcovers for drier climates. Full sun. Propagate by division. Zone 5.

'Jughandle'. Compact, with bluish leaves. A California selection by David Amme.

'Molate'. Leaves bluish. Heat and drought tolerant. A California selection by David Amme.

Festuca valesiaca Schleicher ex Gaudin.
Wallis fescue.

Native to Europe. Similar in most practical respects to the common blue fescue. Represented in cultivation mostly by the following selection. Zone 5.

'Glaucantha'. Leaves blue-green, fine textured, less than 6 in. (15 cm) tall.

Festuca rubra in mid-October at the University of California, Berkeley, Botanical Garden.

Glyceria R. Brown.
Grass family, Poaceae.
Manna grass, sweet grass, sweet hay, reed sweet grass.

From the Greek *glykys* (sweet), referring to the sweetness of the grain, which is attractive to waterfowl, and the foliage, which is favored by grazing livestock. Comprised of nearly 40 perennial species, native to wet places in temperate zones throughout the world. Most are strongly rhizomatous.

Glyceria maxima (Hartman) Holmboe.
[*Glyceria aquatica* Linnaeus].
Manna grass, great water grass, reed sweet grass, sweet hay.

Native to wet soils and shallow water in marshes and at the edges of rivers, ponds, and lakes in Europe and temperate Asia. Green-leaved, with erect, airy flower panicles 6–8 ft. (2–2.4 m) tall, appearing mid to late summer. Spreads aggressively by stout rhizomes, covering large areas if unchecked. Attractive to waterfowl. Requires full sun and moisture. Not particular about soils. Propagate by seed or by division in spring. Usually grown for the following cultivar. Zone 6.

Glyceria maxima in late August at the Munich Botanic Garden in Germany.

'Variegata' Variegated manna grass. Differs from the species in having bright cream-yellow-striped leaves, often tinted pink during cool periods in spring and autumn. Smaller-growing than the species, to only 20 in. (50 cm) tall, and rarely flowering. Not as aggressive a runner, especially in drier soils, but still strong enough to overpower companions in a flower border. Best used in garden places that offer natural checks, such as pond edges and streambanks. Easily tolerates poorly drained soils or standing water. Properly sited, this grass can provide an attractive trouble-free mass of brightly colored foliage. Also effective mixed with other plants in container displays. Deciduous in winter, the foliage becoming an unkempt, light brown mass. Propagate by division in spring or fall. Cut back yearly. Zone 5.

Glyceria obtusa (Muhlenberg) Trinius.

Blunt manna grass.

Native to bogs and marshy places from Nova Scotia south along the coast through the New Jersey pine barrens to North Carolina. Interesting for the bright yellow-green color of its foliage and for its erect, dense flower panicles, 2–3 ft. (60–90 cm) tall, which turn deep brown by late summer. An excellent food source for native waterfowl. Runs by rhizomes. Propagate by seed or by division in spring. Zone 6.

Glyceria maxima 'Variegata' at Longwood Gardens in mid-May.

Hakonechloa Makino ex Honda.

Grass family, Poaceae. Hakone grass, urahagusa.

Comprised of one highly ornamental species, native to Japan.

Hakonechloa macra (Munro) Makino.

Hakone grass, urahagusa.

Native to wet, rocky cliffs in the mountains of Japan's main island, Honshu, including the region near Mt. Hakone, from which the genus name is derived. The graceful, arching stems of this slow spreader form loose, cascading mounds 1–3 ft. (30–90 cm) tall. The soft foliage is rich green and quite reminiscent of bamboo. Plants

Bright green bands of *Glyceria obtusa* contrast with waterlilies in the New Jersey pine barrens, mid-August.

spread by rhizomes and stolons, enough to warrant use as a groundcover but never invasive. The mid- to late-summer inflorescences appear between the leaves and are subtly attractive. Although a warm-season grower, Hakone grass requires a cool, moist environment similar to its native habitat for best growth. In warm dry climates it should be grown in substantial shade. In cooler moist climates, including England and the U.S. Pacific Northwest, it is luxuriant even in nearly full sun. Compared to its strikingly variegated cultivar 'Aureola', it is more sun tolerant, drought tolerant, cold-hardy, faster growing, and much easier to propagate. It turns exquisite copper-orange tones in autumn. Hakone grass has historically been a favorite pot-plant in Japan, and several cultivated variants exist. These are slowly making their way to Western gardens. Superb for accent, groundcover groups or sweeps, and container subjects. All require moist, organic, well-drained soils. Best divided or transplanted in spring. The roots are shallow, and fall transplants are doubly prone to cold damage and frost-heaving. Although generally disease-free, a fungal blight afflicting the genus has been observed on plants growing in Maryland and warrants further research. Zone 4.

Glyceria obtusa seeds are rich brown in mid-September in coastal New Jersey.

Hakonechloa macra in mid-June in Barry Yinger's garden, Lewisberry, Pennsylvania.

Hakonechloa macra in early November in Kurt Bluemel's garden in Fallston, Maryland.

'Albovariegata' ('Albostriata'). White-variegated Hakone grass. Similar to the species except the rich green foliage is accented by fine longitudinal white stripes. Larger and much more vigorous than 'Aureola', growing 3 ft. (1 m) tall in zone 6. Also more tolerant of warm, sunny sites, including gardens in the southeastern United States. Easy to propagate by division in spring. Introduced to the West from the private garden of Masato Yokoi, a Japanese specialist in variegated plants. Similar but distinct white-striped clones are in collector's gardens in Japan and North America but are not yet named or available commercially. Zone 4.

Hakonechloa macra 'Albovariegata' at Longwood Gardens in early June.

Hakonechloa macra 'All Gold' in mid-June in Barry Yinger's garden, Lewisberry, Pennsylvania.

'All Gold'. This introduction, named by variegated plant specialist Masato Yokoi of Japan, has all-gold leaves, without any green stripes. Growth rate and size are similar to those of 'Aureola'. Requires partial shade in warm climates. Zone 6.

'Aureola' ('Albo-aurea'). Golden-variegated Hakone grass. The leaves are almost entirely variegated with only a few slender stripes of green remaining, especially at the margins. The variegation is affected by siting and climatic conditions. When grown in deep shade, the variegation is a lime green. When grown in part sun in warm regions, such as the eastern United States, the variegation is a strong golden-yellow. When grown in sun in cool climates, such as England and the Pacific Northwest, the variegation is more cream-white than yellow. Cool temperatures in spring and in autumn, especially, induce beautiful suffusions of pink and red to the foliage. 'Aureola' is shorter, to 14 in. (35 cm), much slower growing, and less easy to propagate than the green-leaved form. It makes a striking color accent or container subject. Zone 6.

'Beni Fuchi'. Foliage is chocolate-brown in summer and red in autumn, especially toward the tips. There is more than one clone in Japan with these characteristics. Still rare in cultivation outside Japan. Zone 5.

Hakonechloa macra 'Aureola' in part shade in late May at Fred and Mary Ann McGourty's Hillside Gardens in Connecticut.

Hakonechloa macra 'Aureola' in full sun in mid-August at the Royal Horticultural Society Wisley Garden, Surrey, England.

Hakonechloa macra 'Aureola' in mid-October in full sun in Japan.

Helictotrichon Besser ex Roemer & Schultes.

Grass family, Poaceae.
Oat grass.

From the Greek *heliktos* (twisted) and *trichos* (hair, bristle), referring to the shape of the awn. Includes nearly 100 perennial species, mostly native to dry hillsides, meadows, and margins of woods in temperate Eurasia, but extending to other temperate regions throughout the world, including North America. Only the following species is an important ornamental.

Helictotrichon sempervirens (Villars) Pilger.

[*Avena sempervirens* Pilger].
Blue oat grass.

A western Mediterranean native. The best of the mid-sized blue-leaved grasses. Strictly clump-forming, producing a dense tuft of erect, silver-blue foliage to $2^1/_2$ ft. (80 cm) tall, evergreen in mild climates and semi-evergreen even in cold climates. Delicate inflorescences appear in late spring, held more than 2 ft. (60 cm) above the foliage on slender, arching stems. A cool-season grower, flowering best if plants are provided fertile, well-drained soil and if springtime conditions are cool and steadily moist. Flowering is often sparse if conditions are hot and humid; however, this grass is worth growing just

Helictotrichon sempervirens in late May in the author's garden.

for the foliage. Susceptible to disfiguring foliar rusts if late-summer humidity is high, especially if soils are poorly drained. Poor winter drainage can cause root rots. Superb as a specimen, color accent, or container specimen. Propagate the species by seed, the cultivars by division in spring. Zone 4.

'Pendula'. Heavy blooming, inflorescence more nodding.

'Robust'. Rust-resistant. Selected by Eckhard Schimana of Germany.

'Saphirsprudel'. (sapphire fountain). Folliage a bright steel-blue. Improved rust-resistance. Selected and introduced in 1982 by Heinz Klose Nursery of Germany and now available in the United States.

Hesperostipa (Elias) Barkworth.

Grass family, Poaceae.
Needle grass.

Genus name means "western *Stipa*." Comprised of four perennial North American species, segregated from *Stipa*, all with conspicuous, long awns.

Hesperostipa spartea (Trinius) Barkworth.

[*Stipa spartea* Trinius].
Porcupine grass.

Native to open hillsides and prairies in central North America. Clump-forming, upright, to 3 ft. (1 m) tall in flower, the inflorescences nodding at the tops of the culms. Remarkable for the flowing awns, which are to 8 in. (20 cm) long. Threadlike and translucent, they shimmer and sparkle in strong sun as breezes blow across the surface of the prairie. Of easy culture in full sun on most soils of average moisture. Propagate by seed. Self-sows manageably. Zone 3.

Hierochloe R. Brown.

Holy grass, sweet grass, vanilla grass.

From the Greek *hieros* (sacred, holy) and *chloe* (grass). The fragrant leaves have been used to scent churches on holy days and as incense by Native Americans. Scarcely ornamental from a visual standpoint, but perhaps of interest to those who consider scent an ornamental aspect of the garden.

Hierochloe occidentalis Buckley.

California sweet grass.

Native in moist and dry coniferous forests in California and Washington. Crushed leaves wonderfully sweet-fragrant. Upright, to 3 ft. (1 m) tall in flower, running by rhizomes. Prefers light or dense shade and moisture. Propagate by seed or division. Zone 7.

Hierochloe odorata (Linnaeus) P. Beauvois.

Vanilla grass, sweet grass, holy grass, Seneca grass (Native Americans).

Native to wet sites and meadows in North America and Eurasia. Upright, to 2 ft. (60 cm) tall in flower, running aggressively by rhizomes. Of easy culture in sun or part shade on moist soils. Propagate by seed or division. Crushed leaves strongly sweet-fragrant. Used by Native Americans to make fragrant baskets. Zone 4.

Holcus Linnaeus.

Grass family, Poaceae.

From the Greek word for sorghum. Comprised of six annual and perennial species native to woods and open grasslands in Europe, temperate Asia, and Africa.

Holcus lanatus Linnaeus.

Yorkshire fog, velvet grass.

Native to moist or dry meadows and open woodlands throughout the British Isles, in Europe, temperate Asia, and Africa, and introduced and naturalized in North and South America. The leaves and stems of this grass are

Hesperostipa spartea in a Minnesota prairie in mid June.

densely covered with fine hairs and feel like the softest velvet when touched. Strictly clump-forming, producing an erect flower panicle to 3 ft. (1 m) tall in spring or early summer, which opens white to pale green, often with pink or purple tints, and dries narrower but fluffy and cream-white. An attractive native constituent of English meadows. Easy to grow in full sun on any soil, but self-sows readily. A cool-season grower, often semi-dormant in midsummer. The melic grasses, particularly *Melica ciliata,* are similar in producing fluffy white inflorescences but are easier managed in the garden. Zone 5.

Holcus mollis Linnaeus.

Creeping soft grass.

Native to woods and poor grasslands in Europe, especially on acid soils. Superficially similar to *Holcus lanatus* but not quite as soft-hairy, and creeping extensively by rhizomes. Self-sows. Because of its aggressive spread, the green-leaved species form is rarely cultivated for ornament.

'Variegatus' ('Albovariegatus'). Leaves heavily striped white. Creeping by rhizomes, but manageable. Foliage usually less than 8 in. (20 cm) tall, at its best in cool spring and autumn weather. Benefits from midsummer shearing in hot, humid climates. Not a strong bloomer. Grow in full sun in cool climates or part shade in warmer zones. Quite showy and much less vigorous than the species. Makes a fine, near-white groundcover in cool climates. Propagate by division in spring or fall. Zone 6.

Hordeum Linnaeus.

Grass family, Poaceae.

Barley.

From the Latin *hordeum* (barley). Comprised of approximately 40 annual and perennial species distributed throughout temperate regions of the world, mostly on dry soils. Includes cultivated barley, *Hordeum vulgare,* an extremely important cereal crop valued for its short growing season and salt tolerance. Only *H. jubatum* is cultivated for ornament.

Hordeum jubatum Linnaeus.

Foxtail barley.

The most ornamental of the wild barleys, native to meadows and open ground from Newfoundland to Alaska, south to Maryland, Texas, California, and Mexico, and widely introduced and naturalized elsewhere. Though a perennial, this species is often short-lived, behaving more like an annual in the garden. Its long-awned, salmon-pink inflorescences are unquestionably showy and make su-

Holcus lanatus naturalized in a West Virginia meadow, in early June.

Holcus mollis 'Variegatus' in early October in the Christchurch Botanical Garden, New Zealand.

perb cut flowers, but this species self-sows so prolifically it should be introduced only with caution. It is a noxious weed in irrigated pastures in the western United States. A cool-season grower to $2^1/2$ ft. (80 cm) tall, flowering in June and July, and usually unkempt in later season. Easily grown from seed in full sun on any soil, even on salt-laden coastal sands. Zone 4.

Hordeum jubatum in early August along the Maine coast.

Hystrix Moench.

Grass family, Poaceae.
Bottle-brush grass.

From the Greek *hystrix,* (porcupine), referring to the long-awned, bristly flower spikes. Includes up to nine perennial species native to woodlands and meadows in North America, temperate Asia, and New Zealand. Closely related to and sometimes included in *Elymus.*

Hystrix patula Moench.

[*Elymus hystrix* Linnaeus].
Bottle-brush grass.

Native to moist or rocky woods in eastern North America, from Nova Scotia to North Dakota, south to Georgia and Arkansas. Clump-forming, upright, to 3 ft. (1 m) tall. Grown for the attractive bottlebrush-like inflorescences, to 6 in. (15 cm) long, first appearing in mid-June and produced intermittently through August, after rains. Opening green, bleaching to tan, they often remain attractive into autumn, when the deciduous forest foliage is at its color peak. Useful green or dried for cut flower arrangements. One of relatively few true grasses adapted to dry shaded conditions. Responds well to moist fertile garden soils but suffers in hot sun except in colder climates. This subtle woodland native is best in informal settings. The foliage is coarse-textured, and though the flowers are dramatic up close, they are easily lost in the overall landscape picture. Self-sows but easily managed. Ideal for naturalizing in shaded gardens. Propagate by seed. Zone 4.

Hystrix patula in early June in its native habitat at a deciduous woodland edge in Missouri.

Hystrix patula inflorescence resembles a bottlebrush.

Imperata Cyrillo.

Grass family, Poaceae.

Comprised of eight rhizomatous perennial species, native throughout the tropics, extending to warm temperate regions.

Imperata brevifolia Vasey.

Satin-tail.

Native to arid regions in western Texas to Utah, southern California, and Mexico. Green-leaved, upright, usually less than 3 ft. (1 m) tall, running by rhizomes. Inflorescences narrow, terminal, white, satin-textured. Of subtle ornamental value in dry climates. Zone 8.

Imperata cylindrica (Linnaeus) P. Beauvois.

There are two botanical varieties (or phases) of this species, one a mild-mannered ornamental, the other a serious pest in tropical and subtropical climates. Controversy over their relationship threatens to restrict the sale and distribution of the ornamental plant in the United States.

Imperata cylindrica 'Red Baron' at Longwood Gardens in mid-September.

Imperata cylindrica var. *koenigii* (Retzius) T. Durand & Schinz.

Common to lowlands in Japan, China, Korea, and Manchuria. Represents the temperate phase of the species and is sufficiently distinct from the tropical phase that it has been sometimes designated a separate species, *I. koenigii* (Retzius) P. Beauvois. It spreads at a moderate pace by rhizomes.

'Red Baron' ('Rubra'). Japanese blood grass. This red-leaved garden form has been well-known for more than a century in Japan (although not, certainly, as 'Red Baron', a name coined by Kurt Bluemel's nursery), where it is usually grown in shallow containers as a companion plant to specimen bonsai. It spreads very slowly by shallow rhizomes. Leaves are upright, to 20 in. (50 cm), emerging green at the base and red at the tips in spring, the color increasing over summer, becoming solid and intense in later summer and autumn. Occasional reversions to solid green are easily removed and show no change in other characteristics, such as size or rate of spread. Color fades with hard frosts. Winter interest is negligible, and plants are best cut to the ground. Rarely blooms, but when present inflorescences are narrow, silky white, to 2 ft. (60 cm) tall. No seedlings have been observed from such flowering in North America. Grows most luxuriant in moist, fertile soils in full sun. Drought tolerant once established

Imperata cylindrica 'Red Baron' flowering in Delaware in mid-May.

and tough enough for groundcover use in challenging sites, such as parking lots and traffic islands. A strong color accent, dramatic in sweeps and masses. Propagate by division and transplant in spring. Fall transplants are likely to heave out of the ground due to frost action in colder climates. Due to this cultivar's relation to the species' noxious tropical phase, its sale and distribution is sometimes restricted by legislation in the United States. There is no conclusive evidence at this time, however, to determine if 'Red Baron' is capable of mutating or reverting to acquire the invasive characteristic of the tropical phase. Zone 6.

Imperata cylindrica* var. *major (Nees) C. Hubbard.

Represents the tropical phase of the species. Is much larger, more aggressive, and notoriously invasive in warm tropical and subtropical climates.

Isolepis R. Brown.
Sedge family, Cyperaceae.

Includes approximately 30 species of cosmopolitan distribution, mostly in moist habitats. Closely related to and sometimes included in *Scirpus.* Only the following species is commonly grown in gardens.

Isolepis cernua (Vahl) Roemer & Schultes.
[*Scirpus cernuus* Vahl].
Mop-sedge, fiber-optics plant.

Native in the British Isles to open peaty or sandy soils, often near the coast. Also native to Europe and northern Africa. Forms an extremely dense, moplike tuft of fine green stems. Similar in appearance to the spike-rushes, *Eleocharis,* having small terminal spikes. Interesting when grown in a pot, elevated planter, or between rocks at water's edge, highlighting the plant's pendent, spilling form. Easily grown in well-drained soil with moisture, in sun or part shade. Often grown under glass, where it remains fully evergreen. Propagate by division or seed. Zone 8.

Juncus Linnaeus.
Rush family, Juncaceae.
Rush.

Comprised of more than 200 mostly perennial, rhizomatous species, native to moist or wet habitats mainly through the world's temperate zones. Their leaves are most often cylindrical and green, carrying on photosynthesis in the absence of typical, broad-bladed leaves. Flowers are subtle, contributing in only a minor way to the plants' ornamental value. Rushes are most beautiful in their strong, vertical form and fine texture, providing stunning contrast to broad-leaved companions in moist and wet garden areas and in native landscapes. Although they generally form clumps, they also spread by rhizomes and tend to self-sow freely, sometimes requiring control in small-scale designs. In cold climates, they often die to the ground each year and are renewed by fresh, clean growth in spring. In milder climates, old stems tend to accumulate and gradually discolor, resulting in messy appearance. Occasional cutting to the ground is recommended. Most rushes prefer sunny, wet sites, but can be grown on normal garden soils if provided regular moisture. Propagate by division in spring or by seed.

Juncus effusus Linnaeus.
Common rush, soft rush.

Widely native in moist or wet sunny habitats in temperate regions, including Europe and North America. A striking, architecturally interesting plant with dark forest-green stems, upright and arching in a broad fan, to 4 ft. (1.2 m) in height. This species has been employed in Japan for centuries to make the split-rush mats called "tatami." The cold-hardiness varies between plants of different provenance, but the hardiest are reliable in zone 4.

'Carman's Japanese'. Selected by Ed Carman of California. Medium-green stems and slightly finer texture than the type. Zone 6.

'Cuckoo'. Has longitudinal gold stripes. A vigorous grower.

Isolepis cernua in Chip Lima's garden, San Francisco, California, in late November.

'Spiralis'. Stems dark green, twisted, and spiraled. Less than 14 in. (35 cm) tall. Often retains twisted character when grown from seed. Zone 5.

Juncus inflexus Linnaeus.
Hard rush.

Widely native in moist or wet sunny habitats in temperate regions, including Europe and North America. The stems are more narrowly upright and gray-green than those of the common rush, 2–4 ft. (60–120 cm) tall. Zone 6.

'Afro'. Stems gray-green, twisted, and spiraled. Similar in appearance to *Juncus effusus* 'Spiralis' but more vigorous and drought tolerant. Less than 14 in. (35 cm) tall. Usually retains twisted character when grown from seed. Zone 6.

Juncus patens E. Meyer.
California gray rush.

Native to marshy places in California and Oregon. Differs from the common rush mostly in stem color, which is conspicuously gray-green to gray-blue, and in

Juncus effusus 'Spiralis' at Longwood Gardens in early June.

Juncus inflexus 'Afro' at Longwood Gardens in early June.

Juncus effusus flowering in early June in its native habitat in northern Delaware.

the stiffer, more vertical stance. To 2 ft. (60 cm) tall. More heat and drought tolerant than the common rush. Prefers full sun, best on moist soil or in shallow water. Zone 7.

'Carman's Gray'. Selected by Ed Carman of California. Fairly typical of the species. Zone 7.

Juncus polyanthemus Buchenau.

Australian gray rush.

Native to swampy habitats, mostly near the coast, in Australia. Much larger than the common rush, growing to 5 ft. (1.5 m) tall, with cylindrical gray-green to gray-blue stems to 3/8 in. (9 mm) in diameter, evergreen in mild climates. Forms large clumps and increases slowly by rhizomes. A dramatic vertical element for the margins of water gardens, also a superb container specimen. Best in full sun on wet soil or in shallow water. Introduced to California gardens from Australia by Gary Hammer. Propagate by seed or by division in spring. Zone 8.

Koeleria Linnaeus.

Grass family, Poaceae.

Hair grass.

Named for botanist G. L. Koeler (1765–1806), who specialized in grasses. Comprised of approximately 30 annual and perennial species native to temperate North America and Eurasia. Only the two below are significant ornamentals, and these are so similar to each other, except for foliage color, that they are sometimes included in the same species, *Koeleria macrantha.* They are cool-season growers, usually flowering in June and then going partly or fully dormant in areas where summers are hot and humid. In cooler climates they remain presentable through autumn. They tend to be short-lived perennials. Upright in growth, with fine-textured tufts of leaves topped by narrow erect flower panicles. Inflorescences open light green and translucent, and dry to a pleasing buff color. Blooming earlier than many grasses, they make fine companions for flowering perennials. In hot climates, organize borders to mask the grasses' summer dormancy. Ideal for naturalizing in a meadow garden. Easily grown in full sun on moist or moderately dry soils. Propagate by seed or by division in spring. Cold-hardiness varies with seed provenance.

Juncus patens at Longwood Gardens in late June.

Juncus polyanthemus in the conservatory at the New York Botanical Garden in late May.

Koeleria glauca (Schrader) De Candolle.
[*Koeleria macrantha* subsp. *glauca* (Schrader) P. D. Sell].
Blue hair grass.

Native to Europe and north temperate Asia, particularly on sandy soils. To 2 ft. (60 cm) tall in bloom. Leaves strongly greenish blue. Zone 6.

Koeleria macrantha (Ledebour) Schultes.
[*Koeleria cristata* auct. p.p., non Persoon, *Koeleria pyramidata* auct. p.p., non (Lamarck) P. Beauvois].
Hair grass, June grass (United States), prairie June grass (United States), crested hair grass.
Native to prairies and open woods over much of the western, central, and northeastern United States. Also native to temperate Europe and Asia. To 2 ft. (60 cm) tall in bloom. Leaves medium to bright green. Plants of northern prairie provenance are cold-hardy to zone 4, others to zone 6.

Leymus Hochstetter.
Grass family, Poaceae.
Wild rye, blue wild rye, lyme grass, blue lyme grass.

Approximately 40 perennial species, native to sands, dunes, and other saline or alkaline habitats, stony slopes, and steppes, mostly in northern temperate zones. Many species formerly included in *Elymus* have been transferred to this genus.

Koeleria macrantha in early June at the Shaw Arboretum, Missouri Botanical Garden, St. Louis.

Koeleria glauca in mid-July at the University of Washington Center for Urban Horticulture, Seattle.

Leymus arenarius (Linnaeus) Hochstetter.
[*Elymus arenarius* Linnaeus, *Elymus glaucus* hort., non Buckley].
Lyme grass, blue lyme grass, sea lyme grass, blue wild rye, sand wild rye, European dune grass.
Native on shifting sands and dunes around the coasts of the British Isles, northern and western Europe. An important native dune stabilizer. Long popular with gardeners for the bluish foliage, despite invasive tendencies, and a particular favorite of England's Gertrude Jekyll. Spreads aggressively by stout rhizomes. Stems erect or lax, 3–4 ft. (1–1.2 m) tall in bloom. Inflorescence a narrow spike, at first colored like the leaves, drying to light beige, not ornamental. Appearance is often improved by cutting plants back after flowering, ensuring a flush of new growth for the autumn garden. Leaves flat, to 1/2 in. (12 mm) wide. The bluish gray color of the foliage varies in intensity between seedlings and populations of differing provenance, yet all plants are distinctly glaucous. Foliage attractive year-round in mild climates. A cool-season grower, but fairly tolerant of warm summers and above-average humidity. The running growth habit is most pronounced in looser soils, but can be contained with moderate effort. Useful as a groundcover, and often stunning as a color accent, especially in combination with deep blue or purple flowers or maroon foliage. Of easy culture in any soil, in full sun or light shade. Extremely drought tolerant and fairly salt tolerant, adapted to use in traffic islands and other challenging urban sites. Best propagated by division in spring. *Leymus arenarius* is sometimes slightly smaller than *L. racemosus* but the two are so similar they are frequently confused in gardens. Zone 4.

'Findhorn'. Compact, shorter growing.

'Glaucus'. A superfluous name applied to this typically glaucous-leaved species. It should not be used.

Leymus cinereus (Scribner & Merrill) Á. Löve.
[*Elymus cinereus* (Scribner & Merrill) Á. Löve].
Gray wild rye, basin wild rye.

Native to meadows, canyons, streamsides, sagebrush scrub, and open woodland from Minnesota to British Columbia, south to Colorado, Nevada, and California, typically at higher elevations than *Leymus condensatus*. Stems and foliage gray-green, erect or slightly lax, to 6–8 ft. (2–2.4 m) tall in bloom. Clump-forming or spreading very slowly by rhizomes. Mostly evergreen in mild climates. Perhaps too large for modest-sized gardens, best in large drifts or sweeps in broad meadows or clearings. Prefers full sun, cool summer night temperatures, low humidity. Grows well in northern continental Europe. Drought tolerant. Propagate by seed or by division in spring. Zone 7.

Leymus arenarius in Berlin, Germany, in late August.

Leymus cinereus in mid-June at the Santa Barbara Botanic Garden, California.

Leymus cinereus detail.

Leymus condensatus (Presl) Á. Löve.
[*Elymus condensatus* J. Presl].
Giant wild rye.

Native to sands and dunes, rocky slopes, and moist ravines along the southern California coast to San Diego, and on the adjacent Channel Islands. Clump-forming or spreading slowly by rhizomes. Mostly evergreen in mild climates. Typically green-leaved, the largest plants growing to 9 ft. (2.7 m) tall in bloom. Inflorescences narrowly cylindrical, appearing in June. Needs full sun. Drought tolerant. Bold and somewhat coarse-textured. Propagates readily by seed or by spring division. Zone 7.

'Canyon Prince'. A handsome introduction by the Santa Barbara Botanic Garden in California, from Ralph Philbrick's original collection of native material from Prince Island, one of the Channel Islands off the southern California coast. Foliage flushed green at first, becoming extremely silver-blue on maturing. Shorter than the type, growing 4 ft. (1.2 m) tall in flower. Spreads steadily by rhizomes, but not invasive. Propagate by division in spring. Zone 7.

Leymus mollis (Trinius) Hara.
[*Elymus mollis* Trinius, *Elymus arenarius* var. *villosus* E. May].
Sea lyme grass, American dune grass.

Native to sand dunes along coasts, Alaska to Greenland, south to New York and central California, also along the Great Lakes, and from Siberia to Japan. Similar in most respects to *Leymus arenarius* but foliage usually bluish green, less glaucous, much less frequently cultivated for ornament. Zone 4.

Leymus racemosus (Lamarck) Tzvelev.
[*Elymus racemosus* Lamarck, *Elymus giganteus* Vahl, *Elymus glaucus* hort., non Buckley].
Giant blue wild rye, mammoth wild rye, Volga wild rye.

This Eurasian native is so similar in appearance and growth habit to *Leymus arenarius* that the two are frequently confused in gardens. Despite one of its common names, this wild rye is not appreciably larger than *L. arenarius.* The foliage may be very slightly wider but is not necessarily bluer, and the plant grows to the same maximum blooming height of 4 ft. (1.2 m). All cultural de-

Leymus condensatus in mid-June in coastal California scrub above San Diego.

A young plant of *Leymus condensatus* 'Canyon Prince' in mid-June at the Santa Barbara Botanic Garden, California.

tails and design applicability the same as for *L. arenarius*. Zone 4.

'Glaucus'. A superfluous name applied to this typically glaucous-leaved species.

Luzula De Candolle.

Rush family, Juncaceae.
Wood-rush.

Approximately 80 mostly perennial species of cosmopolitan distribution but mainly in cold temperate regions of the Northern Hemisphere. Closely related to the rushes, *Juncus*, but common to dry or moist woodland environments, as the common name implies. Leaves mostly in basal tufts, the plants clump-forming or spreading by rhizomes. All have open clusters of brown or light tan flowers in spring, but these are usually only subtly attractive. Wood-rushes are grown mostly for their foliage, which is often lustrous and evergreen, sometimes variegated, and for their durability as groundcovers in woodland gardens and on various soil types. Many wood-rushes have distinct whitish hairs along their leaf margins. All can be propagated by division in spring or early autumn, the species also by seed.

Luzula acuminata Rafinesque.

Hairy wood-rush.

Native to woods, clearings, and bluffs in North America, from Canada south to upland Georgia, west to Illinois and South Dakota. Basal leaves deep green and lustrous, broad, to 1/2 in. (12 mm) wide, hairy at margins, remaining evergreen through winter. Inflorescences in April and May, to 14 in. (35 cm) tall, the umbels simple and unbranched, the flowers brownish. An attractive, slowly rhizomatous woodland groundcover. Spreads less vigorously than the European *Luzula sylvatica*. Does not tolerate dense deciduous shade, moist or moderately dry conditions. Not particular about soils. Zone 4.

Luzula acuminata in late August at Mt. Cuba Center, Greenville, Delaware.

Leymus racemosus in late August at the Munich Botanical Garden in Germany.

Leymus racemosus detail at Longwood Gardens, late July.

Luzula acuminata var. _carolinae_ (S. Watson) Fernald.

Differs from the species in having a more southern distribution, common to calcareous wooded slopes, with slightly broader leaves and inflorescences with branched umbels. Zone 5.

Luzula luzuloides (Lamarck) Dandy & Willmott.
Wood-rush.

Native to central and southern Europe. Loosely tufted, slowly rhizomatous, basal leaves narrow, to 1/4 in. (6 mm) wide, gray-green, hairy. Foliage evergreen in milder climates. Inflorescences to 2 ft. (60 cm) tall, flower clusters dense, off-white to light tan, becoming pendulous. Attractive in mass. A useful groundcover for sun or part shade. Of easy culture on most soils, moist or moderately dry. Zone 6.

Luzula nivea (Linnaeus) De Candolle.
Snowy wood-rush, snow rush.

Native to central and southern Europe into the Alps. Very similar to *Luzula luzuloides* but often with clearer white flowers. Loosely tufted, slowly rhizomatous, basal leaves narrow, to 3/16 in. (4 mm) wide, green, hairy. Foliage evergreen in milder climates. Inflorescences to 2 ft. (60 cm) tall, flower clusters dense, off-white to near white, becoming pendulous. Attractive in mass. A useful groundcover for sun or part shade. Of easy culture on most soils, moist or moderately dry. Zone 6.

'Schneehäschen' (little snow hare). Flower heads near-white. Zone 6.

'Snowbird'. Flower heads near-white. Zone 6.

Luzula pilosa (Linnaeus) Willdenow.
Hairy wood-rush.

Native to Eurasia. Nearly identical to the North American *Luzula acuminata* and considered synonymous with it by some authorities. Zone 5.

Luzula sylvatica (Hudson) Gaudin.
[*Luzula maxima* (Richard) De Candolle].
Greater wood-rush.

Native to oak woodlands, open moorlands, streamsides, and other acid habitats in the British Isles, and in western, central, and southern Europe, the Caucasus, and Turkey. The largest and finest of the wood-rushes for groundcover use, especially in shaded settings. Forms large tussocks and spreads strongly by rhizomes, eventually making a virtually weed-proof mass. Basal leaves to 3/4 in. (2 cm) wide, dark green and glossy, hair especially at margins. Foliage evergreen in milder climates, semi-evergreen through zone 6. Flowers in early May, in light green masses to 2 ft. (60 cm) tall. An excellent companion for ferns, woodland wildflowers, and shrubs. Easy to grow on most soils, including heavy clays. Prefers moisture but very drought tolerant. Zone 4.

'Aurea'. Leaves yellow-green. Zone 6.

'Höhe Tatra' (high Tatra). Leaves green. From the Tatra Mountains of Europe. Zone 5.

'Marginata'. The best garden wood-rush. The dark green glossy leaves, to 5/8 in. (15 mm) wide, have cream-white edging 1/32 in. (1 mm) wide. The overall effect is crisp and refined. A much under-appreciated woodland groundcover. Zone 4.

'Tauernpass'. Compact with broad leaves. Zone 6.

'Wäldler' (woodsman). Leaves light green. Zone 6.

Luzula acuminata var. *carolinae* in early May at Springwood, the eastern Pennsylvania garden of Dick and Sally Lighty.

Luzula nivea 'Schneehäschen' in mid-July in Alan Bloom's garden in Bressingham, England.

Melica Linnaeus.

Grass family, Poaceae.
Melic.

Comprised of approximately 70 perennial species, native to woodland shade and dry slopes in temperate regions throughout the world excluding Australia. Melic grasses are cool-season growers, adding their delightful, showy cream-white flowers to the garden in spring, then mostly going dormant or semi-dormant in summer. Foliage is generally coarse and unremarkable, and it is best to plan for other plantings to mask it, especially in dormancy. Partly for this reason, the more compact *Melica ciliata* is a superior, more manageable garden plant than the taller *M. altissima*, which is no showier in bloom and less attractive later. Besides these European species, a few California natives, such as *M. imperfecta*, are worth exploring for use in regional gardens in hot, dry climates. Summer-dormant plants may be cut back to the ground. Propagation by seed is usually best. Divide or transplant in spring.

Luzula sylvatica at Longwood Gardens in early June.

Luzula sylvatica 'Marginata' flowering in early May at Springwood, the eastern Pennsylvania garden of Dick and Sally Lighty.

Melica altissima Linnaeus.

Siberian melic.

Native to shrubby thickets and forest borders from central and eastern Europe to Siberia. Mostly upright, to 3 ft. (1 m) or more in flower, the stems leafy. Blooms May to June. Inflorescence a narrow terminal panicle, fluffy and white, fading to cream, useful in bouquets if cut before fully open. Prefers sun or light shade, moist or moderately dry. Summer dormant in hot climates. Self-sows manageably. Zone 5.

'Alba'. Spikelets nearly white.

'Atropurpurea'. Spikelets mauve-colored.

Melica ciliata Linnaeus.

Hairy melic grass, silky-spike melic.

Native to Europe, northern Africa, and Southwest Asia. The showiest, most manageable melic grass. Leaves mostly basal, the flowering stems rising above and arching over the foliage to 30 ft. (9 m). The narrow flower panicles are silky-white, fading to cream, useful for bouquets if cut before fully open. A delightful addition to the spring garden.

Melica altissima is partly summer dormant by mid-August at the Royal Botanic Gardens, Kew, England.

Melica ciliata in early June at Longwood Gardens.

Melica imperfecta with poppies in late February in the meadow at the Santa Barbara Botanic Garden, California.

Compact and suited to smaller spaces, or effective in sweeps and masses. Prefers sun or light shade, moist or moderately dry. At least partly summer dormant in hot climates. Individual plants are often relatively short-lived. Self-sows pleasantly. Zone 6.

Melica imperfecta Trinius.
Coast range melic, foothill melic.

Native to dry hillsides, chaparral, and open woodlands at low and moderate elevations in the coastal ranges of California. Foliage tufted, mostly basal. To 2 ft. (60 cm) tall in flower. Flower panicles long, narrow, cream-white. Summer dormant if dry, but turns green quickly with winter rains, attractive in early spring. Ideal for meadow gardens. Zone 8.

Merxmuellera Conert.
Grass family, Poaceae.

Named for German botanist Hermann Merxmüller. Comprised of 16 species native to open habitats in southern and southwestern Africa.

Merxmuellera macowanii (Stapf) Conert.
[*Danthonia macowanii* Stapf].

Native to southern Africa. A large, tussock-forming perennial to 5 ft. (1.5 m) tall in bloom. Inflorescences arching gracefully over the blue-green, fine-textured foliage. Evergreen in mild climates. Though little-known in cultivation, this beautiful species has been cultivated in the grass garden at the Royal Botanic Gardens, Kew, England, for several years. It deserves wider attention. Zone 8.

Milium Linnaeus.
Grass family, Poaceae.
Millet.

Includes six annual and perennial species native to temperate woodlands in Eurasia and North America.

Milium effusum Linnaeus.
Wood millet.

A widespread native of damp or rocky woods in northeastern North America, of damp oak and beech woods in the British Isles and Europe, and of moist mountain woods in Japan. A pronounced cool-season grower, as evidenced by habitat preference. Only the golden form is important in gardens.

'Aureum'. Golden wood millet, Bowles' golden grass. The new spring foliage is among the brightest chartreuse-yellow of all garden plants. Makes a superb color companion to spring-blooming flowers. This cool-season, woodland plant is at its best in light shade in cooler climates, and always best in spring. The foliage darkens to light green by summer and in hotter climates it goes partly summer dormant. Heavier shade relieves summer stress but diminishes the vibrancy of the spring foliage color. 'Aureum' is smaller than the species, the foliage rarely topping 18 in. (45 cm). The open flower panicles are sparsely produced. Self-sows mildly, and seedlings are usually yellow-leaved, though there may be some variation. Tolerant of a range of soils, but appreciates moisture. Propagated by division. Zone 6.

Merxmuellera macowanii in mid-August at the Royal Botanic Gardens, Kew, England.

Milium effusum 'Aureum' in late May in Connecticut.

Miscanthus Andersson.
Grass family, Poaceae.
Eulalia, Japanese silver grass, miscanthus, susuki zoku (Japan).

From the Greek *mischos* (stalk) and *anthos* (flower), referring to the stalked spikelets. Comprised of approximately 20 usually large perennial species native to marshes, slopes, mountainsides, and other open habitats, mainly in eastern Asia, but extending west into Africa. They are much celebrated in Japan in traditional art and as a symbol of autumn, along with the coloring of Japanese maples. There, too, they are the source of thatching material for temple roofs and traditional residences.

To the uninitiated Western gardener, miscanthus sometimes seems to be all there is to ornamental grasses, with more than 100 named cultivars to date. As a group among grasses, miscanthus is unrivaled in the diversity and beauty of its flowers, foliage, autumn colors, and winter presence; in its extraordinary adaptability to myriad purposes in the garden; and in its ability to survive and prosper in some of the most challenging cultural conditions imaginable. Though it has been grown in Western gardens for more than a century, it has never before enjoyed the attention given it in current decades. Its winning attributes, greatly enhanced by horticultural selection and development in the late twentieth century, have boosted it to a level of popularity bordering on ubiquity. While most of this acclaim is well deserved, there are a few caveats. Although once pest-free and disease-free, miscanthus now has at least two problems worthy of attention: miscanthus mealybug and miscanthus blight (see Chapter 6).

The most serious problem with miscanthus concerns its invasive potential. Many of the same strengths that make it a durable, adaptable garden plant also qualify it for naturalizing in a diversity of habitats far beyond its origins. It is especially competitive in moist, sunny environments in warm temperate regions. Near-monocultures in its native habitats, such as coastal Japan, speak of the vigor of this grass and hint at its potential under similar conditions elsewhere. This risk of encroachment is a regional matter, of serious consequence in some areas and irrelevant in others. For example, because miscanthus is a warm-season grower, it poses no threat in cool climates, such as England, where the growing season lacks the warmth and sunny duration required for prolific flowering and seed development. Conditions in the southeastern United States, however, most closely approximate ideal conditions for miscanthus, and it is here, especially near moist, sunny bottomlands, that caution is warranted.

Ironically, the invasive potential of *Miscanthus* has been enhanced by horticultural development. Antique cultivars, including 'Gracillimus', 'Variegatus', and 'Zebrinus', require very long, hot seasons if they are to flower at all, and their seeds rarely mature in regions where they flower very late in autumn. Many modern cultivars, including some of the most beautiful, such as 'Graziella' and 'Malepartus', were developed and selected for their ability to flower in short seasons. These are superb new choices for northern Europe, England, and colder zones in the United States, finally allowing gardeners in these places to enjoy their plumy magnificence. Unfortunately these selections bloom early enough to be prolific self-sowers in some warmer zones up into the mid-Atlantic states. They readily naturalize in and out of the garden, and can be a real nuisance in managed meadow gardens. Although California is warm, miscanthus appears to be little if any problem there. The dry conditions associated with that state's mediterranean climate provide a natural check for the genus, which is dependent upon moisture combined with heat for self-sowing. Gardeners should use common sense when selecting miscanthus and considering its use in gardens adjacent to vulnerable native habitats.

Being warm-season plants, miscanthus are late-starting in spring but grow strongly in summer heat. They are most luxuriant in hot, moist situations and are unaffected by summer humidity. They grow well on most soils, from loose sands to heavy clays. Their root systems, adapted to marshy conditions, are very tolerant of poorly drained soils with low aeration. Except on the poorest sands, fertilization is not necessary. Excess nitrogen causes over-lush growth and weak, floppy stems, especially on plants in moist or shady sites. All species and most cultivars prefer full sun sites; however, there are selections with limited shade tolerance.

The genus includes clump-formers, such as *Miscanthus sinensis*, and strongly rhizomatous types, such as *M. sacchariflorus*. Individual plants live for many years, but older clumps eventually die out in their centers and should be renewed by taking divisions from the perimeter of the clump. This should be done in spring or early summer, or in autumn only in the mildest climates. Fully mature plants are often too large for residential gardens, and periodic division is a frequently employed method of reducing the plants' size while retaining the desirable attributes of form and flowering. A sharp spade is an indispensable tool for such tasks (see page 128). Be cautious of the often sharp-edged leaves, especially common to *M. sinensis*, which can cause minor but irritating cuts to hands and face. Seed propagation is easy but is not appropriate for the clonal cultivars.

Miscanthus blooms from midsummer through autumn, varying with species and cultivars. The flowers open silvery or with red tints, becoming fluffy on drying, and usually remaining attractive through winter. The inflorescences are made up of many slender racemes, usually clustered at their bases in a digitate (like fingers on a hand) arrangement to form fan-shaped plumes (see Figure 2-9). This is particularly true of the Asian species. Inflorescences of the African species typically have a dominant, elongated axis and are sometimes separated partly based on this character and placed in the related genus *Miscanthidium*. The distinction between the two genera is

Miscanthus floridulus in mid-July in Japan. Note extended central rachis in inflorescence. (Photo: Hideaki Tatsumi, from *Wildflowers of Japan*, reproduced courtesy of YAMA-KEI publishers, Japan.)

blurred by intermediates, such as *Miscanthus floridulus,* which has rarely, if ever, been grown in Western gardens.

The modern array of cultivated selections will fulfill a multitude of design purposes, including specimen focal points, massing, and screening. Despite their generally large size, miscanthus vary in foliage texture from coarse to very fine. The variegated-leaved cultivars are specially effective choices for use in decorative containers, and most miscanthus make superb cut flowers. At the turn of the nineteenth century, miscanthus (then known as eulalia, from the old genus name) were frequently recommended in books on water gardens. Indeed, many are quite at home in wet soils and even tolerate periodic standing water. They can be stunning when placed at the edges of pools and ponds. Many newer selections offer significant autumn foliage coloration, and almost all are graceful additions to the garden in winter. Cold-hardiness varies considerably between species and cultivars.

Miscanthus floridulus (Labillardière) Warburg.

Tokiwa susuki.

Native to lowlands in Japan, Taiwan, and the Pacific islands. A large grass, growing more than 8 ft. (2.4 m) tall, with broad, coarse leaves to 1 1/4 in. (32 mm) wide. Blooms July to August. The large inflorescences have a dominant central rachis, a character that distinguishes this species from all other Asian miscanthus. *Miscanthus floridulus* has rarely, if ever, been grown for ornament in Western gardens; but this name has often been erroneously applied to a superficially similar, commonly cultivated clonal cultivar that has the tall stature and clump-forming habit of this species and the awnless florets typical of *M. sacchariflorus.* This cultivar is possibly a hybrid, but is of uncertain garden origin and is correctly referred to simply as *Miscanthus* 'Giganteus' (see separate entry). It is easily distinguished from *M. floridulus* by its lack of a dominant rachis in the inflorescence and its late-season flowering period.

Miscanthus 'Giganteus'

Giant miscanthus.

Although frequently listed as belonging to *Miscanthus floridulus, M. sacchariflorus,* or *M. sinensis,* this venerable cultivar does not fit any of these species precisely. It is of obscure garden origin, possibly a hybrid, but certainly a great garden plant. Upright in form, with a maximum height approaching 10 ft. (3 m). The 1-in. (25-mm) wide leaves are deep green with the white midvein common to most miscanthus. The leaves are pendant, giving the overall effect of a large fountain. Mostly clump-forming, only slightly rhizomatous. Blooms very late summer or not at all in short growing seasons. Inflorescences opening with

Miscanthus 'Giganteus' in early August in the garden of Dr. and Mrs. Elliott Harris, Baltimore, Maryland.

Miscanthus 'Giganteus' in mid-October at Kurt Bluemel's nursery in Maryland.

pink tints, quickly turning silver on drying. The lowest foliage, to 3 ft. (1 m), frequently turns brown or dies in late summer, so it is often best to place companion plantings in front to mask this. Does well at water's edge. Generally does not self-sow. Propagate by division. Zone 4.

Miscanthus 'Herbstfeuer'

Autumn fire.

Similar to *Miscanthus* 'Purpurascens' (which see) but shorter and slower-growing. Of obscure parentage, possibly a hybrid, but certainly not *M. sinensis.* Zone 5.

Miscanthus 'Little Big Man'

From a seedling of *Miscanthus* 'Giganteus' selected by Jim Waddick. Similar to 'Giganteus' in most respects but smaller. Propagate by division. Zone 5.

Miscanthus nepalensis (Trinius) Hackel.

Himalaya fairy grass.

Native to the Himalayas and Burma. Attractive as grown in the conservatories at the Royal Botanic Gardens, Kew, England, but not reliably cold hardy outdoors even in England. Green-leaved and less than 5 ft. (1.5 m) tall in full flower.

Miscanthus nepalensis in mid-August in the Temperate House at the Royal Botanic Gardens, Kew, England.

Miscanthus oligostachyus Stapf.

Kari yasu modoki.

Native to mountains on the Japanese islands Honshu, Shikoku, and Kysuhu. Much smaller than *Miscanthus sinensis,* usually less than 4 ft. (1.2 m) tall in bloom, with a more open habit. Leaves shorter, approximately 1/2 in. (12

Miscanthus oligostachyus beginning to flower in mid-August in the Westpark, Munich, Germany.

Miscanthus oligostachyus in early October at Longwood Gardens.

mm) wide, relatively soft and thin in substance, very flat, with a less pronounced white midrib than *M. sinensis.* Inflorescence sparsely branched, with only two to five erect racemes, not nearly as full and fluffy as larger species. Blooms in August. Fall color often includes bronze-red tones. Useful for its compact size, tolerance of light shade, and exceptional cold-hardiness. Unnamed variegated selections are well known in Japan but are rarely encountered in Western gardens. The cultivar 'Purpurascens', though often labeled incorrectly as belonging to *M. sinensis,* is much closer to this species. Generally does not self-sow. Propagate by seed or division. Zone 4.

An unnamed variegated selection of *Miscanthus oligostachyus* in early November in Japan.

Miscanthus 'Purpurascens'

Usually has the most reliable red-orange fall foliage color of any miscanthus grown in the United States, an attribute combined with small size, upright stature, early flowering, and extreme cold-hardiness to make this a superb choice. Does not belong to *Miscanthus sinensis,* although often listed as such. Possibly a hybrid involving *M. oligostachyus,* but ultimate origin is obscure. Selected in the 1960s by Hans Simon of Germany, from seed obtained from Japan. Ironically, the fall color is not reliable in Germany, and the plant is not widely grown there. It colors well but often does not flower in England. Blooms in warm climates in late July or August, to 5 ft. (1.5 m) tall, the inflorescences narrow and vertical, with few raceme branches, opening with slight pink tints and drying silvery. Leaves to 1/2 in. (12 mm) wide, slightly gray-green

Miscanthus 'Purpurascens' in early September at the U.S. National Arboretum, Washington, D.C.

Miscanthus 'Purpurascens' fall foliage in full sun in early October at Longwood Gardens.

in summer. Never needs staking and performs satisfactorily even in light shade, in which case the fall foliage colors are various pastels. Not drought tolerant, suffers in extreme heat. Rarely if ever self-sows. Zone 4.

Miscanthus sacchariflorus (Maximowicz) Bentham. Silver banner grass, Amur silver grass, ogi.

Native and common to wet places in lowlands of Japan. Also native to Manchuria, Ussuri, Korea, and northern China. Primarily distinguished by its stout rhizomes and strongly running habit, and by the lack of awns in the flower spikelets. Blooms in August, to 8 ft. (2.4 m) tall, the flowers held well above the foliage, opening silver and becoming fluffy-white upon drying. The inflorescences are narrower and more upright than those of *Miscanthus sinensis,* and remain attractive through most of winter. Leaves to 1 1/4 in. (32 mm) wide, with pronounced white midrib, turning yellow in autumn. Often loses lower foliage during summer dry periods. The spreading habit is useful for colonizing large sites, such as parking lot berms or banks of ponds, but can be difficult to control in smaller gardens. Spreads more slowly on heavy soils. Self-sows. A very beautiful but strongly rhizomatous

Miscanthus sacchariflorus at Longwood Gardens in late August.

Miscanthus 'Purpurascens' fall foliage in half shade in mid-October in the author's former Delaware garden.

An unnamed yellow-variegated form of *Miscanthus sacchariflorus* at Barry Yinger's nursery in Pennsylvania, early September.

yellow-variegated selection has been introduced from Japan by Barry Yinger, but is unnamed at the time of this writing. Zone 4.

'Interstate 95'. A very vigorous runner, promoted for stabilization of difficult, disturbed sites. Propagate by division. Zone 4.

'Robustus'. Supposedly larger than the type, but often without distinction as sold. Zone 4.

Miscanthus sinensis Andersson.
[*Eulalia japonica* Trinius].
Miscanthus, eulalia, Japanese silver grass, susuki.

Native to slopes in the lowlands and mountains of Japan, from Hokkaido south through Yaku-shima and the Ryukus to Taiwan. Also native to the southern Kuriles, Korea, and China. The premier *Miscanthus* species, of exceptional beauty and variability, but always strictly clump-forming. The typical form of the species is rarely grown, having medium-green leaves to 3/4 in. (2 cm) wide with prominent white midrib. Produced from August to October, the inflorescences are full and dense, each with numerous racemes, opening reddish-colored and fading to silver-white upon drying. Typical fall foliage color is yellow. Stouter plants, more common near seashores, have been distinguished botanically as *M. sinensis* var. *condensatus* (see below). In gardens, *M. sinensis* is represented by myriad cultivated varieties differing significantly in size, height, texture, summer and autumn foliage color, flowering times and colors, and cold-hardiness. The following are among the best or most widely available; this is not a complete listing. All prefer full sun unless otherwise noted. Heights are for mature specimens under best conditions; many grow much smaller in colder or drier conditions. Hardiness zones listed are based on observed performance; some cultivars may prove more cold hardy with further evaluation. Unless otherwise stated, all are propagated by division. Figure 2-9.

A typical form of *Miscanthus sinensis* in mid-September at Brookside Gardens in Maryland.

'Adagio'. A diminutive introduction by Kurt Bluemel, similar to 'Yaku Jima', but superior for its consistent production of inflorescences that extend beyond the tops of the foliage. Leaves green, very narrow. Blooms in August, to 5 ft. (1.5 m) tall. Inflorescences open with red tints. A good fine-textured choice for smaller gardens. Yellow autumn color. Zone 6.

'Aethiopien'. A compact, slow-growing selection with strong burgundy-red foliage tints in autumn. Introduced by Ernst Pagels. Zone 6.

'Altweibersommer'. Blooms in late summer, to 7 ft. (2.1 m) tall. Introduced by Ernst Pagels. Zone 6.

'Arabesque'. Compact, to 5 ft. (1.5 m) tall, with green leaves. Blooms in August. Introduced by Kurt Bluemel. Zone 6.

'Autumn Light'. Tall, to 8 ft. (2.4 m) tall, with green, narrow leaves. Blooms in September. Introduced by Kurt Bluemel. Zone 5.

Miscanthus sinensis 'Adagio' in early October at Kurt Bluemel's nursery in Maryland.

'Blondo'. Green-leaved, somewhat coarse-textured, but very cold-hardy. Grows 6 ft. (2 m) tall in the U.S. Midwest. Introduced by Bluebird Nursery of Nebraska. Zone 4.

'Bronceturm' (bronze tower). Leaves broad, green, very coarse textured. Tall, to 9 ft. (2.7 m). Flowers copper-bronze when first appearing in midsummer, not elevated much above the foliage. Introduced by Ernst Pagels. Zone 6, likely colder.

Miscanthus sinensis 'Aethiopien' in late August at Ernst Pagels' nursery in Leer, Germany.

Miscanthus sinensis 'Bronceturm' in late August at Ernst Pagels' nursery in Leer, Germany.

'Dixieland'. Similar to 'Variegatus' but more compact. Introduced by Kurt Bluemel. Zone 6.

'Ferner Osten' (far east). Inflorescences with a very pronounced red color when first opening in mid to late summer. Slightly wider-leaved and earlier blooming than 'Gracillimus'. Introduced by Ernst Pagels. Zone 6, likely colder.

'Flamingo'. Large, loosely open, pink-tinted inflorescences with relatively few raceme branches, which are slightly pendent. Blooms late summer, to 6 ft. (2 m) tall. Introduced by Ernst Pagels. Zone 5.

'Goldfeder' (gold feather). One of the most distinct and beautiful variegated miscanthus, with leaves to 3/4 in. (2 cm) wide, longitudinally striped light golden-yellow. Little-known only because it is slow to propagate and has been somewhat difficult to obtain commercially. Named by German nurseryman and ornamental grass specialist Hans Simon, who discovered it in the late 1950s as a sport on 'Silberfeder'. It is similar to 'Silberfeder' in being somewhat open-growing, with midsummer inflorescences held well above the foliage, opening silver, rather than red-tinted. To 7 ft. (2.1 m) tall. The variegation darkens to light yellow-green by late summer. Zone 6.

'Goliath'. Leaves green, late-summer flowers opening with pink tints, to 9 ft. (2.7 m). Introduced by Ernst Pagels. Zone 5.

'Gracillimus'. Maiden grass. One of the oldest and perhaps the best known *Miscanthus* cultivars, valued for its

Miscanthus sinensis 'Ferner Osten' in late August at Ernst Pagels' nursery in Leer, Germany.

Miscanthus sinensis 'Flamingo' in mid-August in Germany.

fine-textured foliage and gracefully rounded overall form. It is among the last to bloom, the copper-red inflorescences opening in late September or October, or not at all in regions with short growing seasons. To 7 ft. (2.1 m) tall in bloom. Fall foliage color golden-yellow. Garden reference books from the late 1800s often refer to 'Gracillimus' as *Eulalia japonica* var. *gracillima* or *E. gracillima* var. *univittata*, horticultural names formulated before the advent of cultivar nomenclature. Seedlings of 'Gracillimus' are often indistinguishable from the parent, and this cultivar has been propagated both by seed and division over the decades. It is not truly a clonal cultivar. Plants purchased as 'Gracillimus' should have narrow leaves, rounded form, and late-season reddish flowers, but they may not all be identical. Mature specimens tend to flop, especially if at all shaded, too moist, or if fertility is high. Though many earlier-blooming, green narrow-leaved alternatives to 'Gracillimus' are now available, not all possess the

Miscanthus sinensis 'Goldfeder' foliage detail in late August.

Miscanthus sinensis 'Goldfeder' at Longwood Gardens in late August.

graceful rounded form. Three that come close are 'Ferner Osten', 'Graziella', and 'Silberspinne'. Zone 5.

'Graziella'. Leaves narrow, green. Blooms in August or early September, the inflorescences opening mostly silver, held high above the foliage, very fluffy when dry, to 7 ft. (2.1 m) tall. Slightly more upright in form than 'Gracillimus'. Fall foliage color usually rich copper red and orange. Very beautiful and refined. Introduced by Ernst Pagels. Zone 5.

'Grosse Fontäne' (large fountain). Leaves green, midsummer flowers, to 8 ft. (2.4 m) tall. Introduced by Ernst Pagels. Zone 5.

'Helga Reich'. Green fine-textured foliage, flowering in September, to 6 ft. (2 m) tall. Zone 6.

'Hinjo' (Little Nicky®). Compact zebra grass. A superb cultivar with much of the character of 'Zebrinus' but significantly smaller in all aspects, to 6 ft. (2 m) tall in full flower, and never flops. The horizontal bands of yellow variegation are quite vivid and are more closely spaced than those of 'Zebrinus' or 'Strictus', making a stronger impression, especially from a distance. The best choice in banded-leaved miscanthus for smaller gardens. Introduced by Hines Nurseries of California. Zone 5.

Miscanthus sinensis 'Graziella' flower detail in early November in the author's garden.

Miscanthus sinensis 'Gracillimus' in mid-October at Longwood Gardens.

Miscanthus sinensis 'Graziella' in mid-January in the author's garden.

Miscanthus sinensis 'Graziella' color in early November at Kurt Bluemel's nursery in Maryland.

Miscanthus sinensis 'Hinjo' at Longwood Gardens in mid-August.

'Juli' (July). Broad green leaves, early summer flowering. Upright and somewhat coarse-textured. Few branches to the inflorescence, an indication that this is a likely hybrid involving *Miscanthus oligostachyus*. Introduced by Ernst Pagels. Zone 6.

'Kascade' (cascade). Named for the large, loosely open, pink-tinted inflorescences, which have relatively few raceme branches, and these are slightly pendent. Blooms midsummer, to 7 ft. (2.1 m) tall. Upright and slightly narrow in form, with flowers held high above the foliage. Introduced by Ernst Pagels. Zone 5.

'Kirk Alexander'. Leaves with horizontal bands of yellow variegation. Free-flowering and more compact than 'Zebrinus', but leaf banding not nearly as vivid as 'Hinjo'. Named for landscape architect Kirk Alexander. Zone 6.

'Kleine Fontäne' (little fountain). Similar to 'Grosse Fontäne' but smaller. Introduced by Ernst Pagels. Zone 5.

'Kleine Silberspinne' (little silver spider). Upright, narrow-leaved, to 6 ft. (2 m) tall, flowers opening silvery in August. Introduced by Ernst Pagels. Zone 5.

'Little Kitten'. Narrow-leaved and extremely compact, under 3 ft. (1 m) tall in flower. Originated as a seedling from 'Yaku Jima'. Leaves green, flowers sparsely. Zone 6.

Miscanthus sinensis 'Kascade' in late August at Ernst Pagels' nursery in Leer, Germany.

Miscanthus sinensis 'Juli' in late August at Ernst Pagels' nursery in Leer, Germany.

Miscanthus sinensis 'Kleine Fontäne' in late August at Ernst Pagels' nursery in Leer, Germany.

Miscanthus sinensis 'Kleine Silberspinne' in late August at Ernst Pagels' nursery in Leer, Germany.

'Malepartus'. Blooms early September. Leaves wider than those of 'Graziella' but similar in form. Flowers open silver, become very fluffy-white when dry, to 7 ft. (2.1 m) tall. Fall foliage color gold, often with strong infusions of orange and red. Introduced by Ernst Pagels. Zone 5.

'Morning Light'. Arguably the best all-around garden plant of all the *Miscanthus* species and cultivars. It has the narrow foliage, fine texture, and rounded form of 'Gracillimus', with leaf margins cleanly and uniformly white-

Miscanthus sinensis 'Morning Light' in late October at Longwood Gardens.

Miscanthus sinensis 'Malepartus' at Longwood Gardens in late August.

Miscanthus sinensis 'Morning Light' foliage detail in mid-July.

variegated. Blooms late, with reddish flowers like 'Gracillimus' and is not inclined to self-sowing. Unlike 'Gracillimus', it never flops. Known to cultivation in Japan for at least a century, but first introduced to Western gardens in 1976 by Sylvester March and John Creech of the U.S. National Arboretum, Washington, D.C., who obtained propagations from variegated plant specialist Masato Yokoi. Named by Kurt Bluemel. Of great refinement and elegance, this versatile selection is especially beautiful near water or grown in a container. Tolerates light shade. Zone 5.

'Mt. Washington'. Similar to 'Graziella' but slightly more upright and narrow in form, with consistently deep red-burgundy autumn foliage. Originated as a seedling in the garden of Jacqueline and Eric Gratz, in the Baltimore, Maryland, community of Mt. Washington. Zone 5.

'Nippon'. Compact and narrowly upright, midsummer blooming, to 5 ft. (1.5 m) tall. Leaves green, often with good red autumn tones. Introduced by Ernst Pagels. Zone 5.

Miscanthus sinensis 'Mt. Washington' fall foliage detail in early November at Longwood Gardens.

Miscanthus sinensis 'Nippon' in mid-August in Germany.

Miscanthus sinensis 'Puenktchen' in late August at Ernst Pagels' nursery in Leer, Germany.

'November Sunset'. Leaves green, narrow. Blooms in late summer, reddish flowers on opening. Introduced by Kurt Bluemel. Zone 5.

'Puenktchen' (little dot). Has banded variegation similar to 'Strictus' with leaves even more stiffly held. Very spiky texture. Introduced by Ernst Pagels. Zone 5.

'Rigoletto'. Similar to 'Variegatus' but more compact. Introduced by Kurt Bluemel. Zone 6.

'Roland'. Tall-growing, with pink-tinted flowers in mid to late summer. Introduced by Ernst Pagels. Zone 5.

'Roterpfeil' (red arrow). Strong red autumn foliage color. Flowers open with red-pink tints, to 6 ft. (2 m) tall. Introduced by Ernst Pagels. Zone 5.

'Rotsilber' (red-silver). Inflorescences open pink-red. Leaves green with orange-red autumn color. Introduced by Ernst Pagels. Zone 5.

'Sarabande'. Similar to 'Gracillimus' but narrower-leaved and finer textured overall. Golden-copper colored inflorescences in August, to 6 ft. (2 m) tall. Introduced by Kurt Bluemel. Zone 5.

Miscanthus sinensis 'Sarabande' in mid-August at Kurt Bluemel's nursery in Maryland.

'Silberfeder' (silver feather). Name refers to the large feathery flowers that emerge silver with only the slightest pink tint. Leaves green, 3/4 in. (2 cm) wide. Inflorescences held very high above the foliage, to 7 ft. (2.1 m), appearing in August. Stems often slightly lax and may flop even in sun, but do this so gracefully the effect is often quite attractive. Selected in Germany in the early 1950s by Hans Simon, from seedlings growing at the Munich Botanic Garden. Free-flowering, even in England, where it has long been a favorite. Zone 4.

Miscanthus sinensis 'Silberfeder' in early October at Longwood Gardens.

Miscanthus sinensis 'Silberfeder' in mid-September at Ashland Hollow, the northern Delaware garden of Mr. and Mrs. W. H. Frederick, Jr.

'Silberpfeil' (silver arrow). Promoted as being more upright than 'Variegatus' but has not proved so, and is nearly impossible to distinguish since the foliage is identically white-striped. Zone 6.

'Silberspinne' (silver spider). Narrow green leaves, upright form, flowers opening silver with pink tints in midsummer, to 6 ft. (2 m) tall. Particularly graceful. Introduced by Ernst Pagels. Zone 5.

'Silberturm' (silver tower). Tall-growing, to 9 ft. (2.7 m), leaves green. Introduced by Ernst Pagels. Zone 6.

'Strictus' ('Zebrinus Strictus'). Porcupine grass. Known in Western gardens for a century and identical to 'Zebrinus' but significantly more upright in stature and less inclined to flop. Leaves are held more erect, like porcupine quills, increasing the effectiveness of the variegation and making for an overall more spiky effect. Blooms in September, opening reddish, to 9 ft. (2.7 m) tall. Zone 5.

'Undine'. Similar to 'Graziella' but taller. Introduced by Ernst Pagels. Zone 5.

'Variegatus'. The white-striped foliage of this antique cultivar still provides the strongest white landscape effect of all the miscanthus; unfortunately mature specimens usually need staking. Blooms in mid-September, opening strongly red-tinted, to 7 ft. (2.1 m) tall. Young plants make superb container specimens. Zone 5.

Miscanthus sinensis 'Strictus' in early August in the Cyr garden in Maryland.

A young plant of *Miscanthus sinensis* 'Silberspinne' in mid-August in Germany.

Miscanthus sinensis 'Variegatus' in early July in Mervyn Feesey's garden in England.

'Wetterfahne' (weathervane). Leaves green, broad, held somewhat horizontally, flowers pink-red in midsummer. Introduced by Ernst Pagels. Zone 6.

'Yaku Jima'. Not a clonal cultivar, but a name used for several very similar, compact, narrow-leaved plants, usually less than 5 ft. (1.5 m) tall. Diminutive forms of *Miscanthus sinensis* are common on the Japanese island of Yaku Jima (or Yakushima). Staff of the U.S. National Arboretum, Washington, D.C., first brought 'Yaku Jima' seedlings to the United States that were variable but similar in being small-sized and narrow-leaved. The name 'Yaku Jima' has been used by nurseries as a catch-all for these seedlings and their progeny. Zone 6.

'Zebrinus'. Zebra grass. The lax green leaves have irregularly spaced horizontal

Comparison of *Miscanthus sinensis* 'Variegatus' (right rear) and *Miscanthus sinensis* 'Morning Light' (left front) in late July at Kurt Bluemel's garden in Maryland.

Miscanthus sinensis 'Wetterfahne' in late August at Ernst Pagels' nursery in Leer, Germany.

Miscanthus sinensis 'Yaku Jima' next to *Panicum virgatum* 'Heavy Metal' in late September at Longwood Gardens.

bands of yellow variegation. Flowers copper tinted in mid-September, to 8 ft. (2.4 m) tall. Although the foliage is more graceful and the overall effect less formal than that of 'Strictus', this venerable old cultivar usually requires staking. It has been surpassed by the more compact 'Hinjo'. Zone 5.

'Zwergelefant' (little elephant). Broad green leaves, very coarse textured and open, flowers open red-pink in midsummer, to 6 ft. (2 m) tall. Zone 6.

Miscanthus sinensis var. *condensatus* (Hackel) Makino.

[*Miscanthus condensatus* Hackel].
Hachijo susuki.

This botanical variety most frequently occurs in coastal areas in Japan, including Hachijo island off Honshu, but is also found at higher elevations in Japan as well as in Korea, China, Indochina, and the Pacific islands. It has been recognized as a separate species by some taxonomists. Plants representing this botanical variety are sometimes labeled 'Condensatus', implying cultivar status, but this is improper nomenclature. Taller, more robust, and wider-leaved than typical *Miscanthus sinensis*, this variety usually produces an extra flush of growth late in autumn, and the foliage remains green longer in winter. Blooms in late summer, opening red-copper tinted. There is usually no significant fall foliage color other than yellow; however, the two following cultivars have the most dra-

Miscanthus sinensis var. *condensatus* in mid-September at Springwood, the eastern Pennsylvania garden of Dick and Sally Lighty.

Comparison of *Miscanthus sinensis* 'Zebrinus' (left) and *Miscanthus sinensis* Strictus' (right) at Longwood Gardens in early August.

Miscanthus sinensis 'Zebrinus' foliage detail in late July at Longwood Gardens.

Miscanthus foliage comparison, late September at Longwood Gardens. From top: *M. sinensis* var. *condensatus* 'Cosmopolitan'; *M. sinensis* var. *condensatus* 'Cabaret'; *M. sinensis* 'Variegatus'; *M. sinensis* 'Goldfeder'; *M. sinensis* 'Morning Light'; *M. sinensis* 'Gracillimus'; *M. sinensis* (typical species form); *M. sinensis* 'Strictus'.

matically variegated summer foliage of all the miscanthus. Good near water. Zone 5.

'Cabaret'. Arguably the boldest, most spectacular of all the variegated miscanthus. To 1 1/4 in. (32 mm) wide, the leaves are cream-white in the center with wide dark green margins. 'Cabaret' requires a long warm season for flowering, but is worth growing just for the foliage. Cut stems make stunning additions to fresh bouquets. Blooms in late September, mature specimens to 9 ft. (2.7 m) tall. Flowering stems are often suffused deep pink in late summer and autumn. Sturdy and upright, rarely requiring staking or support. Individual stems occasionally revert to solid green and should be removed. Originally found by Kokin Watanabe of Mishima, Japan, and first introduced to Western gardens in 1976 by Sylvester March and John Creech of the U.S. National Arboretum, Washington, D.C., who obtained propagations from variegated plant specialist Masato Yokoi. Named by Kurt Bluemel. Tony Avent of Plant Delights Nursery has found that 'Cabaret' is seed-sterile. Germinating seedlings routinely lack chlorophyll and do not survive. A superb container subject. Tolerates light shade. Propagate by division. Zone 6.

'Cosmopolitan'. Leaves to 1 1/2 in. (4 cm) wide, with mostly green centers and wide cream-white variegated margins, in a pattern nearly the reverse of 'Cabaret'. 'Cosmopolitan' flowers much more freely and slightly earlier than 'Cabaret', opening copper-red in early September, to 10 ft. (3 m) tall. Individual stems occasionally revert to solid green and should be removed. Originally found in Japan in the 1940s by Toyoichi Aoki of Tokyo. First introduced to the United States in 1976 by staff of the U.S. National Arboretum, Washington, D.C., who obtained plants from variegated plant specialist Masato Yokoi.

Miscanthus sinensis var. *condensatus* 'Cabaret' in late October against *Rhus typhina* 'Laciniata' in the author's garden.

Miscanthus sinensis var. *condensatus* 'Cabaret' foliage detail in late September.

Named by Kurt Bluemel. A superb container subject. Tolerates light shade. Propagate by division. Zone 6.

'Cosmo Revert'. All-green plants segregated from 'Cosmopolitan'.

Miscanthus tinctorius (Steudel) Hackel.

Kari yasu.

Native to mountains on Japan's central island, Honshu. Very similar to *Miscanthus oligostachyus* in most respects, but slightly larger, with a few more branches in each inflorescence. Rare in Western gardens. Hardiness not established though it should be reliable at least through Zone 5.

Miscanthus transmorrisonensis Hayata.

Taiwanese miscanthus, evergreen miscanthus.

A 1979 introduction from Taiwan by Paul Meyer of the Morris Arboretum and C. Ferris Miller of Chollipo Arboretum, who collected seed of plants growing at 9500 ft. (2900 m) elevation on Mt. Daxue. This species is frequent on exposed mountain slopes at medium to high altitudes throughout Taiwan. It is closely related to *Miscanthus sinensis* but horticulturally quite distinct, with narrow green foliage rarely topping 3 ft. (1 m) and late July or early Au-

Miscanthus sinensis var. *condensatus* 'Cosmopolitan' in late September at Longwood Gardens.

Miscanthus transmorrisonensis in early October at Kurt Bluemel's nursery in Maryland.

Miscanthus sinensis var. *condensatus* 'Cosmopolitan' foliage detail in late September at Longwood Gardens.

gust flowers held high above the foliage on long graceful stems. The foliage often stays green into late December as far north as zone 6 and is fully evergreen in southern California. A beautiful, distinct miscanthus. Propagate by seed or division. Zone 6.

Molinia Shrank.

Grass family, Poaceae.
Moor grass.

Named for Juan I. Molina (1740–1829), who studied the natural history of Chile. Comprised of two to three clump-forming perennial species, native to wet moorlands and heaths in Europe, western Russia, Turkey, China, and Japan. Only *Molinia caerulea* is grown for ornament, and it is usually separated into two subspecies. The typical subspecies is the shorter of the two.

One variegated purple moor grass is prized for its foliage; the others are essentially green plants valued for their strong architectural forms and airy inflorescences. They are cool-season growers that grow best in moist, cool climates.

Molinia caerulea (Linnaeus) Moench.

Purple moor grass.

Native to moist places, including heaths, moors, bogs, fens, mountain grasslands, and lake shores in the British Isles as well as continental Europe and Asia. Strictly clumping, producing a low mound of basal foliage, with leaves to 3/8 in. (9 mm) wide, usually green, typically turning golden-yellow in autumn. Blooms in midsummer, the narrow panicles held above the foliage on slender stalks varying from strictly upright to strongly arched, to 3 ft. (1 m) tall. Flower spikelets are purple-colored, but this color is subtle due to their small size. Requires moist, cool summer conditions for best growth. Flowering is minimal in regions with hot summers, especially if conditions are dry. Partly shaded conditions and plentiful moisture can partly offset heat stress. Tolerates low soil fertility and acid conditions, but also grows on alkaline soils common to the north-central United States. Propagate the species by seed or by division in spring, the cultivars only by division. Zone 4.

'Dauerstrahl' (faithful ray). Green-leaved and arching. Zone 4.

'Heidebraut' (heather bride). Green-leaved and upright-divergent. Zone 4.

'Moorhexe' (moor witch). Green-leaved and narrowly erect. Zone 4.

'Rotschopf'. Green-leaved and upright-divergent, with foliage tinted dark red during growing season and especially in autumn. Zone 4.

'Strahlenquelle' (source of rays). Green-leaved with

Molinia caerulea 'Dauerstrahl' in late August in northern Germany.

Molinia caerulea 'Strahlenquelle' in late August at the Sichtungsgarten in Wiehenstephan, Germany.

strongly arching-pendant inflorescences that are bowed under the weight of the delicate purplish flowers. Zone 4.

'Variegata'. Leaves dramatically striped light yellow to cream-white. In regions where flowering is heavy, the bright yellow stalks of the inflorescences are attractive, but this plant is worth growing just for the foliage. Zone 5.

Molinia caerulea subsp. *arundinacea* (Schrank) H. Paul.

[*Molinia arundinacea* Schrank, *Molinia litoralis* Host, *Molinia altissima* Link]. Tall purple moor grass.

Differs from the typical subspecies dramatically in height and in other less obvious characters: subspecies *caerulea* usually grows less than 3 ft. (1 m) tall, while subspecies *arundinacea* grows to 8 ft. (2.4 m) tall. These taller plants have been recognized in the past as a separate species, as the various synonyms indicate. Native

Molinia caerulea 'Heidebraut' in late August in northern Germany.

Molinia caerulea 'Moorhexe' in late August in northern Germany.

Molinia caerulea 'Variegata' in late August in northern Germany.

Molinia caerulea subsp. *arundinacea* in mid-August in Kurt Bluemel's garden in Maryland.

Molinia caerulea subsp. *arundinacea* 'Karl Foerster' in early September at the U.S. National Arboretum in Washington, D.C.

to fens, fen scrub, and along rivers in the British Isles as well as to continental Europe and Asia. Produces mounded basal foliage 2–3 ft. (60–90 cm) tall, topped by stately inflorescences to 8 ft. (2.4 m) tall, either upright or arching. Leaves green or gray-green in summer, to 1/2 in. (12 mm) wide. The entire plant turns rich golden-yellow in autumn. The appeal of this large grass is in its strong sculptural form and in the graceful way the inflorescences move with the wind. Most effective when side-lit or backlit by the sun, especially against a contrasting background. Needs a few seasons to reach mature size and beauty, but will last for many years with minimal maintenance. Best in cool climates, but grows strongly even in areas with fairly hot summers as long as it is kept moist. Not particular about soils. Tolerates low soil fertility and acid conditions, but also grows on alkaline soils common to the north-central United States. The flower stalks begin to break off at the ground by early winter, at which time the plant is best cut back. The cultivars below are all quite similar, differing mostly in the height of the flowers and the relative stiffness or arching aspect of the inflorescences. Propagate the subspecies by seed or by division in spring, the cultivars only by division. Zone 4.

'Bergfreund' (mountain friend). To 5 ft. (1.5 m) tall. Zone 4.

'Fontäne' (fountain). Arching form, to 6 ft. (2 m) tall. Zone 4.

'Karl Foerster'. Arching form, to 7 ft. (2.1 m) tall. Named for the famous German nurseryman and ornamental grass pioneer. Zone 4.

'Skyracer'. Upright and unusually tall, to 8 ft. (2.4 m) tall. Introduced by Kurt Bluemel. Zone 4.

'Staefa'. Mostly upright, to 5 ft. (1.5 m) tall. Named for the Swiss city. Zone 4.

'Transparent'. Arching form, to 6 ft. (2 m) tall. The name refers to the transparent section between the top of the basal foliage and the point on the inflorescence stalks where the flowers begin. Zone 4.

'Windspiel' (wind's game). Slender and upright, to 7 ft. (2.1 m) tall. The name alludes to the wind playing with the supple and responsive inflorescences. Zone 4.

Muhlenbergia Schreber.

Grass family, Poaceae.
Muhly.

Named for botanist G. H. E. Muhlenberg (1753–1815), a specialist in grasses. Comprised of more than 125 primarily perennial species, most native to the southern United States and Mexico. Important range grasses, they form a large portion of the grass flora of semi-arid and arid regions in the Southwest. For example, *Muhlenbergia* is the largest genus of grasses native to Arizona. Tolerant to sun and drought, many muhly grasses have attractive, fine-textured basal foliage in shades of green to glaucous-blue, topped by airy inflorescences, some of which are strongly colored pink, purple-red, or purple-gray. Little known to ornamental horticulture, they are increasingly attracting attention as gardeners search for water-conserving ornamentals suited to the many hot, dry regions across the southern United States. A few species are wide-

Molinia caerulea subsp. *arundinacea* 'Skyracer' fall color in early November at Longwood Gardens.

Molinia caerulea subsp. *arundinacea* 'Transparent' in mid-August in southern Germany.

ranging, and provenance will likely prove an important factor in selecting plants with greater cold-hardiness for garden use.

Muhlenbergia capillaris (Lamarck) Trinius.
[*Muhlenbergia capillaris* var. *filipes* (M. A. Curtis) Chapman ex Beal, *Muhlenbergia filipes* M. A. Curtis].
Pink muhly, pink hair grass, Gulf muhly, purple muhly.

Native mostly on sandy or rocky soils, in prairies, pine barrens, and openings in woodlands from Massachusetts to Indiana and Kansas, south to Florida and Texas and Mexico. Plants of moist coastal barrens have been segregated by some taxonomists as a separate botanical variety or even a separate species, but there seems to be no clear delineation and they are considered here to be synonymous with *Muhlenbergia capillaris*. The most highly ornamental of the muhly grasses, with dark green, glossy basal foliage overtopped by masses of delicate open flower panicles in vibrant pink or pink-red, drying to light buff. Blooms September to November, to 3 ft. (1 m) tall, remaining attractive into winter. Clump-forming. Effective singly, but especially dramatic in groups and sweeps. Tough enough for groundcover use and in challenging settings, such as traffic islands, even in the warm southeastern United States. Drought tolerant, best in full sun or very light shade. Propagate by seed or by division in spring. Zone 6, possibly colder.

'Lenca' (Regal Mist™). An exceptionally deep-pink-flowered clonal selection made by Mountain States Nursery of Arizona.

Muhlenbergia capillaris in early November at Longwood Gardens.

Muhlenbergia dubia Fournier ex Hemsley.
Pine muhly.

Native to canyons and rocky hills at elevations to 7000 ft. (2100 m) in western Texas, New Mexico, and northern Mexico. Clump-forming and densely tufted with light green, fine-textured leaves. Blooms August to November, the inflorescences stiff, narrow, purplish gray fading quickly to light cream color, 2–3 ft. (60–90 cm) tall. Drought tolerant. Prefers full sun. Propagate by seed or by division in spring. Zone 7.

Muhlenbergia capillaris in mid-November at Yucca Do Nursery in Waller, Texas.

Muhlenbergia dubia in mid-November at the National Wildflower Research Center in Austin, Texas.

Muhlenbergia dubioides C. O. Goodding.
Southwestern muhly, weeping muhly.

Native to canyons and rocky slopes in southern Arizona. Clump-forming with basal leaves in a draping mound. Inflorescences narrow, purplish gray, erect, to 3 ft. (1 m) tall. Drought tolerant. Prefers full sun. Zone 7.

Muhlenbergia dumosa Scribner ex Vasey.
Bamboo muhly.

Native to rocky canyon slopes and valleys at low altitudes in southern Arizona, also northwestern Mexico. Very distinct from the other muhly grasses, with billowing, lacy, bright green foliage and leafy, erect or arching stems to 4 ft. (1.2 m) tall that move gracefully with the slightest breeze. The overall effect is quite bamboolike. Spreads slowly by creeping rhizomes. Blooms March to May, flowers insignificant. Drought tolerant, but not as much as other species; best with occasional moisture. A fine companion for cacti and other bold-textured succulents. Makes a superb container specimen or conservatory subject in areas where it is not cold-hardy. Propagate by seed or division. Zone 8, possibly colder.

Muhlenbergia dumosa in early November at Longwood Gardens.

Muhlenbergia emersleyi Vasey.
Bull grass.

Native to rocky slopes, woods, canyons, and ravines in Arizona, New Mexico, and Texas. Clump-forming with medium-textured gray-green leaves in a dense basal mound. Blooms August to November, the inflorescences mostly erect, to 3 ft. (1 m) tall, purplish gray, dense, not airy like *Muhlenbergia capillaris.* Drought tolerant. Best in full sun or light shade. Propagate by seed or division. Zone 7, possibly colder.

Muhlenbergia involuta Swall.
Edwards Plateau Muhly.

Native to rocky prairies and uplands, usually near small streams, only on the Edwards Plateau of Texas. Clump-forming with green, mostly basal leaves. Blooms in fall, the inflorescences loose and airy, to 4 ft. (1.2 m) tall. Propagate by seed or division. Zone 7, possibly colder.

Muhlenbergia lindheimeri Hitchcock.
Lindheimer's muhly.

Native to Mexico and Texas. A stunning clump-former with fine-textured, semi-evergreen blue-gray basal leaves. Inflorescences upright, to 5 ft. (1.5 m) tall, vaguely reminiscent of *Calamagrostis.* Drought tolerant and summer-heat tolerant, does well even in the southeastern United States. Blooms September to October, the inflorescences light purplish gray, lasting mostly through winter. Prefers full sun. Propagate by seed or division. Zone 7, possibly colder.

'Lenli' (Autumn Glow™). A clonal selection made by Mountain States Nursery of Arizona. Inflorescences yellowish in autumn.

Muhlenbergia lindheimeri in late May at Plant Delights Nursery in Raleigh, North Carolina.

Muhlenbergia lindheimeri in late October at Longwood Gardens.

Muhlenbergia reverchonii Vasey & Scribner.
Seep muhly.

Native to limestone soils and periodic seep areas in Texas and Oklahoma. Clump-forming and densely tufted with green leaves. Blooms August to October, the inflorescences to $2^1/2$ ft. (80 cm) tall, open and airy. Propagate by seed or division. Zone 6, possibly colder.

Muhlenbergia reverchonii in mid-November at the National Wildflower Research Center in Austin, Texas.

Muhlenbergia involuta in mid-November at the National Wildflower Research Center in Austin, Texas.

Muhlenbergia rigens (Bentham) Hitchcock.
Deer grass.

Native to dry or open ground, hillsides, gullies, and open forest to 7000 ft. (2100 m) elevation in California, as well as Arizona, Nevada, New Mexico, Texas, and southern Mexico. Clump-forming with gray-green leaves forming a large basal mound, semi-evergreen. Blooms in late summer, the inflorescences narrow, whiplike, to 5 ft. (1.5 m) tall, soon drying to light straw color, remaining upright and attractive long through winter. A stunning vertical accent, especially when side-lit or back-lit by the autumn or winter sun. Very drought tolerant. Prefers full sun. Propagate by seed or division. Zone 7, possibly colder.

Muhlenbergia rigida (Kunth) Trinius.
Purple muhly.

Native to sunny, rocky slopes in Texas, Arizona, and northern Mexico. Clump-forming with green leaves. Blooms late August to early November, the inflorescences brownish purple to dark purple, to 3 ft. (1 m) tall. Zone 7.

Nashville™. A strongly purple-flowered clonal selection made by Mountain States Nursery of Arizona.

Nassella Barkworth.
Grass family, Poaceae.
Needle grass.

Comprised of more than 80 species native to the Americas. Many, including those below, were formerly included in *Stipa*. All are graceful, cool-season growers with long, showy awns.

Nassella cernua (Stebbins & Á. Löve) Barkworth.
[*Stipa cernua* Stebbins & Á. Löve].
Nodding needle grass.

Native to sandy, dry slopes in grasslands, chaparral, and juniper woodlands in California. Clump-forming and tufted. A true cool-season grower, dormant in summer. Blooms in late winter to early spring, inflorescences delicate and open, to 3 ft. (1 m) tall, with awns to $4^1/2$ in. (11 cm) long, purplish at first, drying silvery, usually nodding. Similar in appearance to *Nassella lepida* and *N. pulchra*, and all were once a conspicuous part of California native grasslands. Prefers full sun, best on well-drained soil but broadly tolerant. Ideal for naturalizing in meadows and meadow gardens, but needs open ground for seeds to establish. Self-sows but not invasive. Propagate by seed. Zone 8.

Nassella lepida (Hitchcock) Barkworth.
[*Stipa lepida* Hitchcock].
Foothill needle grass.

Native to dry slopes in oak grasslands, chaparral, and coastal scrub in California. Clump-forming and tufted. A true cool-season grower, dormant in summer. Blooms in late winter or early spring, inflorescences delicate and open, with awns nearly 2 in. (5 cm) long. Prefers full sun,

Muhlenbergia rigens in mid-December at the University of California, Berkeley, Botanical Garden.

Muhlenbergia rigens in late February in southern California.

best on well-drained soil but broadly tolerant. Ideal for naturalizing in meadows and meadow gardens, but needs open ground for seeds to establish. Self-sows but not invasive. Propagate by seed. Zone 8.

Nassella pulchra (Hitchcock) Barkworth.
[*Stipa pulchra* Hitchcock].
Purple needle grass.

Native to dry grasslands, chaparral, and coastal scrub in California. Delicately beautiful; an emblem of the dry native grasslands that once covered much of California but which are now mostly eradicated or displaced by introduced exotic species. Blooms in late winter or early spring. Inflorescences on erect stalks, to 3 ft. (1 m) tall. Spikelets with graceful long awns, to 4 in. (10 cm), purple at first, turning silvery and translucent. A cool-season grower, dormant in summer, resuming growth in fall and usually green through winter. Prefers full sun, best on well-drained soil but broadly tolerant. Ideal for naturalizing in meadows and meadow gardens, but needs open ground for seeds to establish. Self-sows but not invasive. Propagate by seed. Zone 8.

Nassella tenuissima (Trinius) Barkworth.
[*Stipa tenuissima* Trinius].
Mexican feather grass.

Native to dry open ground, open woods, and rocky slopes in Texas, New Mexico, Mexico, and Argentina.

Nassella pulchra in late February with California poppies, *Eschscholzia californica*, at the Santa Barbara Botanic Garden, California.

Nassella tenuissima in early August near Seattle, Washington.

Among the finest textured of all ornamental grasses, producing a dense green fountain of hairlike leaves and threadlike stems ending in silvery inflorescences with awns more than 3 in. (7.5 cm) long. Blooms June to September, to 2 ft. (60 cm) tall, the inflorescences becoming light straw-colored and remaining attractive into winter. Stunning in contrast to rocks or bold-textured companion plantings. Delicate and easily moved by breezes. Easily grown on well-drained soil in full sun or light shade. Very drought tolerant. A cool-season grower that remains evergreen in cool climates but goes dormant during hot summers. Self-sows readily and can be a minor nuisance. May be capable of naturalizing in areas such as California and the Pacific Northwest. Propagate by seed. Zone 6.

Panicum Linnaeus.
Grass family, Poaceae.
Panic grass.

Includes nearly 500 annual and perennial species native to deserts, savannas, swamps, and forests, widely distributed in tropical regions, and extending to temperate North America. The inflorescences are panicles with narrow or more often widespreading branches. The following species is important ornamentally.

Panicum virgatum in early July in its native habitat in coastal New Jersey.

Panicum virgatum Linnaeus.
Switch grass, panic grass.

Native to prairies and open ground, open woods, and brackish marshes, from eastern Canada through most of the United States except for California and the Pacific Northwest, south to Mexico and Central America. Once a major component of the great American tallgrass prairie, this large, variable species was for many decades greatly appreciated in German gardens and ignored at home. This pattern has ended, and now an increasing array of fine horticultural selections, both American and European, is available. Switch grass is quite diverse in size, growing from 4 to 8 ft. (1.2 to 2.4 m) tall. Although always forming recognizable clumps, it may also run by rhizomes, sometimes slowly, sometimes with moderate speed. It may be erect-stemmed and narrow, or lax and billowing in form. Summer foliage color ranges from typical deep green to bright powder-blue, and autumn tones vary from typical golden-yellow to deep burgundy. Like many North American prairie grasses, switch grass is a long-lived, warm-season grower. It begins growth late in spring, grows strongly in the heat of summer, and flowers in July or August. The profuse, airy panicles are often pink or red-tinted when first opening. All parts of the plant are quite sturdy even when dry and dormant, standing through winter unless snows are heavy, and providing important cover for birds. Versatile in the garden, effective as a speci-

Panicum virgatum in mid-October in its native habitat in coastal New Jersey.

Panicum virgatum growth from the previous season is still attractive in mid-May, at water's edge, with *Orontium aquaticum* in the New Jersey pine barrens.

men, in sweeps or masses, for screening, at the edges of pools or ponds, or in a large decorative container. Of easy culture in full sun on almost any soil from quartz sands to fertile, heavy clays. Drought tolerant once established and withstands soggy soils or periodic inundation. Self-sowing is usually minimal but can be prolific on open moist soil; this can be valuable for naturalizing, but can be a problem when attempting to maintain uniform sweeps of clonal cultivars, since seedlings often differ noticeably from parents. Requires little maintenance except cutting back annually in late winter or early spring. The extremely blue-leaved cultivars generally do not have the strong golden autumn color typical of green-leaved plants, and none turn red in fall. Some, such as 'Heavy Metal', are prone to foliar rust diseases in hot, moist summers. Propagate the species by seed or by division in spring, the cultivars by division only. Zone 4.

'Blue Tower'. Tall blue switch grass. Leaves glaucous-blue, to 8 ft. (2.4 m) tall in flower. A selection from a native population in Princeton, Illinois, by Crystal Palace Perennials of Illinois. Zone 4.

'Cloud Nine'. Tall switch grass. Leaves glaucous blue-green, to 8 ft. (2.4 m) tall in flower, erect, and usually upright through winter, a pleasing dark gold in autumn. Introduced by Bluemount Nursery of Maryland. Zone 4.

'Hänse Herms'. Red switch grass. Leaves green in summer, taking on dark red tones by August, and turning

Panicum virgatum 'Cloud Nine' in early August at Firefly Farm, the eastern Pennsylvania garden of Mary and Tom Shea.

Panicum virgatum 'Hänse Herms' in late August at the Westpark, Munich, Germany.

Panicum virgatum 'Prairie Sky' is glaucous-blue in late June at Longwood Gardens.

mostly burgundy in autumn. Among the best for this trait. Just over 4 ft. (1.2 m) tall in flower. Stems bend gracefully during rains, usually returning to upright position upon drying, but may lodge permanently after prolonged rainy periods. Zone 4.

'Heavy Metal'. Blue switch grass. Leaves strongly glaucous-blue and strictly upright. Stems never lean or flop, even in heavy rains. To 5 ft. (1.5 m) tall in bloom, with strong pink tones in the inflorescences. Introduced by Kurt Bluemel. Zone 4.

'Prairie Sky'. Blue switch grass. Leaves noticeably bluer than that of 'Heavy Metal'. Not as sturdy-stemmed and sometimes flops in wet seasons common to the eastern United States. Stands upright in drier, western regions. Selected by Roger Gettig of Wisconsin. Zone 4.

'Red Cloud'. Red switch grass. Leaves green in summer, purplish in autumn. Flowers strongly red tinted, to $5\frac{1}{2}$ ft. (1.7 m) tall. Zone 4.

'Rotbraun' (red-brown). Red switch grass. Similar to 'Hänse Herms', but the autumn burgundy-red tones are not as pronounced. To 4 ft. (1.2 m) tall in flower. Zone 4.

Panicum virgatum 'Heavy Metal' (two clumps, front left) is strictly upright, while *P. virgatum* 'Hänse Herms' (front right) is lax-stemmed and arching in early August, after a moist season, at Longwood Gardens.

Panicum virgatum 'Strictum' in mid-August in southern Germany.

Panicum virgatum 'Shenandoah' is mostly burgundy in mid-October at North Creek Nurseries in eastern Pennsylvania.

'Rotstrahlbusch'. Red switch grass. Leaves red-burgundy in autumn, but not nearly as pronounced as 'Hänse Herms'. To 4 ft. (1.2 m) tall. Zone 4.

'Shenandoah'. Red switch grass. Unmatched for burgundy fall color. Leaves green in early summer, taking on dark red tones by July and turning wholly wine-colored by September. Approximately 4 ft. (1.2 m) tall in flower. Selected by Hans Simon of Germany, from his evaluations of more than 500 seedlings of 'Hänse Herms'. Zone 4.

'Squaw'. Leaves green, with strong pink tones in the inflorescences, to 4 ft. (1.2 m) tall in flower, some red foliage tones in fall. Introduced by Kurt Bluemel. Zone 4.

'Strictum'. Leaves blue-green, to 6 ft. (2 m) tall in flower. Zone 4.

'Warrior'. Leaves green, to 5 ft. (1.5 m) tall in flower, some red foliage tones in fall. Introduced by Kurt Bluemel. Zone 4.

Pennisetum Richard ex Persoon.

Grass family, Poaceae.
Fountain grass.

From the Latin *penna* (feather) and *seta* (bristle), referring to the bristlelike inflorescences. Approximately 80 species, mostly perennials, native to both open and woodland habitats, widely distributed in the tropics and in warm temperate regions. Aptly named, these grasses are characterized by a fountain of flowers flowing out of a cascading mound of basal foliage. They are warm-season growers, unperturbed by hot, humid summers, flowering from late June to October. Most are clump-forming, though a few are strong runners. They range in size from less than 1 ft. (30 cm) to more than 5 ft. (1.5 m) tall. Most prefer full sun or light shade and are best divided or transplanted in spring. Many self-sow readily, and a few have escaped from cultivation and have become serious weeds in warm regions, such as southern California and Australia. Though the following species are true perennials, a few are tender tropicals that are grown as annuals in cold-temperate regions.

Pennisetum alopecuroides (Linnaeus) Sprengel.

[*Pennisetum japonicum* Trinius].
Fountain grass, chikara shiba.

Native to sunny open lowlands and grassy places in Japan and over much of eastern Asia. Of uncertain nativity in western Australia. This extremely variable species is the most commonly grown of the truly cold-hardy fountain grasses. Typically 2–3 ft. (60–90 cm) tall, but cultivated selections range from less than 1 ft. (30 cm) to more than 5 ft. (1.5 m). Leaves are narrow, to 1/2 in. (12 mm) wide, green in summer turning golden-yellow in autumn. Inflorescences are spikelike racemes, usually dense and

Pennisetum alopecuroides foliage in late June at Longwood Gardens.

Pennisetum alopecuroides in mid-August in Kurt Bluemel's garden in Maryland.

cylindrical, resembling large foxtails. They are superb as cut materials for fresh bouquets. Flower color varies from dark purple (most common) to cream-white, and flowering period begins as early as June or as late as September. Inflorescences remain attractive only into late fall or early winter, then begin to shatter. Easily grown in full sun or light shade on most soils. Moderately drought tolerant, best with regular moisture. Especially effective when planted in groups or masses, or in decorative containers. Self-sows manageably usually; however, the wider-leaved fall-blooming varieties, such as 'Moudry' and 'National Arboretum', are particularly fertile and can be invasive if conditions are suitably moist in and beyond the garden. Propagate the species by seed or by division in spring, the cultivars by division only. Zone 6, sometimes colder.

'Cassian'. With dusky light brown flowers beginning in August, to 3 ft. (1 m) tall. Foliage turns rich gold with red tints in autumn. Introduced by Kurt Bluemel. Named for German horticulturist Cassian Schmidt. Zone 6.

'Caudatum' (*Pennisetum caudatum* hort.). White-flowering fountain grass. Flowers are nearly white, beginning in August, to 4 ft. (1.2 m) tall. A beautiful, underused cultivar. Zone 6.

'Hameln'. Flowers cream-white, beginning in late July. To 3 ft. (1 m) tall, which is at least 1 ft. (30 cm) shorter than the average species height. Excellent for groundcover massing. Zone 6.

Pennisetum alopecuroides fall color in mid-October in eastern Pennsylvania.

Pennisetum alopecuroides 'Caudatum' in early September in northern Delaware.

Pennisetum alopecuroides 'Hameln' in early August at Longwood Gardens.

'Little Bunny'. A true miniature, only 18 in. (45 cm) tall in bloom. Flowers in August. Originated as a seedling of 'Hameln', found by Jack Weiskott of Ornamental Plantings Nursery in Greenport, Long Island, New York. Zone 6.

'Little Honey'. Leaves longitudinally striped white. Originated as a sport of 'Little Bunny' and is slightly smaller, usually only 1 ft. (30 cm) tall in bloom. Named by Cliff Russell of Russell Nurseries, Richboro, Pennsylvania. Zone 6.

'Moudry'. Leaves relatively wide, to 7/16 in. (11 mm), dark green, and very glossy, forming a neat, lustrous basal mound to 2 ft. (60 cm) tall. A striking addition to the autumn garden. Blooms September to November, flowers exceptionally dark purple, extending on stiff stalks in late September. In some years, the inflorescences do not fully emerge from the foliage. This cultivar originated from seed introduced by the U.S. National Arboretum, Washington, D.C., from Japan, where populations of wide-leaved, late-blooming, dark-flowered plants are commonly native. Though horticulturally distinct, these types have not been distinguished botanically from the species. Kurt Bluemel's nursery received plants grown from U.S. National Arboretum seed, which was received from Baltimore City horticulturist G. Moudry. Moudry's name inadvertently came into use as the cultivar's name. Though highly ornamental, 'Moudry' self-sows prolifically, especially if conditions are moist. It can seed heavily into lawns adjacent to flower beds. If grown near turf, it is advisable to cut back before seed is produced. Zone 6.

'National Arboretum'. Similar to 'Moudry' in all re-

Pennisetum alopecuroides 'Little Bunny' in late August at Longwood Gardens.

Pennisetum alopecuroides 'Little Honey' in August at North Creek Nurseries in eastern Pennsylvania. (Photo: Dale Hendricks.)

Pennisetum alopecuroides 'Moudry' in early October in northern Delaware.

Pennisetum alopecuroides 'Moudry' covered in morning dew in late October in the author's former Delaware garden.

spects, but the inflorescences are consistently held out from the foliage. Zone 6.

'Paul's Giant'. Unusually large, reaching 5 ft. (1.5 m) tall. Blooms in August, flowers cream-white to tan. Fall foliage a strong yellow-orange. Discovered as a seedling by horticulturist Paul Skibinski of Hockessin, Delaware. Zone 6.

'Weserbergland'. Very similar to 'Hameln' but slightly larger, wider. Zone 6.

'Woodside'. Early blooming, flowers well in England. To 2 ft. (60 cm) tall. A selection from Woodside, the garden of Mervyn Feesey of Barnstaple, England. Zone 6.

Pennisetum alopecuroides 'Paul's Giant' in early October at Longwood Gardens.

Pennisetum alopecuroides 'National Arboretum' in early November at Longwood Gardens.

Pennisetum alopecuroides 'Paul's Giant' in late October at Longwood Gardens.

Pennisetum 'Burgundy Giant'

Giant burgundy fountain grass.

The boldest-textured fountain grass, with bronze-burgundy leaves to 1 3/8 in. (35 mm) wide. Upright, clump-forming, to 6 ft. (2 m) tall. Blooms July to September, inflorescences colored like the foliage. Named at Longwood Gardens in cooperation with Marie Selby Botanical Gardens in Florida, from plants growing at Selby of unknown garden origin. Probably a variant of *Pennisetum macrostachyum* (Brongniart) Trinius, a large species native to New Guinea, Borneo, and adjacent islands. Taxonomic description and classification of the tropical *Pennisetum* species are incomplete and existing literature sometimes contradictory, making it difficult to identify garden plants with certainty. 'Burgundy Giant' is very tender, requiring temperatures above 40°F (4°C). Makes a superb summer annual, planted in the ground or grown in a pot. Rapid-growing, reaching full height in a single summer even in zone 6. Prefers full sun, regular moisture. Usually does not set viable seed, but can easily be propagated from stem cuttings rooted in sand under mist. Zone 10.

Pennisetum incomptum Nees ex Steudel.

[*Pennisetum flaccidum* Griesbach].

Spreading fountain grass.

Native to northern China and the Himalayas. Spreads aggressively by rhizomes to form large masses to 4 ft. (1.2 m) tall. Leaves green to gray-green. Blooms late June, often continuing through August into September. Flowers greenish, drying light tan, on nearly upright stems. Racemes longer and much more slender than those of *Pennisetum alopecuroides*. Needs full sun but adapted to a wide range of soil and moisture conditions. Spreads too aggressively to be manageable in a mixed flower border, but is relatively early flowering, has good fall and winter presence, and can be an appropriate choice for a mass planting in difficult sites, such as traffic islands or in contained areas around buildings. Rhizomes persistent, can be difficult to eradicate once established. Zone 4.

Pennisetum 'Burgundy Giant' in late July at Longwood Gardens.

Pennisetum macrourum Trinius.

Fountain grass.

Native to South Africa. Similar in most respects to *Pennisetum incomptum* but with even longer racemes. Zone 6.

Pennisetum orientale Richard.

Fountain grass.

Native from central and southwestern Asia to northwestern India. One of the most striking hardy fountain grasses. Low growing, compact, and exceptionally floriferous when well grown. Blooms over an unusually long period from late June into October. Inflorescences fluffy, nearly white with strong pearlescent-pink tints in cool seasons. Requires well-drained soil, full sun and warmth for best growth and flowering, but can be grown in part shade in warm regions. Insufficient summer sun reduces winter hardiness. Leaves green to gray-green. Densely clump-forming. When transplanting, take care that the

Pennisetum incomptum in mid-August in Newark, Delaware.

Pennisetum macrourum in mid-August at the Royal Botanic Gardens, Kew, England.

crown of the plant is not at all below grade. Showy enough for specimen use, also superb in groups or masses, or in a container. Rarely self-sows. Does not propagate easily by division, best from seed. Zone 6.

Pennisetum setaceum (Forsskål) Chiovenda.
[*Pennisetum ruppelii* Steudel, *Pennisetum ruppelianum* Hochstetter, *Pennisetum macrostachyum* Fresenius, non (Brongniart) Trinius].
Tender fountain grass.

Native to tropical Africa, southwestern Asia, and Arabia. An old-fashioned garden favorite, perennial but usually treated as an annual grown from seed each year. Clump-forming, erect to arching, to 5 ft. (1.5 m) tall, with purplish pink racemes nearly 15 in. (38 cm) long. Blooms July to September, superb for cut flowers. Leaves typically green. Taller and narrower than *Pennisetum alopecuroides*, this species sometimes requires staking in late summer, especially on moist, rich soils. Requires full sun. Self-sows in warm climates, and has escaped and naturalized in various parts of the world. In cold zones, propagate by seed sown indoors in late winter. New plants should not be set out until after danger of frost is past. There is some doubt whether the red-leaved cultivars, such as 'Eaton Canyon' and 'Rubrum', belong to this species. Zone 9.

'Eaton Canyon' ('Cupreum Compactum', 'Rubrum Dwarf'). Compact purple fountain grass. Leaves, stems,

Pennisetum orientale in full sun in late June in northern Delaware.

Pennisetum orientale in light shade in early August at Pauline Volmer's garden, Baltimore, Maryland.

Pennisetum setaceum in late August at Longwood Gardens.

Pennisetum setaceum 'Eaton Canyon' in mid-August at Longwood Gardens.

and inflorescences a rich red-burgundy color, like 'Rubrum' in miniature, with a maximum height of 30 in. (75 cm) in flower. Blooms late summer to frost. Originated as a seedling of 'Rubrum' at Magic Growers nursery in Pasadena, California. Tender and, like 'Rubrum', does not survive prolonged temperatures below 40°F (4°C). Rarely sets seed. Propagate by division.

'Rubrum' ('Atropurpureum', 'Cupreum', 'Purpureum') Purple fountain grass. All parts of the plant a rich red-burgundy color. Leaves to 3/4 in. (2 cm) wide. Upright, to 5 ft. (1.5 m) tall. Blooms late summer to frost, with racemes more than 1 ft. (30 cm) long. Tender, does not survive prolonged temperatures below 40°F (4°C). Treated as a summer annual from plants held over in a greenhouse or purchased annually, the dramatically colorful grass is stunning as a specimen or in groups or masses. Rarely sets seed. Propagate by division. Zone 9.

Pennisetum villosum R. Brown ex Fries.

Feathertop.

Native to mountains in northeastern tropical Africa. Flowers nearly pure white, the racemes shorter, fuller, and more rounded than most fountain grasses. Prized by florists as a cut flower and equally pretty in the garden. Stems often lax. Tender, but more cold-hardy than *Pennisetum setaceum*, occasionally surviving winters in zone 7. Best in full sun with regular moisture. Dramatic in mass or in a container. Propagate by seed. Zone 8.

Phalaris Linnaeus.

Grass family, Poaceae.

Canary grass.

About 15 annual or perennial species, native to cool north-temperate zones, including North America and Eurasia. Also native to Mediterranean regions and South America. One species, *Phalaris canariensis* Linnaeus, canary grass, is widely cultivated for birdseed. A native of Medi-

Pennisetum setaceum 'Rubrum' in late August in eastern Pennsylvania.

Pennisetum villosum in early August in northern Delaware.

terranean Europe, this annual has escaped and naturalized in various warm regions. It has short, wide flower panicles that are readily distinguished from the long, narrow panicles of reed canary grass, *P. arundinacea*, a perennial and the only species cultivated ornamentally, most often in its variegated-leaved forms.

Phalaris arundinacea Linnaeus.

Reed canary grass.

This grass is a good example of how behavior differs among plants of different provenance, even though they may belong to the same species. It is a cool-season, perennial species native to both North America and Eurasia, usually in moist places, including marshes and riverbanks. Plants of European origin (which may be referred to as European genotypes or European ecotypes) were widely planted for forage and erosion control in North America, where they were found to be much more vigorous than the American genotype. The European genotype has since naturalized and become a major threat to marshes and other native wetlands in northern North America. It is capable of completely displacing native wetland and wet prairie species, forming huge monocultures that spread by seed and by strong rhizomes. Unfortunately, there is no reliable method for distinguishing Eu-

Phalaris arundinacea in early July growing wild in northern Delaware.

ropean genotypes from American genotypes, since they are identical in appearance. Control is difficult since it may result in inadvertent destruction of native plants; there are no herbicides available that are specific to the invasive forms. Frequent burning is one method of controlling *Phalaris arundinacea* in high quality native wetlands. Since the species is favored by moist but not constantly wet conditions, the draining and artificial lowering of water levels in native wetlands have resulted in conditions favorable to it. Restoring water to higher levels is another possible means of control. Typically green-leaved, reed canary grass is attractive but not showy. Stems are mostly upright, to 5 ft. (1.5 m) tall, flowering in June. The variegated cultivars, which are all derived from European genotypes, are quite distinct and are among the most dramatically variegated ornamental grasses. They are true cool-season growers, often going partly or fully dormant in midsummer in hot climates. If cut back midseason, they produce a strong new flush of leaves that remains crisply attractive into early winter. Flowers of the variegated cultivars often detract from their overall appeal and are best cut back. Not particular about soils, but best with regular moisture, in full sun in cool climates or in part shade in hot regions. Self-sowing is very minor in the garden; however, all spread aggressively by rhizomes and require regular maintenance to keep contained. When properly sited, they are striking additions to the garden, useful as accents or groundcovers, and are worth the effort required to control their spread. Also superb when grown in pots. Tawny blotch, a disease caused by *Stagonospora foliicola* fungi, was previously only known from typical green-leaved plants of *P. arundinacea* planted for forage purposes. It has subsequently been observed on variegated ornamental plants in cultivation in the mid-Atlantic United States. Symptoms appear in July, characterized by a browning of the foliage that ruins the ornamental appeal of the plants. It should respond to treatment with fungicides. Propagate cultivars by division in spring or fall. Zone 4.

'Feesey' ('Strawberries and Cream'). Named for British horticulturist and ornamental grass specialist Mervyn Feesey. Leaves green with prominent longitudinal stripes. Compared to the old standard, 'Picta', the variegation is much stronger and clearer white, especially during cool periods of spring and autumn, when the foliage and stems are frequently and conspicuously pink-tinted. More of a

Phalaris arundinacea 'Picta' in late May at Fred and Mary Ann McGourty's Hillside Gardens in Connecticut.

Phalaris arundinacea 'Feesey' in mid-July at Alan Bloom's garden in Bressingham, England.

Phalaris arundinacea 'Luteopicta' in mid-April at Longwood Gardens.

cool-season grower than 'Picta' and often suffers worse in extreme heat. Zone 4.

'Luteopicta' ('Aureovariegata'). Leaves attractive cream-yellow-striped, especially in spring, darkening mostly to green in the heat of summer, especially in full sun. Zone 4.

'Picta' ('Elegantissima', var. *picta*, f. *picta*, var. *variegata*). Gardener's-garters, ribbon grass. A popular favorite since the Victorian era, often persisting in gardens through successions of owners. Leaves green with dramatic cream-white stripes, never pink-flushed. Zone 4.

'Tricolor'. Similar to 'Feesey' in having pink-flushed foliage in cool periods. The pink tones often persist into warmer weather, but the variegation is not quite as clear-white as that of 'Feesey'. Zone 4.

'Woods Dwarf' ('Dwarf's Garters'). Similar to 'Picta' but more compact, shorter. Zone 4.

Phragmites Adanson.

Grass family, Poaceae.
Reed.

From the Greek *phragma* (fence, screen), referring to the fencelike, screening effect created by dense stands of this large grass. Comprised of up to four very similar species of cosmopolitan distribution. Warm-season growers, all are strongly rhizomatous perennials of wet or moist habitats.

Phragmites australis (Cavanilles) Trinius ex Steudel.

[*Phragmites communis* Trinius].
Common reed, carrizo.

A huge, variable grass, found on every continent except Antarctica and especially common in freshwater and brackish wetlands in the world's temperate zones. In the synonym, the specific epithet *communis* refers to the extensive communities formed by this strongly rhizomatous species. Sturdy and upright, it usually grows 10–13 ft. (3–4 m) tall. The canes have been widely used for thatching. Leaves are gray-green, to 2 in. (5 cm) wide. The large terminal inflorescences appear in August or September, opening golden-tan to bronze-purple, drying to translucent silver. At its best, it provides a stunning, luminous balance to the brilliant autumn foliage tones of deciduous trees and shrubs, and colorful fall flowers. Unfortunately, an appreciation of the beauty of this grass must be tempered by an awareness of its great invasive potential. In places where it is indigenous, including North America, this species can be a stable component of native wetlands if the habitat is relatively undisturbed; however, during the twentieth century the species has spread aggressively in countless temperate wetlands, including many within its native range. The apparent reasons for much of this invasion can be traced to human activity, including dredging, channeling, salting of roads, and waste discharge, which have created conditions destructive to other native species but still tolerable to the reed. These invasions may also be partly due to the introduction of *Phragmites australis* plants from other regions, with different genetic makeup disposing them to aggressive behavior in their transplanted locations. The herbicide Rodeo™, containing glyphosate, is licensed for use over water and can be an effective control. Though the usual species form is too aggressive for most gardens, the variegated type is more manageable. Zone 3.

'Variegatus'. Has dramatically yellow-striped leaves. To 8 ft. (2.4 m) tall if grown in full sun in wet soil, but much smaller if conditions are drier or if root growth is restricted. Effective at the edges of water garden pools or small ponds, or grown in a container. Propagate by division in spring. Zone 4.

Phragmites australis subsp. *altissimus* (Bentham) W. D. Clayton.

Differs from the typical subspecies in height of plants, which can reach 18 ft. (5.5 m) tall. These tall-growing forms have often been listed under the illegitimate name 'Pseudodonax'.

Variation in inflorescence color in *Phragmites australis* among plants growing wild in late August in southern New Jersey.

Phragmites australis in mid-October in New York State.

Phragmites australis 'Variegatus' in late August in northern Germany.

Phragmites karka (Retzius) Trinius ex Steudel.

Reed.

Very similar to *Phragmites australis* but not as widely distributed, occurring in Japan, China, India, Burma, Malaysia, and Australia. Leaves narrower, usually less than $1\frac{1}{2}$ in. (4 cm) wide. Cultivated only in variegated form. Zone 4.

'Candy Stripe'. Similar or identical to 'Variegata', with white-striped leaves tinted pink in cool weather. Named by Crystal Palace Perennials of Illinois. Zone 5.

'Variegata'. Leaves with bold, nearly white longitudinal stripes, often pink-tinted in cool seasons. Much smaller than the species, usually less than 4 ft. (1.2 m) tall. Zone 5.

Phyllostachys Siebert & Zuccarini.

Grass family, Poaceae.

From the Greek *phyllon* (leaf) and *stachys* (spike). Comprised of approximately 80 species of medium-sized and large running bamboos native to China, Burma, and India. Characteristically grooved or flattened, the culms of many species and cultivated varieties are beautifully colored in shades of green, yellow, glaucous-blue, and black. Some are dramatically striped or banded. In warm climates, *Phyllostachys* species rapidly form large stands and are frequently employed as living fences. Their running nature is much less pronounced in cooler climates. Many species can be easily maintained as modest-sized clumps when grown in regions approaching the limits of their winter cold-hardiness. Many, even the larger species, can

Phragmites australis 'Variegatus' in mid-August in Oregon.

Phragmites karka 'Variegata' in New England in late August.

also be enjoyed as container specimens, as is common in Japanese bonsai tradition. Although these will be dramatically diminished in the height and diameter of their culms, many container-grown species will still attain their decorative colorations. Plants in pots can be held indoors over freezing winters, situated in a greenhouse, sunroom, or even near a large south-facing window. All the species are best propagated by division in spring and should be replanted quickly and provided with generous moisture until re-established. The following species exhibits exceptional beauty and adaptability, whether planted in the ground or in decorative containers.

Phyllostachys nigra (Siebert ex Miquel) Makino.
Black bamboo, kuro chiku.

Culms to 1½ in. (4 cm) in diameter, green at first, becoming ebony-black in their second or third year and remaining so for many seasons. In warm, moist climates it runs rapidly and can reach 30 ft. (9 m), but its spread is quite manageable in cooler climates and height is much reduced. Makes a superb container specimen and can be held over winter indoors in a conservatory or sunroom. Zone 7, root hardy to zone 6.

Pleioblastus Nakai.
Grass family, Poaceae.

From the Greek *pleios* (many) and *blastos* (buds), referring to the many branches that occur at each node. Comprised of approximately 20 species of small to medium-sized bamboos native to China and Japan, many of which spread rapidly by rhizomes. The following two were selected for inclusion because of their dramatically variegated foliage and adaptability to pot culture. Both have been long cultivated in Japan but are not known as wild populations. Although diminutive, they can be very aggressive spreaders in warmer climates if provided fertile soil and plentiful moisture. They can completely over-run beds and borders, but make ideal groundcovers in contained situations, such as traffic islands or parking lot islands. Generally best when limited by sturdy walls or when grown in containers in full sun with moisture or up to half shade. Propagate by division in spring. Drought tolerant once established but requiring generous moisture after transplanting. Cut back annually in spring.

Phyllostachys nigra in early August at the Rakusai Bamboo Garden in Kyoto, Japan.

Pleioblastus auricomus (Mitford) D. McClintock.
[*Pleioblastus viridistriatus* (Regel) Makino, *Arundinaria viridistriata* (Regel) Makino ex Nakai].
Compact golden-striped bamboo, kamuro zasa.

Leaves bright yellow with green longitudinal stripes of varied width. To 3 ft. (1 m) tall. Zone 5.

Pleioblastus variegatus (Siebold ex Miquel) Makino.
[*Arundinaria fortunei* (Van Houtte) Nakai, *Arundinaria variegata* (Siebert ex Miquel) Makino].
Compact white-striped bamboo, chigo zasa.

Leaves dark green with cream-white longitudinal stripes. Usually under 2 ft. (60 cm) tall. A less aggressive spreader than *Pleioblastus auricomus*. Zone 5.

Pleioblastus auricomus in early June at Ashland Hollow, the Delaware garden of Mr. and Mrs. W. H. Frederick, Jr.

Poa Linnaeus.
Grass family, Poaceae.
Blue grass, meadowgrass.

Approximately 500 annual and perennial grasses native mostly to cool temperate regions throughout the world. Includes the familiar lawn species, *Poa pratensis* Linnaeus, known as Kentucky blue grass, although not native to North America but to Eurasia and northern Africa. Besides the relatively wide-leaved lawn species, there are several blue grasses with very fine textured leaves, some quite glaucous-blue and similar in appearance to their close relatives in the genus *Festuca*. Most are cool-season growers, best in full sun on well-drained soils. Propagate by seed or by division in spring.

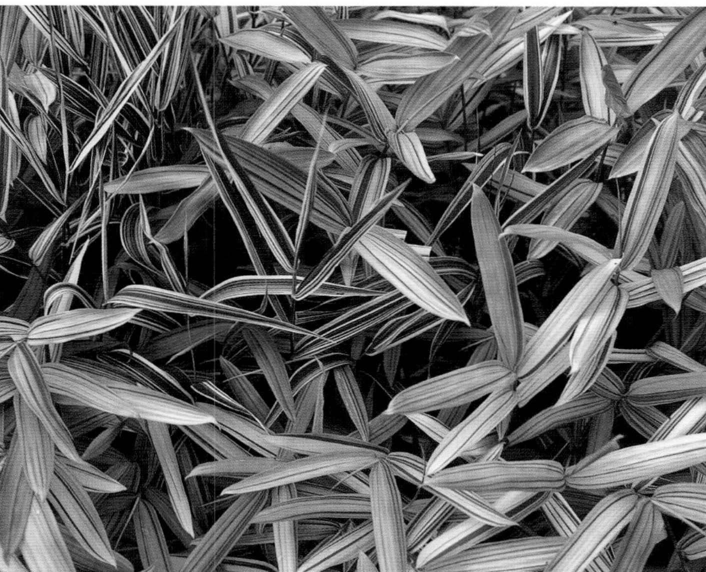

Comparison of *Pleioblastus auricomus* (yellow) and *Pleioblastus variegatus* (green with white stripes) in early summer in New York.

Pleioblastus variegatus in mid-May at the Rakusai Bamboo Garden in Kyoto, Japan.

Poa arachnifera Torrey.
Texas blue grass.

Native to Texas, Kansas, and Oklahoma. Leaves blue-green, 3/16 in. (4 mm) wide, forming tufted mounds and spreading by rhizomes. Similar to Kentucky blue grass, but more drought tolerant and a more water-conserving alternative for lawns or groundcover in dry areas, including California. Zone 6.

Poa chaixii Villars.
Broad-leafed meadowgrass, forest blue grass.

Native mostly to mountainous regions in central and southern Europe. Naturalized in woodlands in northern parts of the British Isles. Leaves bright green, to 3/8 in. (9 mm) wide. Blooms spring or early summer, to 3 ft. (1 m) tall. Zone 5.

Poa colensoi Hooker f.
New Zealand blue grass.

Native to New Zealand. Densely tufted, clumping. Foliage very fine textured and glaucous-blue, to 1 ft. (30 cm) tall, easily mistaken for blue fescue. Blooms late spring to early summer. Zone 7.

Poa colensoi in mid-July at the Royal Botanic Garden, Edinburgh, Scotland.

Poa costiniana in mid-June at Lotusland in southern California.

Poa labillardieri in mid-August at the Royal Botanic Gardens, Kew, England.

Poa costiniana Vickery.
Australian blue grass.

Native to moist alpine or subalpine areas in Australia. Densely tufted, clumping. Foliage fine-textured, mostly green. Blooms in late spring or early summer, to 2 ft. (60 cm) tall. Zone 8, possibly colder.

Poa labillardieri Steudel.
Australian blue grass, New Zealand blue grass.

Native to moist river flats and open areas in forests in Australia, also New Zealand. Densely tufted, clumping. Foliage fine-textured, glaucous-blue. Blooms in late spring or early summer, to 4 ft. (1.2 m) tall. Zone 8, possibly colder.

Restio Linnaeus.
Restio family, Restionaceae.
Restio.

Comprised of nearly 100 mostly dioecious, rushlike species native to South Africa and Australia. The South African species form the majority and are mostly restricted to the southwestern Cape region. Part of the fynbos plant community, which is characterized by natural burning, they are generally found on well-drained soils low in fertility. They are cool-season growers, most active in spring and autumn, but with an evergreen presence. New growth appears after winter rains. Many are quite beautiful but little known in cultivation. Research at the National Botanical Garden, Kirstenbosch, in Cape Town, South Africa, has found that smoke treatment of seeds often dramatically increases germination rates, making it possible to propagate various restios readily enough that they will become more common in gardens in mediterranean and warm temperate regions.

Restio festucaeformis Masters.
Restio.

Native to hills and lower mountains between Bredasdorp and Somerset West in the South African Cape, sometimes growing along streambanks or forming vast sweeps in marshy areas. Tufted and clump-forming, to 18 in. (45 cm), stems sparsely branched, attractively lax. Germinates readily from smoke-treated seed, growing quickly and flowering within two years. Golden-brown bracts on inflorescences are quite showy and long-lasting. Difficult to divide, the roots do not like to be disturbed. Requires sharp drainage, resents high fertility. Best planted in spring or autumn in mediterranean climates. An excellent seasonal container subject in areas beyond its winter cold-hardiness. Zone 8.

Rhynchelytrum Nees.

Grass family, Poaceae.

Includes 14 annual and perennial species native to savannahs and other open habitats in tropical Africa, Madagascar, and Southeast Asia. Only the following is commonly grown ornamentally. It is a common, though usually innocuous weed of wide distribution in tropical regions.

Rhynchelytrum repens (Willdenow) C. Hubbard.

[*Rhynchelytrum roseum* (Nees) Stapf & C. Hubbard].
Natal ruby grass.

Native to open habitats in tropical Africa. Clumping, the narrow blue-green leaves forming a fine-textured mound. A tender and often short-lived perennial grown for its showy, pink to purple-red flowers, usually produced in summer or early autumn, to 2 ft. (80 cm) tall. Blooms through winter in mild climates or when grown under glass if provided sufficient moisture. The inflorescences are deeply colored when first opening, fading to light sandy-pink. Easily grown on almost any soil. Best in full sun or very light shade. An innocuous weed of disturbed places in the tropics, this species is also naturalized on open sandy places in the southern United States, including Florida, Texas, and Arizona. Easily grown as an annual in cold zones and especially attractive as a potted specimen. Most easily propagated by seed but may also be divided. Self-sows manageably in gardens in warm regions. Zone 8.

Rhynchospora Vahl.

Sedge family, Cyperaceae.
Beak-rush, white-top sedge, star sedge.

From the Greek *rhynchos* (beak) and *sporos* (seed), referring to the elongated, beaklike seeds. This large genus includes more than 200 mainly perennial species native mostly to wet or moist habitats in warm regions of both hemispheres. The scope of this genus has been broadened to include species formerly in *Dichromena*, an exclusively American genus. Derived from the Greek *dis* (double) and *chroma* (color), the latter genus name alluded to the green and white bracts of the inflorescences. All *Rhychospora* species, often called white-top sedges or star sedges, are distinct in having conspicuously long, leafy bracts radiating from their inflorescences in a starlike pattern. The bracts are nearly white except at their tips and are quite ornamental, remaining attractive for months. Useful for fresh cut flowers or for drying. Perennial, spreading by rhizomes, these sedges make unusual, attractive additions to aquatic gardens and can also be grown in tubs or pots. They must not be allowed to dry out, or the bracts will scorch and turn brown. Propagate by seed or division.

Restio festucaeformis in early March, grown under glass at Longwood Gardens.

Rhynchelytrum repens in mid-December in John Greenlee's garden, Pomona, California.

Rhynchospora colorata (Linnaeus) H. Pfeiffer.
[*Dichromena colorata* (Linnaeus) Hitchcock].
White-top sedge, white-bracted sedge, star sedge, umbrella grass, star rush.
Native to moist sand, swamps, and pond edges in the eastern United States, mainly coastal, from Virginia to Florida and Texas, and into Mexico. To 20 in. (50 cm) tall, blooming in summer, sometimes into winter in the warmer regions, with three to seven bracts of unequal lengths, white at their bases. Easily grown in full sun or light shade on moist soils or in shallow water to 2 in. (5 cm) deep. Tolerates brackish conditions. Runs by rhizomes to produce dense clusters. Zone 8.

Rhynchospora latifolia (Baldwin ex Elliott) Thomas.
[*Dichromena latifolia* Baldwin ex Elliott].
White-top sedge, white-bracted sedge, star sedge, star rush.
Native to moist sand, savannahs, pine woods, swamps, and pond edges in the southeastern United States, from the Carolinas south to Florida and Texas. Slightly taller and showier than *Rhynchospora colorata*. To 32 in. (80 cm) tall, blooming in summer, sometimes into winter in the warmer regions, with six to ten bracts of unequal lengths, white at their bases. Easily grown in full sun or light shade on moist soils or in shallow water to 2 in. (5 cm) deep. Runs by rhizomes to produce dense clusters. Zone 8.

Rhynchospora nervosa (Vahl) Böckeler.
[*Dichromena nervosa* Vahl].
White-top sedge, star sedge.

A tropical native of Central and South America and the Caribbean. Similar to *Rhynchospora colorata* and *R. latifolia* but larger, taller, to 5 ft. (1.5 m), and more tender. Zone 10.

Rhynchospora latifolia in mid-December in southern California.

Saccharum Linnaeus.
Grass family, Poaceae.
Plume grass, sugarcane.

From the Greek *sakchar* (sugar). Comprised of more than 40 perennial species native throughout the tropics and subtropics, extending into warm temperate regions. Most are found in moist habitats, including riverbanks and valley bottomlands, though some occur on open hillsides. Sugarcane, *Saccharum officinarum*, is widely cultivated in warm regions for the production of sugar, and selections with colored stems are also occasionally grown for ornament. The genus *Saccharum* is now generally accepted as including all species formerly in the genus *Erianthus*, which was originally split from *Saccharum* based on the presence of awns. Among these awned species are ravenna grass, now *S. ravennae*, which is widely grown in temperate gardens, and several North American natives that are still largely unknown in gardens but have genuine ornamental potential and deserve further experimentation and evaluation. The North American species are similar in their narrow, upright form and can be used to make a strong vertical impact even in relatively small spaces. They are mostly clump-forming. All have large, plumy inflorescences that remain translucent and attractive throughout winter, and many have rich autumn foliage color. All are warm-season growers. Propagate by division in spring or by seed.

Saccharum alopecuroidum (Linnaeus) Nuttall.
[*Erianthus alopecuroides* (Linnaeus) Elliott].
Silver plume grass.

Native to open, moist, sandy woods, uncommon in coastal southern New Jersey but increasingly frequent southward on the piedmont and inner coastal plain in the Carolinas, south to Florida. Also occurs westward to Illinois and Missouri. Distinct from many other North American natives in its strong preference for shaded habitats. The inflorescences also differ, being strongly silver even when first opening in August or September, to 1 ft. (30 cm) long. To 10 ft. (3 m) tall, leaves green, to 1 in. (25 mm) wide, with little significant autumn color. An interesting choice of vertical accent for woodland gardens. Self-sows manageably. Zone 7.

Saccharum arundinaceum Retzius.

Native to India and Southeast Asia, where it is sometimes used in paper manufacture. Relatively little-known to gardens, but with strong ornamental potential. Material collected in China by Jim Waddick has proved hardy in zone 6. Leaves broad, gray-green. Blooms in late summer or early autumn, the large open panicles light pink at first, fading to silver, to 9 ft. (2.7 m) tall or more. Best in full sun. Zone 6.

Saccharum contortum (left) and *S. alopecuroidum* (right) in late October in the author's garden.

Saccharum baldwinii Sprengel.
[*Erianthus strictus* Elliott].
Narrow plume grass.

Native to marshes and wet places on the coastal plain from Virginia south to Florida and Texas, and north into Tennessee and Missouri. Strictly upright, blooming late summer, to 7 ft. (2.1 m) tall, the inflorescence narrow, to 16 in. (40 cm) long, very silvery on drying. Awns straight. Prefers full sun, well-drained soil, with regular moisture. Fall foliage deep purple-red to dark orange. Self-sows readily in warmer zones, which may be a nuisance in small gardens but is ideal for naturalizing in regional meadow gardens. Zone 7.

Saccharum brevibarbe (Michaux) Persoon.
[*Erianthus brevibarbis* Michaux].
Short-awn plume grass, brown plume grass.

Native to damp soils in the eastern United States. Nearly identical to *Saccharum contortum*, but lacking the characteristic twisted awns. Inflorescences also tend to be more brownish, often with purple tints. Zone 7.

Saccharum contortum (Elliott) Nuttall.
[*Erianthus contortus* Elliott, *Saccharum brevibarbe* var. *contortum* (Elliott) R. Webster].
Bent-awn plume grass.

Native to open ground on the coastal plain or in moist sandy pinelands from Delaware south to Florida and Tex-

Saccharum arundinaceum in late summer at Plant Delights Nursery in Raleigh, North Carolina. (Photo: Tony Avent.)

Saccharum contortum in early September in the author's garden.

as, north to Tennessee and Oklahoma. Clump-forming and narrowly upright to 10 ft. (3 m) tall. Leaves to 3/4 in. (2 cm) wide, green in summer turning various shades of purple, bronze and orange-red in autumn. The foliage has a distinct reddish coloration even in winter, when most grasses have bleached to straw color. The narrow, strictly upright plumes appear in September, standing about 2 ft. (60 cm) above the uppermost leaves. Reddish brown at first, the flower clusters become lighter colored upon drying. The awns have a characteristic twist. Best in full sun or light shade on moist soils. Grows in clay or even periodically wet soil. Self-sows to a minor extent in northern zones, heavily in southern zones. Zone 6.

Saccharum giganteum (Walter) Persoon.
[*Erianthus giganteus* (Walter) C. Hubbard, non Muhlenberg].
Sugarcane plume grass, giant plume grass.

Native on moist soil, mainly on the coastal plain from New York south to Florida and Texas, north to Kentucky. The largest of the North American native species but still considerably smaller than ravenna grass, *Saccharum ravennae*. Stems mostly upright, to 10 ft. (3 m) tall or more,

Saccharum contortum in late October in the author's garden.

Saccharum contortum in late October in its native habitat in coastal Maryland.

Saccharum giganteum dried, in late winter in Mississippi.

spreading modestly by rhizomes. Blooms in late summer or early autumn, the inflorescences strongly pink-red at first, drying to light pink, eventually translucent and silvery in winter. Plumes large and fluffy, the fullest of the North American natives. Autumn foliage colors include dark red and bronze-purple. Zone 6.

Saccharum officinarum Linnaeus.

Sugarcane.

Native origin unknown, possibly Southeast Asia. Grown for centuries and still the primary source of the world's sugar, this large, tender tropical is increasingly finding its way into ornamental gardens as selections with colored leaves and stems become more available. Capable of reaching 20 ft. (6 m) tall in tropical climates, it rarely grows more than 8 ft. (2.4 m) when planted as a summer annual in cooler zones. Usually does not bloom under these conditions. This warm-season grower thrives in full sun and warm, moist conditions, and is easily grown in a large container, providing an interesting tropical accent. Culms are to 2 in. (5 cm) in diameter. Many colored selections are without reliable names. Propagate by division or by rooting stem sections. Zone 10.

'Pele's Smoke'. Purple-stemmed sugarcane. Similar or identical to 'Violaceum'.

'Violaceum'. Purple-stemmed sugarcane. Foliage smoky purple. Stems shiny mahogany-purple with distinct cream-colored bands marking the nodes, remaining attractive into winter in colder zones, after the foliage has died back due to frosts.

Saccharum ravennae (Linnaeus) Linnaeus.

[*Erianthus ravennae* (Linnaeus) P. Beauvois].

Ravenna grass.

Native to northern Africa and the Mediterranean region. Sometimes called hardy pampas grass in areas too cold to sustain the true pampas grass, *Cortaderia selloana.* Among the largest and most striking of the cold-hardy ornamental grasses. Upright and clumping, with leaves to 1 in. (25 mm) wide, gray-green, forming a large basal mound to 4 ft. (1.2 m) tall. Blooms only in regions with long, warm growing seasons. Large, plumy inflorescences are produced in late August or early September, on stout, upright-divergent stems to 14 ft. (4.2 m) tall. The flowers are slightly pink-tinted when first opening, quickly turning lustrous silver, standing tall and remaining attractive

Saccharum giganteum in early November at Longwood Gardens.

Saccharum officinarum 'Pele's Smoke' in early February in John Greenlee's garden, Malibu, California.

through winter. Superb for fresh or dried flower arrangements, best cut before fully expanded. The flowering stems become conspicuously red-tinted in late summer, and in autumn the foliage assumes pleasing orange tones. Requires full sun but is otherwise undemanding as to site and soil conditions. Very drought tolerant once established. Excess moisture or fertility encourages lax growth and causes flowering stems to fall outward to the ground unless staked or tied. This large grass grows for many years with little maintenance other than annual cutting back, but clumps eventually tend to die out in center and should be renewed by division in spring. May also be started from seed. Self-sows in very warm regions. A magnificent specimen for sheer size and the vertical, shining effect of its ample plumes. Also effective in groupings in larger gardens. Zone 6.

Sasa Makino & Shibata.
Grass family, Poaceae.

From *zasa*, the Japanese name for the smaller bamboos. Includes approximately 40 species of small or me-

Saccharum ravennae naturally back-lit in late October at Longwood Gardens.

Saccharum ravennae in late October at Longwood Gardens.

Saccharum ravennae flowering stems in late October at Longwood Gardens.

dium-sized bamboos, native mainly to damp woodlands in Japan, Korea, and China. Most spread rapidly by rhizomes to form open or dense thickets of slender culms topped by broad, horizontal leaves. Some can be extremely invasive in the garden. The following species spreads strongly but manageably, especially in colder zones, and is perhaps the most beautiful of all.

Sasa veitchii (Carrière) Rehder.

Kuma zasa.

Native to moist woodlands in Japan. Uniquely beautiful in late autumn and winter, when the leaf margins dry and become evenly light cream-colored, contrasting boldly with the dark green centers and creating an effect that rivals the best variegated plants. In the coldest winters, the leaves become entirely blanched. Leaves solid green in summer, 4–10 in. (10–25 cm) long and $1^1/_4$–$2^1/_4$ in. (32–56 mm) wide. Culms 32–60 in. (80–150 cm) tall. A superb groundcover for larger areas or an effective accent in smaller garden spots if suitably contained by physical barriers. Of easy culture in light to fairly dense shade on sandy or clay soils if provided regular moisture. New transplants require plentiful moisture until established. An unusually stunning addition to the autumn and winter garden. Propagate by division in spring. Zone 6.

Sasa veitchii in late September in lightly shaded parking lot islands at Longwood Gardens.

Schizachyrium Nees.

Grass family, Poaceae.

Little bluestem, prairie beard grass.

Comprised of a single North American species, split from the genus *Andropogon* primarily on characteristics of the inflorescence. In *Schizachyrium* each raceme is located at the end of a slender peduncle, which extends noticeably from each branching point of the stem (see Figure 2-10). The racemes of *Andropogon* are clustered, two to four on each peduncle, and the peduncles are short and mostly enclosed by the leaf sheaths.

Schizachyrium scoparium (Michaux) Nash.

[*Andropogon scoparius* Michaux].

Little bluestem, prairie beard grass.

Native to prairies and open woods, dry fields and hills from Quebec and Maine to Alberta and Idaho, south to Arizona and Florida. Originally one of the most characteristic grasses of the American tallgrass prairie, wide-ranging and tolerant of moisture conditions varying from average to extremely dry, and able to grow on both acid and alkaline soils. Unlike its close relative, *Andropogon virginicus,* little bluestem is a valuable forage grass and has been widely planted for this reason since the demise of the great prairies. Strictly clump-forming, it is fine-textured but not particularly little, growing from 2 to 4 ft.

Sasa veitchii in late January at Longwood Gardens.

(60 to120 cm) tall. It is little only in comparison to its prairie relative big bluestem, *A. gerardii*, which can reach 8 ft. (2.4 m). Form varies from rigidly erect to lax and arching. Summer foliage color is quite variable. Some populations and individuals are bright green, others are strongly glaucous and light blue, often with conspicuous purple tints. Fall and winter color varies from tan to copper-orange to dark orange-red. Close observation of populations reveals that plants with blue or purplish summer color are often deepest red-colored in winter. Increasingly, ornamental selections with blue or purplish summer foliage are being evaluated, named, and clonally propagated. Blooms in late summer, the inflorescences delicate and inconspicuous until they dry, becoming silvery and noticeably attractive when side-lit or back-lit by the autumn or winter sun. Remains attractive through winter, even after snows. Requires full sun, prefers good drainage or sloping ground. Does not persist on highly fertile soils or in excessively moist conditions, and suffers if the crowns are crowded by mulch. Ideal for managed meadows, where it co-exists happily with prairie wildflowers as long as it is not shaded. The blue-leaved selections are showy enough to merit consideration even in highly designed landscapes. Propagate by seed or by division in spring. Zone 3. Figure 2-10.

'Aldous'. A seed cultivar originally developed for forage, producing a high percentage of tall, blue-leaved plants.

'Blaze'. A seed cultivar originally developed for forage, producing plants that generally have strong reddish autumn and winter hues.

'Cimarron'. A seed cultivar originally developed for forage, producing a high percentage of blue-leaved plants.

'The Blues'. A clonal cultivar with strongly glaucous, light blue stems. Named by Kurt Bluemel's nursery and North Creek Nurseries, selected from seedlings of 'Aldous' provided by Dick Lighty of Pennsylvania. Propagate by division only. Zone 3.

Schizachyrium scoparium in early October in the managed meadow of Longwood Gardens, with native asters (*Aster* species) and goldenrods (*Solidago* species) blooming in background.

In late October, a taller, deeper colored plant of *Schizachyrium scoparium* is easily distinguished among a hillside population at Longwood Gardens.

Schoenoplectus (Reichenbach) Palla.
Sedge family, Cyperaceae.
Bulrush, clubrush.

Comprised of approximately 80 annual and perennial species of cosmopolitan distribution in aquatic and semi-aquatic habitats. Many species have sometimes been included in the closely related genus *Scirpus*. The great bulrush, *Schoenoplectus tabernaemontani*, has long been cultivated ornamentally in water gardens; however, there are many other species that deserve further attention. All are warm-season growers.

Schoenoplectus subterminalis
(Torrey) Soják.
[*Scirpus subterminalis* Torrey].
Swaying-rush.

Aquatic, native to ponds and slow-moving, often acid waters, and to bogs and peaty shores across northern North America. A subtly beautiful plant, growing mostly submersed in up to 5 ft. (1.5 m) of water, the long, threadlike, lime-green leaves and stems float just beneath the water's surface, gently revealing undulations in the current. The specific epithet *subterminalis* refers to the tiny inflorescences, which are just below the tips of stems that extend a few inches out of water at flowering time in midsummer. Runs by rhizomes. Not suited to smaller aquatic gardens, but truly worth establishing, enhancing, or conserving in larger landscapes. Propagate by seed or division. Zone 4.

Schizachyrium scoparium 'The Blues' in mid-August at Longwood Gardens.

The inflorescences of *Schizachyrium scoparium* (right) are individually held out from the stems on slender branches, unlike the densely clustered inflorescences of *Andropogon virginicus* (left).

Schoenoplectus subterminalis in early July, mostly submersed in slow-moving water in the New Jersey pine barrens.

Schoenoplectus tabernaemontani (C. C. Gmelin) Palla.

[*Scirpus tabernaemontani* C. C. Gmelin, *Scirpus validus* Vahl, *Scirpus lacustris* Linnaeus, *Schoenoplectus lacustris* subsp. *tabernaemontani* (C. C. Gmelin) Á. & D. Löve]. Great bulrush, clubrush.

Of cosmopolitan distribution in freshwater and brackish rivers, lakes, and ponds. Mostly clump-forming, with rushlike, upright stems carrying on the usual photosynthetic functions of leaves and bearing clusters of brownish flowers, usually in their upper portion. Though the variegated cultivars are most often grown, the simple grace of the typical, dark green stems can be attractive at the edge of ponds or pools in water gardens, especially as textural foils for broad-leaved waterlilies and other aquatics. Best on neutral to acid soils in shallow water, with full sun exposure. Propagate by division in spring.

'Albescens'. White bulrush. Stems nearly white, with only narrow longitudinal stripes of green, to 5 ft. (1.5 m). Zone 5.

'Golden Spears'. Stems fully yellow in spring, fading to green as the season progresses. Zone 5.

'Zebrinus'. Zebra bulrush. Stems dark green with vivid light yellow horizontal bands. Zone 5.

Schoenoplectus tabernaemontani in its native habitat in northern Delaware.

Schoenoplectus tabernaemontani 'Albescens' in mid-July at the Royal Botanic Garden, Edinburgh, Scotland.

Schoenoplectus tabernaemontani 'Zebrinus' in early June at Longwood Gardens.

Scirpus Linnaeus.

Sedge family, Cyperaceae.

Approximately 100 perennial species of cosmopolitan distribution in moist habitats. Warm-season growers, they usually have well-developed leaves and flowers in terminal panicles, which are sometimes showy. The genera *Isolepis* and *Schoenoplectus* are sometimes included in *Scirpus*, but are treated separately in this book, in keeping with modern convention.

Scirpus atrovirens Willdenow.

Native to moist meadows, bogs, and low thickets in eastern North America. Clump-forming, usually less than 5 ft. (1.5 m) tall, with conspicuous dark green spikelets that turn dark brown by midsummer and remain attractive into autumn. Of easy culture on any moist soil in full sun or part shade. Self-sows. Not for the formal garden, but a pleasant addition to moist meadow gardens and the edges of water gardens. Propagate by seed or division. Zone 4.

Scirpus cyperinus (Linnaeus) Kunth.

[*Scirpus rubricosus* (Linnaeus) Kunth].

Wool grass.

Native to wet meadows and swamps in northeastern North America. Very ornamental, with large woolly inflorescences on erect stems to 5 ft. (1.5 m) tall. Blooms in

Scirpus atrovirens in late June in eastern Pennsylvania.

Scirpus cyperinus in late August with tickseed sunflower, *Bidens* species, in northern Delaware.

midsummer, the flowers green at first, becoming softly woolly and light brown as seeds mature in late summer. Remains upright and attractive throughout winter. Forms dense tussocks, with many arching basal leaves in summer. Easily grown on moist or periodically wet soils in full sun or light shade. Self-sows and thus ideal for naturalizing. Propagate by seed or by division in spring. Zone 4.

Sesleria Scopoli.
Grass family, Poaceae.
Moor grass.

Named for Leonardo Sesler, an eighteenth-century Venetian physician who owned a botanic garden. Includes approximately 27 species native to Europe, often in mountainous areas, centered in the Balkans. Most are densely tufted perennials with evergreen or semi-evergreen foliage. They are frequently overlooked because they lack showy flowers; however, many are tough, long-lived plants of easy culture that are superbly suited for small-scale or large-scale groundcover use, in full sun or in as much as half shade. Most are very drought tolerant once established. They offer a variety of sizes and foliage colors in shades of yellow-green to blue-green. Most are very cold-hardy and tolerant of alkaline soils. Propagate by seed or by division in spring or fall.

Sesleria autumnalis (Scopoli) F. W. Schultz.
Autumn moor grass.

Native from northeastern Italy to Albania. Distinguished from most other species by its late summer to fall flowering period and by its nearly lime-green foliage. Leaves to 3/8 in. (9 mm) wide. The inflorescences are conspicuous and attractive, held erect above the foliage to 20 in. (50 cm), opening silvery-white. Zone 4.

Sesleria caerulea (Linnaeus) Arduino.
[*Sesleria albicans* Kitaibel ex Schultes].
Blue moor grass.

Native to Europe, including the British Isles, often in calcareous grasslands, limestone rock-crevices, and screes. Low-growing, forming basal mounds of strongly blue-green foliage to 8 in. (20 cm) tall. To 3/16 in. (4 mm) wide, the leaves are two-toned: strongly glaucous-blue on their upper surfaces with dark green undersides. Due to the way the foliage lays, both colors are always visible. Blooms April to May, the small spikelike panicles held above the foliage on slender stalks. Flowers are blackish at first, with light yellow pollen sacs, turning mostly green and becoming inconspicuous. The foliage is nearly evergreen even to zone 6. Zone 4.

Sesleria heufleriana Schur.
Blue-green moor grass.

Native to southeastern Europe. Very similar to blue moor grass but larger, taller, and less blue. The upper surfaces of the leaves are mostly green in early spring, becoming noticeably glaucous-blue by early summer and remaining so through autumn and winter. The early spring flowers are black with cream-yellow pollen sacs, held above the foliage on slender stalks that continue to

Scirpus cyperinus in December in northern Delaware.

Sesleria autumnalis in mid-August in the author's garden.

grow taller as the seed matures and then fall to the sides, becoming inconspicuous. The foliage forms neat tufted mounds to 15 in. (38 cm) tall and is semi-evergreen even in colder climates. Zone 4.

Sesleria caerulea in early May at Longwood Gardens.

The bicolored foliage of *Sesleria caerulea* in mid-December in southern California.

Sesleria heufleriana beginning to bloom in mid-April at Longwood Gardens.

Sesleria heufleriana in early May at Longwood Gardens.

Sesleria nitida Tenore.
Gray moor grass.

Native to central and southern Italy and Sicily. Appears strongly gray-blue in the landscape. The leaves are two-toned, like those of *Sesleria caerulea* and *S. heufleriana*, but they lay flat, with the strongly glaucous upper surfaces always visible. Also the tallest of the three species, forming a flowing mound of foliage to 20 in. (50 cm) tall, overtopped in early spring by nearly black flower panicles similar to the other spring-flowering species. Leaves to 1/4 in. (6 mm) wide, the foliage semi-evergreen. Zone 4.

Setaria Palibin.
Grass family, Poaceae.
Foxtail.

From the Latin *seta* (bristle), referring to the bristlelike inflorescence. Includes more than 100 annual and perennial species of open grasslands and woodlands, widely distributed in tropical, subtropical, and temperate zones. Many of the annual foxtails are cosmopolitan weeds, and although sometimes attractive, are only occasionally grown ornamentally. The following perennial species is a tender tropical, grown not for flowers but mostly for its bold, palmlike foliage.

Setaria palmifolia (Koenig) Stapf.
Palm grass.

Native to tropical Asia. A coarse-textured perennial, growing to 10 ft. (3 m) tall in tropical climates. The rich green leaves are 3–5 in. (7.5–12 cm) wide and conspicuously pleated. The inflorescences are only subtly interesting. Cylindrical and green, they extend above or arch outward from the foliage on slender green stems. Palm grass is often displayed as a conservatory specimen, but also makes an interesting tropical accent if grown in a container placed in the garden during warm periods. It may also be planted in the ground for summer and removed to protection in winter. Does not tolerate prolonged temperatures below 40°F (4°C). Grows to 5 ft. (1.5 m) tall in a single summer if provided plenty of sun and moisture. Propagate by division. Zone 9.

Shibataea Makino ex Nakai.
Grass family, Poaceae.
Okamezasa zoku.

Named for Japanese botanist Keita Shibata (1897–1949). Comprised of two or three species of low-growing bamboos native to woodlands in China and Japan. The following species has been cultivated for centuries in

Sesleria nitida in mid-May in Kurt Bluemel's garden in Maryland.

Setaria palmifolia in late summer.

Japan, where it is valued for its beautiful foliage and modest rate of spread.

Shibataea kumasasa (Koenig) Stapf.

Okamezasa.

Native to woodlands in Japan. Low-growing, usually less than 4 ft. (1.2 m) tall, with erect, leafy culms forming a dense groundcovering mass. Leaves dark green, lustrous, usually 3–4 in. (7.5–10 cm) long and to 1 in. (25 mm) wide, clustered at the nodes. Spreads very modestly by rhizomes and can be easily maintained among shrubs or other sturdy perennials in a border. Makes a superb groundcover and may be clipped to maintain shorter heights. Fully evergreen in milder climates. Foliage may desiccate in colder winters, after which the plants are best cut back to the ground. New growth emerges in late spring and is delayed if conditions are dry. Prefers light shade but can be grown in full sun if provided adequate moisture. Easily divided or transplanted in spring, or also in fall in milder zones. Zone 6.

Shibataea kumasasa in late January in the author's garden.

Sorghastrum Nash.

Grass family, Poaceae.

Indian grass, wood grass.

From the genus *Sorghum* plus the Latin suffix *-astrum* (imitation), referring to the resemblance to sorghum. Includes approximately 16 annual and perennial species native to the Americas and tropical Africa. A characteristic North American tallgrass prairie species, *Sorghastrum nutans* is very important ornamentally. Two less-known species from southeastern United States deserve further evaluation in gardens.

Sorghastrum elliottii (C. Mohr) Nash.

Slender Indian grass, Elliott's wood grass.

Native to open, sandy areas and woods from Maryland to Tennessee, south to Florida and Texas. Similar to *Sorghastrum nutans* but more slender and shorter, usually less than 5 ft. (1.5 m) tall when blooming in late summer. Zone 6.

Sorghastrum nutans (Linnaeus) Nash.

[*Sorghastrum avenaceum* (Michaux) Nash, *Chrysopogon nutans* Bentham].

Indian grass.

One of the most beautiful and characteristic grasses of the once-vast North American tallgrass prairie. In the original prairie mix, this clump-former was the second-most prevalent tall grass next to big bluestem, *Andropogon gerardii*. Like many prairie natives, it is a warm-season grower, blooming in late summer. It has a wide native range, occurring on prairies, dry slopes, and open woods from Quebec and Maine to Manitoba and North Dakota, south to Florida, Arizona, and into Mexico. Ultimate height and foliage color vary over this range. Plants of central prairie provenance tend to have broad leaves, to 1/2 in. (12 mm) wide, which are frequently glaucous and bluish. They also tend to be tall-growing, to 7 ft. (2.1 m) or more when in flower. As the species reaches the eastern part of its range the foliage tends to be narrower and completely green, and ultimate height is usually closer to 5 ft. (1.5 m). Narrow green-leaved plants tend to be more upright than wide-leaved glaucous types, especially if conditions are at all shaded. Autumn foliage color is also variable, being yellow on glaucous-leaved plants and bright orange on green-leaved individuals. The showy flower panicles usually appear in August and are copper-colored with conspicuous bright yellow pollen sacs. Loose and open at first, the inflorescences narrow upon drying, becoming light chestnut brown and translucent, and remaining attractive through most of winter. They make good cut flowers, fresh or dried. Easy to grow on a wide range of soils, including heavy clay. Best in full sun. Grows taller with moisture but is drought tolerant once established. Self-sows prolifically, a desirable trait for prairie restorations or meadow gardens, but a nuisance in precise, regimented designs. Requires little maintenance other than cutting back annually, which is best done in late winter or early spring. Indian grass provides high quality forage, and several seed cultivars have been developed for this purpose. Propagate by seed or division.

'Cheyenne'. A seed cultivar developed primarily for forage and pasture use. Of Oklahoma provenance. Zone 4.

'Holt'. A seed cultivar developed primarily for forage and pasture use. Of Nebraska provenance. Zone 4.

'Osage'. A seed cultivar developed primarily for forage and pasture use. Of prairie origin. Leaves relatively wide and often glaucous-blue. Plants are frequently lax-stemmed when mature. Zone 4.

'Sioux Blue'. Blue Indian grass. A clonal cultivar selected and named by the author from a seedling of 'Osage' (see above) after extensive evaluation in Longwood Gardens' research nursery. Chosen for its powder-blue foliage and erect form. When grown in full sun, it remains upright throughout the growing season and through most of winter. Leaves to 1/2 in. (12 mm) wide, flowering stems to 6 ft. (2 m) tall. Foliage turns yellow in late fall. Heat tolerant and free of the foliar rust diseases that sometimes afflict the glaucous-leaved cultivars of *Panicum virgatum*, and a better choice for gardens in the warm southeastern United States. Zone 4.

Sorghastrum secundatum (Ell.) Nash.

Drooping wood grass.

Native to pine and oak-pine barrens, on mostly sandy soils, from South Carolina to Florida and Texas. Similar to *Sorghastrum nutans* but shorter and with strongly one-sided panicles on arching stems usually less than 5 ft. (1.5 m) tall. Blooms in late summer. Zone 7, possibly colder.

Sorghastrum nutans in early September in eastern Pennsylvania.

Sorghastrum nutans 'Sioux Blue' in mid-January at Longwood Gardens.

Sorghastrum nutans fall color in mid-October in eastern Pennsylvania.

Spartina Schreber.
Grass family, Poaceae.
Cord grass.

Includes approximately 15 perennial species native to wet or moist habitats on both coasts of the Americas and to the Atlantic coasts of Africa and Europe, especially in temperate and subtropical zones. All spread by rhizomes to form extensive colonies, often to the exclusion of other plants. They are important soil builders and stabilizers in coastal and interior marshes. Only one species, *Spartina pectinata,* is often grown ornamentally, mostly in its variegated form. Called prairie cord grass, it stands out from most others in its preference for freshwater habitats. Most cord grasses grow in brackish or saline environments. Called marsh hay, salt hay, or saltmeadow cord grass, *S. patens* (Aiton) Muhlenberg is common in salt meadows, marshes, brackish flats, and on low dunes only periodically flooded along the North American Atlantic coast, where huge quantities of this grass were once cut for hay, packing, and bedding. It is still cut to a lesser extent for use as mulch. Other species native to the North American Atlantic coast include smooth cord grass, *S. alterniflora* Loiseleur, growing at midtide to high-tide levels in salt or brackish marshes, and big cord grass, *S. cynosuroides* (Linnaeus) Roth, which grows more than 10 ft. (3 m) tall in brackish or freshwater tidal marshes.

Sorghastrum nutans 'Sioux Blue' (left) and a typical green-leafed plant of *S. nutans* (right) in late August at Longwood Gardens.

Spartina pectinata Link.
Prairie cord grass.

Native to freshwater marshes and wet prairies throughout the northern United States, extending into brackish areas near the Atlantic coast. Spreads rapidly by rhizomes, with strong upright to arching stems. A warm-season grower, blooming in late July and August, producing stiff, open panicles. To 7 ft. (2.1 m) tall in flower. Leaves to 5/8 in. (15 mm) wide, pendent, dark green, and glossy. The usual green-leaved plant is not often grown, but is suited for use at the edges of ponds or water gardens, though its spreading tendency requires containment or periodic control. Best in full sun on moist soils but tolerates average or dry soils, where its spreading is greatly reduced. Also salt tolerant. Propagate by seed or division. Zone 4.

'Aureomarginata' ('Variegata'). Differs from the species only in having bright yellow variegated leaf margins. Propagate by division. Zone 4.

Spartina pectinata 'Aureomarginata' in late June in eastern Pennsylvania.

Spodiopogon R. Brown.
Grass family, Poaceae.

From the Greek *spodios* (ashen, gray) and *pogon* (beard), referring to the gray hairs surrounding the flower spikes and imparting a grayish color to the inflorescences. Includes nine mostly perennial species native to temperate and subtropical Asia. Only the following is commonly cultivated ornamentally.

Spartina pectinata in early August in its native habitat along the Maine coast.

Spartina pectinata 'Aureomarginata' in mid-August in Germany.

Spodiopogon sibiricus Trinius.
Spodiopogon, Siberian graybeard, o abura suzuki.

Native to slopes and mountains in Japan, Korea, Manchuria, and China, also Siberia, where it frequently occurs in forest glades and among shrubs. Clump-forming and upright, to 4 ft. (1.2 m) tall in flower, with a neatly rounded form. Erect terminal panicles are produced in July and August. Though they lack appreciable color, they are covered with small hairs that glow when side-lit or back-lit by the sun. The inflorescences are effective until late October. The thin, flat leaves are medium green, to 5/8 in. (15 mm) wide, held nearly horizontal. In many years the foliage turns rich red and burgundy in autumn; in other years hard frosts may turn it directly from green to brown. Prefers light shade but grows well in full sun if provided adequate moisture. Not drought tolerant, suffering in summers in the extreme southeastern United States. Grows in fairly dense shade, but its form will be much looser, often attractively so. Easily grown in a shrub border. Effective as a specimen or in sweeps and masses. Propagate by seed or by division in spring. Zone 4.

'West Lake'. From material collected in China by Roy Lancaster. Introduced with German nurseryman Hans Simon. Zone 4.

Spodiopogon sibiricus fall color in early October in eastern Pennsylvania.

Spodiopogon sibiricus in early August in Pauline Volmer's garden, Baltimore, Maryland.

Sporobolus R. Brown.
Grass family, Poaceae.
Dropseed.

More than 100 annual and perennial species of cosmopolitan distribution in temperate, subtropical, and tropical regions, in a wide range of habitats but most frequent on open savannas. Only the following two perennial North American species are grown in gardens; however, other related species are probably worth evaluating. Both are warm-season bunchgrasses.

Sporobolus airoides (Torrey) Torrey.
Alkali sacaton, alkali dropseed.

Native to valleys and meadows, especially on alkaline soils, from South Dakota and Missouri west to eastern Washington, south to southern California, Texas, and Mexico. Somewhat similar to *Sporobolus heterolepis*, but coarser-textured, showier in bloom. Clump-forming, with gray-green leaves to 1/4 in. (6 mm) wide, forming a loose flowing mound to 3 ft. (1 m) tall. The foliage turns yellow in autumn, then light tan during winter. Usually blooms April to July, but occasionally as late as October, the open flower panicles upright or arching, to 5 ft. (1.5 m) tall, opening with a strong pink cast, drying to silver. Deep-rooted, durable, and drought tolerant. Easy to grow on a wide range of soils from sands to heavy clays. Tolerates alkaline conditions. Best propagated by seed. Zone 5, probably colder.

Sporobolus heterolepis (A. Gray) A. Gray.
Prairie dropseed.

Native to North American prairies, from Quebec to Saskatchewan, south to Connecticut, Texas, and Colorado. The most elegant and refined of the prairie grasses, with threadlike leaves just over 1/16 in. (<2 mm) wide, producing a dense, flowing mound of the finest texture, to 15 in. (38 cm) tall. Summer color is a glossy, medium green. Every year, in October or early November, the entire clump turns deep orange, then fades to a light copper color during winter. Appearing in August or September, delicate, open panicles are held high above the foliage on very slender stalks to 30 in. (75 cm) tall. The inflorescences are noticeably attractive when back-lit, but most unusually, they are scented. The fragrance has been called delicate, sweet, or pungent, and has been variously described as evoking crushed cilantro (coriander leaves) or slightly burnt buttered popcorn. The scent of a mass planting can be detected from a distance of many yards. Strictly clump-forming, deep-rooted, and extraordinarily drought tolerant once established. Slow-growing, requiring at least four years to attain significant size but worth the wait. This long-lived, trouble-free plant just keeps getting bigger for decades without any center dieback or need

Sporobolus airoides at Plant Delights Nursery in Raleigh, North Carolina. (Photo: Tony Avent.)

Fall color on a three-year-old clump of *Sporobolus heterolepis* at Longwood Gardens in early November.

for renewal. For this reason, it is a superb choice for small-scale or large-scale groundcover use. Easy to grow on most soils, including heavy clay, in full sun or light shade. Plentiful moisture and a fertile soil speed growth but are not necessary. Sufficiently refined to merit a place in the formal garden, but also a natural for prairie and meadow gardens. Best propagated by seed. Division is possible but difficult, since this grass produces an extremely dense crown. Zone 4.

'Wisconsin'. Selected for reliable bloom in Europe, by German nurseryman Hans Simon, from material of Wisconsin provenance supplied by Prairie Nursery. Zone 4.

Sporobolus heterolepis in early September at the U.S. National Arboretum, Washington, D.C.

A ten-year-old clump of *Sporobolus heterolepis* at Longwood Gardens in mid-July.

Stenotaphrum Trinius.

Grass family, Poaceae.

From the Greek *stenos* (narrow) and *taphros* (trench), referring to the depression in the axis of the flower raceme. Comprised of seven annual and perennial, mostly stoloniferous species native to New and Old World tropics. Only the following is significant to gardens.

Stenotaphrum secundatum (Walter) Kuntze.

St. Augustine grass.

Native from South Carolina to Florida and Texas, and into tropical America. Typically green-leaved, this stoloniferous perennial species is widely cultivated as a coarse-textured lawn grass in warm zones, and has naturalized and escaped in some regions. Zone 9.

'Variegatum'. Leaves longitudinally striped cream-white. Often cultivated for use in hanging baskets or planters, treated as an annual in colder climates. Easily rooted from stem cuttings. Rarely used in larger landscapes, though it was used to stunning effect by Brazilian landscape architect Roberto Burle Marx, who created huge undulating sweeps of this variegated selection alternating with the green form. Zone 9.

Stipa Linnaeus.

Grass family, Poaceae.

Needle grass, spear grass, feather grass.

This genus was once defined very broadly and included many diverse species. Taxonomic research now supports a narrower view of *Stipa* and has resulted in transfers of many species to other genera, including *Achnatherum, Austrostipa, Hesperostipa,* and *Nassella.* The species remaining in *Stipa* are mostly sun-loving perennials, native to steppes and rocky slopes in temperate and warm temperate regions. Most have characteristically long awns, which add to the beauty and translucency of their inflorescences. All are tufted clump-formers with primarily basal foliage. They require good drainage, and most are cool-season growers, preferring full sun but low humidity. Propagate by seed.

Stipa barbata in mid-July at Foggy Bottom, Adrian Bloom's garden in Bressingham, England.

Stipa capillata in late August at the Westpark, Munich, Germany.

Stipa barbata Desfontaines.
Feather grass.

Native to southern Europe. Slender and upright-arching, to 30 in. (75 cm) tall, with silvery awns nearly 7$^1/_2$ in. (19 cm) long, streaming from the tips of the flower stems. Blooms July to August. Zone 8.

Stipa capillata Linnaeus.

Native to central and southern Europe, and Asia. Slender and nearly erect, to 32 in. (80 cm) tall, with relatively straight, silvery awns to 5 in. (12 cm) long. Blooms July to August. Zone 6.

Stipa gigantea Link.
[*Macrochloa arenaria* (Brotero) Kunth].
Giant feather grass, giant-oat.

Native to Spain, Portugal, and Morocco. The largest feather grass and one of the most elegant and stately ornamental grasses. Leaves narrow, $^1/_8$ in. (3 mm) wide, forming large tufted of basal foliage to 20 in. (50 cm) tall, evergreen in mild climates. Blooms June to August, the loose, open panicles held high above the foliage on stems to 8 ft. (2.4 m) tall. The spikelets are golden, with awns to 5 in. (12 cm) long, and are especially dramatic when moving with a summer breeze, lit by the sun. Superb for cut or dried arrangements. This cool-season grower is at its best in England, northern Europe, and the U.S. Pacific Northwest, but can be grown satisfactorily in areas with hot humid summers if provided a sunny site and very well

Stipa gigantea in late August at the Berggarten, in Germany.

drained soil. Does not survive waterlogged winter conditions. Zone 6.

Stipa pennata Linnaeus.
European feather grass.

Native from southern and central Europe into the Himalayas. Leaves narrow, gray-green, forming a neat basal mound. Flowering stems to 30 in. (75 cm) tall, with silvery awns to 8 in. (20 cm) long. Zone 6.

Stipa pulcherrima K. Koch.
European feather grass.

Native to central and southern Europe. Similar to *Stipa pennata,* but with even longer, more feathery awns, to 18 in. (45 cm) long. Zone 7.

Stipa tenacissima Linnaeus.
Esparto grass.

This coarse western Mediterranean native is rarely if ever cultivated as an ornamental. The name is sometimes incorrectly used when referring to *Stipa tenuissima* Trinius, a widely cultivated, fine-textured species that is now called *Nassella tenuissima.*

Thamnochortus Berg.
Restio family, Restionaceae.

Approximately 31 dioecious species native to the southwestern and eastern Cape and Namaqualand in South Africa. They are part of the fynbos plant community, which

Stipa pulcherrima in late August at the Hof Botanical Garden in Germany.

Stipa gigantea in mid-August in Roger Raiche's garden in Berkeley, California.

Stipa pulcherrima feathery awns detail in late August at the Hof Botanical Garden in Germany.

is characterized by natural burning, and are generally found on well-drained soils low in fertility. Cool-season growers, active in spring and autumn, but having an evergreen presence. New growth is produced after winter rains. Many are quite beautiful but little known in cultivation. Research at the National Botanical Garden, Kirstenbosch, in Cape Town, South Africa, has found that smoke treatment of seeds often dramatically increases germination rates, making it possible to propagate various restios readily enough that they will become more common in gardens in mediterranean and warm temperate regions. Difficult to divide, since the roots do not like to be disturbed. They resent high fertility. Best planted in spring or autumn in mediterranean climates. Excellent seasonal container subjects in areas beyond their winter cold-hardiness.

Thamnochortus cinereus Linder.

Native to the southern Cape, from Malmesbury to Willowmore and Humansdorp. Upright and clump-forming, more than 5 ft. (1.5 m) tall, with threadlike sterile branches clustered at nodes, and large velvety-pubescent inflorescences arching at the tops of stems. A very beautiful species deserving more attention by gardeners. Zone 8.

Thamnochortus insignis Masters.

Thatching reed, dekriet.

Native along the South African coast between Cape Agulhas and Albertinia, mostly on sandy, limestone-derived soils. Clump-forming, to 6 ft. (2 m) tall, stems unbranched, with relatively inconspicuous flowers clustered at the tops of stems. Male and female flowers on separate plants. Erect and stately, this species was most commonly used in thatching of traditional Cape Dutch houses in South Africa. With a renewed interest in traditional architecture, the thatching industry is again thriving, and dekriet-harvesting areas are again being developed and managed. Zone 8.

Themeda Forsskål.

Grass family, Poaceae.

As many as 19 annual and perennial species native to open savannas mostly in eastern Asia, but also in Old World tropics and subtropics. *Themeda triandra* Forsskål is a tender perennial, native to southern Africa, where it is an important grazing species. Only its hardy relative below is grown ornamentally.

Themeda japonica (Willdenow) C. Tanaka.

[*Themeda triandra* var. *japonica* (Willdenow) Makino].

Themeda, Japanese themeda, megarukaya.

Native to lowlands and low mountains in Japan, from Honshu south to Kyushu, also Korea, Manchuria, China, and India. Often overlooked because it lacks obvious flowers, it possesses a unique sculptural form that can be an intriguing addition to the garden. Strictly clumping, with leafy stems radiating from the base to create a broad fountain of foliage to 5 ft. (1.5 m) tall. Leaves to 1/4 in. (6 mm) wide, bright green in summer turning rich golden-

Thamnochortus cinereus in mid-September in the Cape region of South Africa.

Thamnochortus insignis in late September in the National Botanical Garden, Kirstenbosch, Cape Town, South Africa.

Thamnochortus insignis in mid-August in the National Botanical Garden, Kirstenbosch, Cape Town, South Africa.

orange by early November. By midwinter, the leaves have become light copper-brown and the stems golden-yellow. Blooms in late summer, the flowers clustered along the upper portions of the stems and relatively insignificant. This warm-season grower begins growth late in spring but does not mind strong sun, heat, or humidity. Easy to grow on a broad range of soils and extremely drought tolerant once established. Propagate by seed or by division in spring. Effective singly or in groups or masses, this reliably attractive, long-lived grass is little known and underappreciated. Zone 4.

Thysanolaena Nees.

Grass family, Poaceae.

From the Greek *thysanos* (tassel, fringe) and *laina* (cloak), referring to the fringe on the fertile lemmas. Comprised of one large perennial species native to tropical Asia.

Thysanolaena maxima (Roxburgh) Kuntze.

Native to open habitats, often in the mountains, in tropical Asia. A huge grass, forming a dense clump with upright to arching stems to 10 ft. (3 m) tall and equally wide or wider. It is sometimes grown in tropical regions for screening. The evergreen leaves are deep, glossy green, to 2^3/4 in. (7 cm) wide, tapering to narrow points, clothing the stems up to the base of the large, terminal panicles. This bold tropical species was a favorite of Brazilian landscape architect Roberto Burle Marx, who valued it for its dramatic texture and graceful plumes. A true tropical, it is winter hardy only in frost-free zones but makes a su-

Themeda japonica in mid-August in Kurt Bluemel's garden in Maryland.

Themeda japonica fall color in early November in Kurt Bluemel's garden in Maryland.

perb conservatory specimen in colder regions or can be grown in a large container for summer and removed to protection in winter. Requires regular moisture. Propagate by division or seed. Zone 10.

Tridens Roemer & Schultes.
Grass family, Poaceae.

Includes 18 perennial species native to open woodlands and plains in eastern North America south to Argentina and Angola. Only the following species is grown ornamentally.

Tridens flavus (Linnaeus) Hitchcock.
[*Triodia flava* (Linnaeus) Smyth].
Purpletop, tall redtop.

Native to meadows, fields, and openings and borders of woods, from New Hampshire to Minnesota and Nebraska, south to Florida and Texas. Best known for the purple top it puts on eastern U.S. meadows and old fields in late summer. Upright and clump-forming, usually 4 ft. (1.2 m) tall in flower. The foliage is relatively coarse-textured, with medium-green leaves to $5/8$ in. (15 mm) wide. Blooms August to September, the open panicles initially metallic red-purple, drying to silvery-tan, standing tall

Thysanolaena maxima in the Clemente Gomes garden, Fazenda Vargem Grande, near Areias, Brazil.

Tridens flavus in mid-September in a northern Delaware meadow.

Tridens flavus in late August in eastern Pennsylvania.

Tripsacum dactyloides in late June in Robert Herald's northern Delaware garden.

above the foliage through winter and into the following spring. Attractive as a cut flower. The foliage becomes bronze-purple tinted in autumn. Prefers full sun or light shade. Grows on a wide range of soils and is tolerant of moist or droughty conditions. Self-sows readily and thus is best suited to naturalizing in meadows or meadow gardens, in large sweeps and masses. Propagate by seed or division. Zone 4.

Tripsacum Linnaeus.
Grass family, Poaceae.
Gama grass.

Includes 13 species native mainly to open woodlands and damp edges from North America south to Paraguay, but most common in Central America. None are important ornamentals, but the following species is curiously attractive.

Tripsacum dactyloides (Linnaeus) Linnaeus.
Eastern gama grass.

Native to wet swales, streambanks, and other moist places from Massachusetts west to Michigan, Iowa, and Nebraska, south to Florida, Oklahoma, and Texas. A large, coarse, rhizomatous grass to 8 ft. (2.4 m) tall in flower. Leaves gray-green with a prominent white midrib, to 1 1/8 in. (3 cm) wide, mostly basal. Blooms June to September, the inflorescence consisting of narrowly cylindrical structures with female spikelets in the lower portion and males in the upper. The feathery pink stigmas produced by the female spikelets are long and conspicuous. Easily grown in full sun or light shade and most soils. Prefers moisture but fairly drought tolerant. Use caution when handling; the leaf margins are quite sharp and can cause razorlike cuts. Propagate by seed or division. Zone 5.

Typha Linnaeus.
Cat-tail family, Typhaceae.
Cat-tail, reedmace, bulrush.

The only genus in the cat-tail family, comprised of 10 to 15 species native to marshes and similar wetland habitats throughout the world's temperate and tropical regions. They spread by stout rhizomes to form dense colonies, often excluding other species, but providing important cover for wildlife. They are also critical to the cleansing and nutrient cycles of marshy habitats. The leaves have been used in chair caning and basketry, and the floss from the seed-heads is used in pillow stuffing. The flat, swordlike leaves are thick, slightly spongy, and nearly vertical, arising from the base of the plant. Usually gray-green in summer, they frequently turn bright yellow or gold in autumn. Warm-season growers, cat-tails typically bloom in mid to late summer. Held erect on sturdy stems, the familiar, cylindrical inflorescences are composed of male flowers in the upper portion and females below, sometimes with a sterile section in between. The male flowers are usually golden at the time they shed their pollen, then they quickly wither away leaving the central stalk exposed. The densely packed female spikes turn from green to rich brown in color as the seeds mature and are widely popular for cut flower arrangements. The fruiting spikes usually remain intact until December, then they gradually come apart, each dispersing more than 100,000 seeds attached to tiny hairs that float on winter winds. The dark brown or blackish spikes are often a beautiful part of snowy, winter landscapes. Cat-tail species vary considerably in size, and the larger ones are too aggressive in their spread for all but the grandest landscapes; they can quickly dominate small ponds unless rigorously controlled. All cat-tails, however, can be easily managed by growing in tubs or containers. Propagate by division of the rhizome or by seed.

Typha angustifolia Linnaeus.

Narrow-leaved cat-tail, narrow-leaved reedmace, lesser bulrush.

Native to the Americas, Europe, and Asia. Flowering stems to 6 ft. (2 m) tall. Male and female segments of the inflorescence are separated by a sterile, naked section. Mature female spikes brown, to 5/8 in. (15 mm) in diameter. Generally more slender and graceful than *Typha latifolia*, though intermediate hybrids known as *T.* ×*glauca* Godron occur. These hybrids are mostly seed-sterile but can form large colonies by vegetative spread. Zone 3.

Typha latifolia Linnaeus.

Common cat-tail, broad-leafed cat-tail, great reedmace, bulrush.

Native to North America, Europe, and Asia. Flowering stems to 10 ft. (3 m) tall. Male and female segments of the inflorescence continuous, without a sterile section. Mature female spikes brown to blackish brown, to 1 3/8 in. (35 mm) in diameter. Zone 3.

Typha minima Hoppe.

Miniature cat-tail, miniature reedmace.

Native to Eurasia. Flowering stems to 32 in. (80 cm) tall. Male and female segments of the inflorescence mostly continuous but sometimes separated by a sterile section. Mature female spikes brown, very shortly cylindrical to nearly round, to 2 in. (5 cm) long and often 1 1/4 in. (32 mm) in diameter. A superb choice for smaller pools, ponds, and containers. Zone 5.

Typha angustifolia in late March in Bloomfield Hills, Michigan.

Typha angustifolia in late June in northern Delaware.

Typha latifolia in late October in Virginia.

Typha latifolia fall color in late October in eastern Pennsylvania.

Typha latifolia in late June in northern Delaware.

Uncinia Persoon.

Sedge family, Cyperaceae.
Hook sedge.

From the Latin *uncinatus* (hooked at the end), referring to a tiny hook on the axis of the inflorescence that facilitates seed dispersal. Approximately 50 tufted or rhizomatous perennial species similar and closely related to *Carex*, occurring mostly in the Southern Hemisphere, concentrated in Australasia but extending to New Guinea and South and Central America. The ornamental species are low-growing New Zealand natives, all quite similar, prized for their red to red-brown foliage that is evergreen in mild climates. Growing in cool, moist habitats, they thrive when transplanted to places like England and the U.S. Pacific Northwest but suffer in the excessive heat common to summers over much of North America. Foliage color varies between seedlings of the same species and is often brighter during the winter months. Flowers are generally insignificant. Propagate by seed or division. Most require well-drained soils and regular moisture, and grow best when their roots are kept cool. Grow in full sun in cool climates, in partial shade in warmer zones.

Uncinia egmontiana Hamlin.

Orange hook sedge.

Native to New Zealand. Leaves green with orange tints to bright orange, tufted, to 16 in. (40 cm) tall. Zone 8.

Uncinia rubra Boott.

Red hook sedge.

Native to New Zealand's North and South Islands, mostly in mountainous regions at elevations of 1400 to 4500 ft. (500 to 1400 m), and nearly to sea level on Stewart Island. Leaves narrow, dark red to bronze-green, tufted, to 14 in. (35 cm) tall. Zone 8.

Uncinia rubra in March, grown under glass at Longwood Gardens.

Uncinia uncinata (Linnaeus f.) Kukenthal.

Hook sedge.

Native to New Zealand. Leaves dark bronze-green to brown, tufted, to 18 in. (45 cm) tall. Zone 8.

Uniola Linnaeus.

Grass family, Poaceae.
Sea-oats.

Comprised of two species native to coastal dunes, sand flats, and arid places in southeastern coastal North America and in South America.

Uniola paniculata Linnaeus.

Sea-oats.

Native to sand dunes along the East Coast of North America from Virginia to Florida and Texas. Important in dune stabilization. In most states, preservation measures make it illegal to collect any parts of the plant. Reaching a height of 4 ft. (1.2 m), this grass is known for its attractive panicles of flat, oatlike spikelets, produced through the summer. Related to woodland wild-oats, *Chasmanthium latifolium*, but far less leafy, sea-oats is much stouter-stemmed, and its spikelets are much more densely clustered. Though it is more commonly valued for dune stabilization rather than for ornament, beach-goers often appreciate its unique beauty, and it deserves wider attention as an ornamental in sandy seaside gardens. Seed is sometimes infertile and can be difficult to obtain com-

Uniola paniculata in early February in Sebastian, Florida.

mercially because of environmentally threatened status. Runs strongly by rhizomes and roots readily when covered by sand. Very salt tolerant. Zone 8.

Vetiveria Bory.

Grass family, Poaceae.
Vetiver.

From the Tamil word *vettiveru,* based on *veti* (coarse) and *ver* (grass). Comprised of 10 perennial species native to flood plains and streambanks in Old World tropics. The following species has been used in medicines and perfumes since prehistoric times and is occasionally grown for ornament.

Vetiveria zizanioides (Linnaeus) Nash.

Vetiver, khus khus, khas khas.

Native to the East Indies and escaped from cultivation in the American tropics and the southern United States. An erect, warm-season grower, to 8 ft. (2.4 m) tall in bloom, the inflorescences narrow panicles produced in late summer in warm climates. Leaves light green, narrow, and erect but characteristically bent backwards near their tips. Cultivated for centuries for the aromatic oils concentrated in its rhizomes. Used in medicines, perfumes, and in India for making screens called "vesicaries," which were kept moist and placed in air currents to perfume the atmosphere. It has also been used to make baskets that are aromatic when wetted. Planting for screening effect in warm climates has led to its escape from cultivation; however, it makes a striking container specimen treated as an annual or tender perennial in cold climates, and plants grown in pots rarely flower. The foliage becomes attractively bronze-purple tinted in autumn. Propagate by division. Zone 9.

Vetiveria zizanioides in mid-August at Longwood Gardens.

Zizania Linnaeus.

Grass family, Poaceae.
Wild rice, water rice.

Comprised of three species native to marshes and shallow water in North America and eastern Asia. The following two make bold additions to aquatic gardens.

Zizania aquatica Linnaeus.

Annual wild rice, wild rice, Canada wild rice, water rice.

Native to freshwater and brackish marshes, borders of streams and ponds from Maine to Michigan and Illinois south to Florida and Louisiana. Mostly annual in the northern United States, occasionally perennial in the southern states. Once the source of edible wild rice, now

Zizania aquatica in late October at Longwood Gardens.

an expensive delicacy due to labor costs of harvesting. Seeds once gathered by American Indians for food. Flowers in graceful airy panicles to 9 ft. (2.7 m) tall, from midsummer to fall. The lower spikelets are male and have conspicuous yellow pollen sacs. The upper spikelets are female. A stately addition to water gardens, also suited to naturalizing in wet areas. Important as food and shelter for waterfowl, and sometimes planted for these purposes in refuges and game preserves. For use in formal water gardens, start seedlings each year and plant in place in spring. The inflorescences are superb in large cut or dried flower arrangements. Zone 4.

Zizania latifolia (Griesbach) Turczaninow.
Asian wild rice, Manchurian wild rice, water rice.

Native to ponds and riverbanks in Japan, south through the Ryukyus and Taiwan, Indochina, China, Korea, and eastern Siberia. The Asian counterpart to North American native *Zizania aquatica*, but fully perennial and not as tall-growing. Mostly clump-forming, spreading slowly by rhizomes. Upright to 8 ft. (2.4 m) tall in flower. Leaves vertical, to 1 1/4 in. (32 mm) wide, green in summer, turning yellow in fall. Flowers in relatively dense, upright panicles, from mid-August into October. The lower spikelets in each inflorescence are male, the upper female. Prefers shallow water, is useful in shallow ponds, pools, or large containers. Propagate by seed or by division in spring. Zone 7.

Zizania latifolia in late September at Longwood Gardens.

Zizania aquatica in late June in its native habitat near Madison, Wisconsin.

Glossary

Annual. A plant that completes its entire life cycle (from seed to seed) in one year.

Anther. The pollen-producing part of the stamen, located at the tip of the slender stalk (called the filament).

Apomixis. The process of reproducing without sexual cross-fertilization.

Awn. A slender bristlelike or needlelike appendage extending from the lemma or glume. Awns may be short and barely conspicuous or they may be many inches long, contributing significantly to the beauty and translucency of grass flowers.

Biennial. A plant that completes its life cycle (from seed to seed) in two years. Biennial species usually produce only foliage during the first year. They flower and produce seed in the second year.

Biome. The plants and animals in an ecosystem.

Blade. The flat, expanded portion of the leaf above the sheath. The blade may be reduced or modified in various ways, or be absent altogether.

Bract. A general term for any structure that represents a modified leaf; most commonly used to refer to reduced, leaflike structures associated with inflorescences. In grasses the glumes, lemmas, and paleas are considered bracts.

Caespitose. Tufted, clump-forming. Grasses with a caespitose growth habit are often referred to as bunch grasses.

Calcareous. Containing much higher than average amounts of calcium or lime.

Caryopsis. The single-seeded fruit typical of members of the grass family, Poaceae. A caryopsis, often called a grain, does not open at maturity and is typically hard and dry.

Circumboreal. Around the northern regions.

Crown. The base of the plant.

Culm. The aboveground stem of a grass plant. Culms are usually upright but may be horizontal.

Deciduous. A plant that sheds or otherwise loses all its leaves annually, or at certain periods, as opposed to an evergreen plant.

Dioecious. A plant species with male and female flowers on separate plants.

Endemic. Native and restricted to or occurring only in a particular place. Sometimes used in a broader sense to mean native, not introduced or naturalized.

Endosperm. An energy reserve in the form of starch, present in the grains of grasses and in the seeds of many other types of plants.

Evergreen. Remaining green or living throughout the year.

Filament. The threadlike stalk that bears the anther at its tip. The filament and anther comprise a stamen.

Floret. In grasses, the collective term for an individual flower plus the enclosing palea and lemma.

Forb. A broad-leafed flowering plant, as opposed to the grasses, sedges, and rushes.

Genotype. A group of organisms having the same genetic constitution.

Germ. The embryonic grass plant.

Glaucous. Covered with a thin waxy covering that is easily rubbed off. Glaucous plant parts usually appear blue-gray, blue-green, or gray-green. The term may also be used to denote such coloration.

Glume. A bract located at the base of a grass spikelet. Typically there are two glumes associated with each spikelet.

Grain. The single-seeded fruit of true grasses, Poaceae, technically called a caryopsis.

Herbaceous. Lacking true woody tissue.

Honeydew. A syrupy waste product produced by mealybugs and aphids.

Inflorescence. The flowering portion(s) of a plant, complete with any associated bracts.

Internode. The section of the culm occurring between two consecutive nodes.

Lemma. The lower, outer bract in the grass floret.

Ligule. A thin membranous ridge or small row of hairs located at the juncture of the sheath and blade on the side facing the culm. The function of the ligule is uncertain, although it may serve to keep rain from entering the sheath. The variation in ligules is often very important in the botanical identification of grasses. It is of lesser value to gardeners in distinguishing between cultivated varieties.

Lodicule. One of two small scalelike structures usually present at the base of the ovary in the flowers of true grasses, Poaceae. The lodicules swell before pollination, forcing the palea and lemma apart and exposing the flower. Lodicules may represent the vestiges of sepals or petals, which are otherwise lacking in grass flowers.

Ovary. The enlarged lower portion of the female organ, containing the ovule or ovules.

Ovule. An immature, unfertilized seed, located within the ovary.

Monoculture. A population or planting consisting of only one type of plant.

Monoecious. A plant species with bisexual florets on each plant.

Node. A point on an axis (usually a culm or stem) where a leaf or branch is attached.

Palea. The upper, inner bract in the grass floret.

Panicle. An inflorescence having spikelets attached at the ends of stalks that branch from the rachis (main axis).

Perennial. A plant that lives for more than two years.

Perigynium. A saclike, sometimes inflated structure enclosing the female flower or ovary in members of the sedge family, Cyperaceae, especially the genus *Carex.*

Raceme. An inflorescence having individual spikelets attached to the unbranched rachis (main axis) by short stalks.

Rachis. The main axis of an inflorescence.

Rhizomatous. Spreading by rhizomes.

Rhizome. An underground horizontal stem.

Sheath. The lower part of the leaf, originating at a node, which clasps or encircles the stem. In true grasses, Poaceae, the sheath usually has overlapping margins. In sedges, Cyperaceae, the sheath is usually fused around the stem.

Shoot. A stem or any portion of the plant derived from stem tissue.

Spike. An inflorescence having individual spikelets without stalks, attached directly to the unbranched rachis.

Spikelet. In grasses, a small spike, consisting of one or more florets attached to a small central axis, together with the basal bracts (called glumes).

Sport. An individual showing marked variation from the normal type.

Stamen. The male organ of a flower, consisting of a slender stalk (called the filament) and the pollen-producing anther.

Stigma. The pollen-receiving structure. The stigma may be located directly at the top of the ovary or may be separated from the ovary by a short stalk (called the style).

Stolon. An aboveground horizontal stem.

Stoloniferous. Spreading by stolons.

Style. A short stalk projecting from the top of the ovary, usually terminating in a feathery stigma that receives pollen.

Tepal. A flower part that cannot be distinguished as either a sepal or a petal.

Terminal. Located at the tip or top end.

Tussock. A thick tuft.

Umbel. A type of inflorescence in which all flowering branches arise from a central point.

Utricle. A saclike, sometimes inflated structure enclosing the female flower or ovary in members of the sedge family, Cyperaceae. This term may also be used to refer to the saclike structure and the enclosed fruit.

Woody. Having well-developed woody tissue, as is present in trees and shrubs.

Bibliography

Abrams, Leroy. 1955. *Illustrated Flora of the Pacific States: Washington, Oregon, and California.* Volume 1, *Ophioglossaceae to Aristolochiaceae, Ferns to Birthworts.* Stanford, California: Stanford University Press.

Adams, Whitney R., Jr. 1996. *Hardy Clumping Bamboos from the Mountains of China and the Himalayas.*

Adamson, R. S. 1938. *The Vegetation of South Africa.* London: British Empire Vegetation Committee.

Aiken, S. G., and S. J. Darbyshire. 1990. Fescue grasses of Canada. Publication 1844/E, Biosystematics Research Centre, Research Branch, Agriculture Canada, Ottawa, Canada.

Anderson, Sieglinde. An introduction to some ornamental grasses, rushes, and sedges for the rock garden. *Bulletin of the American Rock Garden Society* 44: 157–173.

Arber, Agnes. 1934. *The Gramineae: A Study of Cereal, Bamboo and Grass.* Cambridge: Cambridge University Press.

Auckland Regional Botanic Gardens. 1991. New Zealand grasses and sedges for Auckland gardens. Regional Parks Department Auckland Regional Council Advisory Leaflet No. 29.

Bailey, L. H. 1933. *The Standard Cyclopedia of Horticulture,* volume 3. London: Macmillan Press.

Bailey Hortorium. 1976 *Hortus Third: A Concise Dictionary of Plants Cultivated in the United States and Canada.* Rev. and exp. by staff of Liberty Hyde Bailey Hortorium. New York: Macmillan Publishing.

Barkworth, Mary E., and Joy Everett. 1986. Evolution in the Stipeae: Identification and relationships of its monophyletic taxa. In *Proceedings, An International Symposium on Grass Systematics and Evolution.* Washington, D.C.: Smithsonian Institution Press. 251–264.

Bews, J. W. 1929. *The World's Grasses: Their Differentiation, Distribution, Economics and Ecology.* London: Longmans, Green.

Bisset, Peter. 1907. *The Book of Water Gardening.* New York: A. T. de la Mare Printing and Publishing Company.

Bitner, R. L. 1997. Hot pruning: Burning of ornamental grasses. *The Green Scene* (March): 27.

Blomquist, H. L. 1948. *The Grasses of North Carolina.* Durham, North Carolina: Duke University Press.

Bond, Pauline, and Peter Goldblatt. 1984. Plants of the Cape flora: A descriptive catalogue. *Journal of South African Botany* 13 (September).

Boyd, Howard P. 1991. *A Field Guide to the Pine Barrens of New Jersey: Its Flora, Fauna, Ecology and Historic Sites.* Medford, New Jersey: Plexus Publishing.

Brown, Lauren. 1979. *Grasses: An Identification Guide.* Boston, Massachusetts: Houghton Mifflin.

Brown, Melvin L., and Russell G. Brown. 1984. *Herbaceous Plants of Maryland.* Baltimore, Maryland: Port City Press.

Brown, Neville. 1995. Where there's smoke. *The Garden* 120(7): 402–405.

Burman, Lee, and Anne Bean. 1985. *Hottentots Holland to Hermanus.* South African Wild Flower Guide 5. Cape Town, South Africa: Botanical Society of South Africa.

Chapman, G. P. 1996. *The Biology of Grasses.* Wallingford, Oxon, United Kingdom: CAB International.

Chapman, G. P., and W. E. Peat. 1992. *An Introduction to the Grasses: Including Bamboos and Cereals.* Wallingford, Oxon, United Kingdom: CAB International.

Chatto, Beth. 1976. Grasses and grass-like plants. *The Garden* 101 (September): 448–453.

Cheeseman, T. F. 1925. *Manual of the New Zealand Flora.* Wellington, New Zealand: n.p.

Christiansen, M. Skytte. 1979. *Grasses, Sedges and Rushes in Colour.* Dorset, United Kingdom: Blandford Press.

Clapham, A. R., T. G. Tutin, and E. F. Warburg. 1952. *Flora of the British Isles, Illustrations.* Cambridge: Cambridge University Press.

______.1965. *Flora of the British Isles, Illustrations,* part 4, monocotyledones. Cambridge: Cambridge University Press.

Clark, Lynn G., and Richard W. Pohl. 1996. *Agnes Chase's First Book of Grasses: The Structure of Grasses Explained for Beginners.* 4th ed. Washington, D.C.: Smithsonian Institution Press.

Clayton, W. D., and S. A. Renvoize. 1986. *Genera Graminum: Grasses of the World.* London: Her Majesty's Stationery Office.

Collier, Gordon. 1993. *Gordon Collier's Titoki Point.* Auckland, New Zealand: Moa Beckett Publishers.

Cooper, R. C., and R. C. Cambie. 1991. *New Zealand's Economic Native Plants.* Auckland, New Zealand: Oxford University Press.

Correll, Donovan Stewart, and Marshall Conring Johnston. 1970. *Manual of the Vascular Plants of Texas.* Renner, Texas: Texas Research Foundation.

Cowling, Richard, ed. 1992. *The Ecology of Fynbos: Nutrients, Fire and Diversity.* Cape Town, South Africa: Oxford University Press.

Cowling, Richard, and Dave Richardson. 1995. *Fynbos: South Africa's Unique Floral Kingdom.* Vlaeberg, South Africa: Fernwood Press.

Crampton, Beecher. 1974. *Grasses in California.* Berkeley: University of California Press.

Darke, Rick. 1987. *Miscanthus sinensis* 'Morning Light'. *The Public Garden* 2(1): 17.

______. 1988. *Pennisetum* 'Burgundy Giant'. *The Public Garden* 3(2): 37.

______. 1993. *Ornamental Grasses at Longwood Gardens.* Kennett Square, Pennsylvania: Longwood Gardens.

______. 1994. A century of grasses. *Arnoldia* 54: 2–11.

______. 1996. *Ornamental Grasses.* Manual from class taught at Longwood Gardens, Kennett Square, Pennsylvania.

Darke, R., and M. Griffiths, eds. 1994. *Manual of Grasses.* London: Macmillan Press.

Deam, C. C. 1940. *Flora of Indiana.* Indianapolis, Indiana: Department of Conservation, Division of Forestry.

DeWolf, Gordon P., Jr. 1987. *Taylor's Guide to Ground Covers, Vine and Grasses.* Rev. Boston: Houghton Mifflin.

Dore, William G., and J. McNeill. 1980. *Grasses of Ontario.* Quebec: Agriculture Canada.

Duncan, Wilbur H., and Marion B. Duncan. 1987. *Seaside Plants of the Gulf and Atlantic Coasts.* Washington, D.C.: Smithsonian Institution Press.

Eastman, John. 1995. *The Book of Swamp and Bog: Trees, Shrubs, and Wildflowers of Eastern Freshwater Wetlands.* Mechanicsburg, Pennsylvania: Stackpole Press.

Feesey, Mervyn T. 1972. Perennial ornamental grasses. In *Extracts from the Proceedings of The Royal Horticultural Society and Wisley Trial Reports, 1971 and 1972* 97: 119–122.

______. 1973. Ornamental grasses. In *Extracts from the Proceedings of The Royal Horticultural Society and Wisley Trial Reports, 1972* 98: 24–25.

______. 1983. *Ornamental Grasses and Bamboos.* London: Royal Horticultural Society.

Fernald, M. L. 1970. *Gray's Manual of Botany.* 8th ed. New York: D. Van Nostrand.

Fitter, Richart, and Alastair Fitter. 1987. *Collins Guide to the Grasses, Sedges, Rushes and Ferns of Britain and Northern Europe.* London: Williams Collins Sons.

Foerster, Karl. 1961. *Einzug der Gräser und Farne in die Gärten.* 2nd ed. Melsungen: Verlag J. Neumann-Neudamm.

______. 1978. *Einzug der Gräser und Farne in die Gärten.* 3rd ed. Melsungen: Verlag J. Neumann-Neudamm.

______. 1988. *Einzug der Gräser und Farne in die Gärten.* 4th ed. Stuttgart: Verlag Eugen Ulmer.

Gardner, C. A. 1952. *Flora of Western Australia.* Volume 1, part 1, *Gramineae.* Perth, Australia: n.p.

Gleason, Henry A. 1952. *The New Britton and Brown Illustrated Flora of the Northeastern United States and Adjacent Canada.* Volume 1, *Pteridophyta, Gymnospermae and Monocotyledoneae.* Lancaster, Pennsylvania: Lancaster Press.

Gould, Frank W. 1967. The grass genus *Andropogon* in the United States. *Brittonia* 19 (January–March): 70–76.

______. 1973. *The Illustrated Flora of Illinois Grasses: Panicum to Danthonia.* Carbondale and Edwardsville, Illinois: Southern University Press.

Great Plains Flora Association. 1986. *Flora of the Great Plains.* Lawrence: University Press of Kansas.

Greenlee, John. 1992. *The Encyclopedia of Ornamental Grasses.* Emmaus, Pennsylvania: Rodale Press.

Gress, Ernest M. 1924. The grasses of Pennsylvania. Bureau of Plant Industry, Harrisburg, Pennsylvania, General Bulletin 384.

Greuter, W., ed. 1987. *International Code of Nomenclature Adopted by the Fourteenth International Botanical Congress, Berlin, July–August 1987.* Königstein, Germany: Koeltz Scientific Books.

Griffiths, D. A. 1983. *Grasses and Sedges of Hong Kong.* Hong Kong: Urban Council.

Grounds, Roger. 1989. *Ornamental Grasses.* Bromley, Kent, United Kingdom: Christopher Helm.

Hansen, Richard, and Friedrich Stahl. 1993. *Perennials and Their Garden Habitats.* Trans. Richard Ward. 4th ed. Portland, Oregon: Timber Press.

Harden, Gwen J. 1993. *Flora of New South Wales,* volume 4. Kensington: New South Wales University Press.

Hatch, Stephan L., and Jennifer Pluhar. 1993. *Texas Range Plants.* College Station: Texas A&M University Press.

Hayashi, Yasaki, ed. 1983. *Wild Flowers of Japan.* Tokyo, Japan: Yama-Kei Publishers.

Heywood, V. H., ed. 1985. *Flowering Plants of the World.* Englewood Cliffs, New Jersey: Prentice Hall.

Hickman, James C., ed. 1993. *The Jepson Manual: Higher Plants of California.* Berkeley: University of California Press.

Hitchcock, A. S. 1950. Manual of the grasses of the United States. Miscellaneous Publication No. 200, United States Department of Agriculture. 2nd ed. Rev. by Agnes Chase.

Hodgkiss, I. J. 1978. *Hong Kong Freshwater Plants.* Hong Kong: Urban Council.

Holmes, Roger, ed. 1997. *Taylor's Guide to Ornamental Grasses.* Boston: Houghton Mifflin.

Hopkins, William G. 1995. *Introduction to Plant Physiology.* New York: John Wiley & Sons.

Hotchkiss, Neil. 1970. *Common Marsh, Underwater and Floating-leaved Plants of the United States and Canada.* New York: Dover Publications.

Hutchinson, J. 1973. *The Families of Flowering Plants.* 3rd ed. Oxford: Clarendon Press.

Hutchison, Max. 1992. Vegetation management guideline: Reed canary grass (*Phalaris arundinacea* L.). *Natural Areas Journal* 12(3): 159.

Ibrahim, Kamal M., and Christiane H. S. Kabuye. 1988. *An Illustrated Manual of Kenya Grasses.* Rome: Food and Agriculture Organization of the United Nations.

Jamieson, Hanneke, Anthony Hitchcock, and Neville Brown. 1995. Growing restios. *Veld and Flora* 81 (December): 129–130.

Jelitto, L., and W. Schacht. 1990. *Hardy Herbaceous Perennials.* 2 volumes. Portland, Oregon: Timber Press.

Johnson, P. N. 1984. *The Homet Area: A Natural History Guide.* New Zealand: Fiordland National Park.

Jones, Samuel B., Jr., and Leonard E. Foote. 1990. *Gardening with Native Wild Flowers.* Portland, Oregon: Timber Press.

Kitamura, Siro, Gen Murata, and Tetsuo Koyama. 1964. *Coloured Illustrations of Herbaceous Plants of Japan.* Volume 3, *Monocotyledoneae.* Osaka, Japan: Hoijusha Publishing.

Knobel, Edward. 1977. *Field Guide to the Grasses, Sedges and Rushes of the United States.* New York: Dover Publications.

Köhlein, Fritz, and Peter Menzel. 1994. *Color Encyclopedia of Garden Plants and Habitats.* Trans. Michael E. Epp. Portland, Oregon: Timber Press.

Komarov, V. L., ed. 1963. *Flora of the U.S.S.R.,* volume 2. Trans. N. Landau. Jerusalem: S. Monson.

Ladd, Doug. 1995. *Tallgrass Prairie Wildflowers: A Falcon Field Guide.* Helena, Montana: Falcon Press Publishing.

Lawrence, George H. M. 1951. *Taxonomy of Vascular Plants.* New York: Macmillan Publishing.

Lawson, A. H. 1968. *Bamboos: A Gardener's Guide to Their Cultivation in Temperate Climates.* New York: Taplinger Publishing.

Lazarides, M. 1970. *The Grasses of Central Australia.* Canberra: Australian National University Press.

Lee, Yong No. 1966. *Manual of the Korean Grasses.* Seoul, Korea: Ewha Women's University Press.

Lester, Robert. 1990. Clump forming mountain bamboos of China. Northeast Chapter of the American Bamboo Society 1(1): 2.

Li, Hui-Lin, Tank-shui Tseng-chieng Huang, Tetsuo Koyama, and Charles E. DeVol, eds. 1978. *Flora of Taiwan,* volume 5. Taipei, Taiwan: Epoch Publishing Company.

Loewer, H. Peter. 1977. *Growing and Decorating with Grasses.* New York: Walker and Company.

______. 1995. *Step-by-Step Successful Gardening: Ornamental Grasses.* Des Moines, Iowa: Meredith Books.

Madison, John. 1992. Pampas grasses: One a weed and one a garden queen. *Pacific Horticulture* 53(1): 48–53.

Makino, Tomitarô. 1954. *The Illustrated Flora of Japan, with the Cultivated and Naturalized Plants.* Tokyo: The Hokuryukan Company.

Mark, A. F., and Nancy M. Adams. 1973. *New Zealand Alpine Plants.* Wellington, New Zealand: A. H. & A. W. Reed.

Marks, Marianne, Beth Lapin, and John Randall. 1994. *Phragmites australis* (*P. communis*): Threats, management, and monitoring. *Natural Areas Journal* 14(4): 285–292.

Mattern, Anke, and Mark Moskowitz. 1994. Staudengärden echt: The life and work of Ernst Pagels. *The Hardy Plant* 16(1): 11–18.

McVaugh, Rogers. 1983. *Flora Novo-Galiciana: A Descriptive Account of the Vascular Flora of Western Mexico.* Ann Arbor: University of Michigan Press.

Meyer, Mary Hockenberry. 1975. *Ornamental Grasses.* New York: Charles Scribner's Sons.

Meyer, Mary Hockenberry, D. B. White, and H. Pellett. n.d. Ornamental grasses for cold climates. North Central Regional Extension Publication 573, Minnesota Extension Service, Department of Horticultural Science, University of Minnesota.

Mohlenbrock, Robert H. 1972. *The Illustrated Flora of Illinois Grasses: Bromus to Paspalum.* Carbondale and Edwardsville, Illinois: Southern University Press.

______. 1973. *The Illustrated Flora of Illinois Grasses: Panicum to Danthonia.* Carbondale and Edwardsville, Illinois: Southern University Press.

Moriarty, Audrey. 1982. *Outeniqua Tsitsikamma and Eastern Little Karoo: South African Wild Flower Guide 2.* Kirstenbosch, Claremont: Botanical Society of South Africa.

Munz, Philip A. 1974. *A Flora of Southern California.* Berkeley: University of California Press.

Niering, William. 1991. *Wetlands of North America.* Charlottesville, Virginia: Thomasson-Grant.

Niering, William A., and R. Scott Warren. 1980. Salt marsh plants of Connecticut. The Connecticut College Arboretum Bulletin No. 25.

Oakes, A. J. 1990. *Ornamental Grasses and Grasslike Plants.* New York: Van Nostrand Reinhold.

Ohwi, Jisaburo. 1984. *Flora of Japan.* Reprint. Washington, D.C.: Smithsonian Institution.

O'Neill, Nichole, and David F. Farr. 1996. Miscanthus blight, a new foliar disease of ornamental grasses and sugarcane incited by *Leptosphaeria* sp. and its anamorphic state *Stagonospora* sp. *Plant Disease* 80(9) (September): 980–983.

Ottesen, Carole. 1989. *Ornamental Grasses: The Amber Wave.* New York: McGraw-Hill Publishing.

Phillips, E. Percy. 1951. The genera of South African flowering plants. Botanical Survey Memoir No. 25, Department of Agriculture, Division of Botany and Plant Pathology, Pretoria, South Africa.

Phillips, Roger. 1994. *Grasses, Ferns, Mosses and Lichens of Great Britain and Ireland.* London: Macmillan Reference.

Plants and Gardens, Brooklyn Botanic Garden Record. 1993. *The Natural Lawn and Alternatives,* volume 49(3). Brooklyn, New York: Brooklyn Botanic Garden.

Plues, Margaret. 1867. *British Grasses: An Introduction to the Study of the Gramineae.* London: Reeve and Company.

Pohl, Richard W. 1986. Man and the grasses: A history. *Proceedings, An International Symposium on Grass Systematics and Evolution.* Washington, D.C.: Smithsonian Institution Press. 355–358.

______. 1968. *How to Know the Grasses.* Dubuque, Iowa: Wm. C. Brown.

Radford, A. E., H. E. Ahles, and C. R. Bell. 1968. *Manual of the Vascular Flora of the Carolinas.* Chapel Hill, North Carolina: University of North Carolina Press.

Reinhardt, Thomas A., Martina Reinhardt, and Mark Moskowitz. 1989. *Ornamental Grass Gardening: Design Ideas, Functions and Effects.* New York: Michael Friedman Publishing Group.

Roe, Roger G., Nancy Howard Agnew, Linda Naeve, and Nick E. Christians. 1996. Ornamental grasses for the Midwest. North Central Regional Extension Publication 461, Iowa State University.

Salisbury, Frank B., and Cleon W. Ross. 1992. *Plant Physiology.* 4th ed. Belmont, California: Wadsworth Publishing.

Salmon, J. T. 1963. *New Zealand Flowers and Plants in Colour.* Reprint. Wellington, New Zealand: A. H. & A. W. Reed.

Samson, Fred B., and Fritz L. Knopf, eds. 1996. *Prairie Conservation: Preserving North America's Most Endangered Ecosystem.* Washington, D.C.: Island Press.

Schenk, George. 1989. New Zealand's changeful carexes. *Pacific Horticulture* 50(1): 48–54.

Scott, Trevor. 1996. Art nouveau—fresh ideas for grass. *The Garden* 121 (May): 250–253.

Sell, Peter, and Gina Murrell. 1996. *Flora of Great Britain and Ireland.* Volume 5, *Butomaceae–Orchidaceae.* Cambridge: Cambridge University Press.

Šikula, Jaromír. 1979. *A Concise Guide in Colour: Grasses.* Trans. Olga Kuthanová. London: Hamlyn Publishing.

Silberhorn, Gene M. 1982. *Common Plants of the Mid-Atlantic Coast: A Field Guide.* Baltimore, Maryland: The Johns Hopkins University Press.

Simpson, David. 1994. *Cyperus prolifer. Kew Magazine* 2: 6–8.

Smith, Clifton F. 1976. *A Flora of the Santa Barbara Region, California.* Santa Barbara, California: Santa Barbara Museum of Natural History.

Smith, James P., Jr. 1977. *Vascular Plant Families.* Eureka, California: Mad River Press.

______. 1981. *A Key to the Genera of Grasses of the Conterminous United States.* 6th ed. Eureka, California: Mad River Press.

Stace, Clive. 1991. *New Flora of the British Isles.* Cambridge: Cambridge University Press.

Steward, V. Bruce, Jim Stimmel, and Rick Darke. 1995. Understanding the miscanthus mealybug. *American Nurseryman* 182(1): 34–40.

Steyermark, J. A. 1963. *Flora of Missouri.* Ames, Iowa: The Iowa State University Press.

Stimmel, James F. 1997. Miscanthus mealybug. *Perennial Plants* (Spring): 37–38.

Stone, Hugh E. 1945. *A Flora of Chester County, Pennsylvania,* volume 1. Philadelphia, Pennsylvania: The Academy of Natural Sciences.

Strausbaugh, P. D., and E. L. Core. n.d. *Flora of West Virginia.* 2nd ed. Grantsville, West Virginia: Seneca Books.

Swink, F., and G. Wilhelm. 1994. *Plants of the Chicago Region.* 4th ed. Indianapolis, Indiana: Indiana Academy of Science.

Tatnall, Robert R. 1946. *Flora of Delaware and the Eastern Shore.* The Society of Natural History of Delaware.

Taylor, Nigel J. 1992. *Ornamental Grasses, Bamboos, Rushes and Sedges.* London: Ward Lock.

Thiselton-Dyer, William T., ed. 1897–1900. *Flora Capensis.* Volume 7, *Pontederiaceae to Gramineae.* Kent, United Kingdom: L. Reeve.

Thomas, G. S. 1990. *Perennial Garden Plants or the Modern Florilegium.* 3rd ed. Portland, Oregon: Sagapress.

Trehane, Piers. 1989. *Index Hortensis.* Volume 1, *Perennials.* Wimborne, Great Britain: Quarterjack Publishing, distributed by Timber Press, Portland, Oregon.

______, ed. 1995. *International Code of Nomenclature for Cultivated Plants.* Wimborne, United Kingdom: Quarterjack Publishing.

Tricker, William. 1897. *The Water Garden.* New York: A. T. de la Mare Printing and Publishing Company.

Tsvelev, N. N. 1983. *Grasses of the Soviet Union,* parts 1 and 2. Trans. B. R. Sharma. New Delhi, India: Amerind Publishing.

Tucker, Gordon C. The genera of Cyperaceae in the southeastern United States. *Journal of the Arnold Arboretum* 68 (October) : 425–437.

USDA, NRCS. 1997. The PLANTS database. (http://plants.usda.gov). National Plant Data Center, Baton Rouge, Louisiana.

Vasey, George. 1890. Grasses of the Southwest. Bulletin No. 12, United States Department of Agriculture, Division of Botany, Washington, D.C.

______. 1892. Grasses of the Pacific slope, including Alaska and the adjacent islands. Bulletin No. 13, United States Department of Agriculture, Division of Botany, Washington, D.C.

Walter, Kerry S., David F. Chamberlain, Martin F. Gardner, Ronald J. D. McBeath, Henry J. Noltie, and Philip Thomas, eds. 1995. *Catalogue of Plants Growing at the Royal Botanic Garden, Edinburgh.* Oxford, United Kingdom: Royal Botanic Garden Edinburgh.

Wasowski, Sally, and Andy Wasowski. 1994. *Gardening with Native Plants of the South.* Dallas, Texas: Taylor Publishing.

Watson, Leslie, and Michael J. Dallwitz. 1992. *The Grass Genera of the World.* Wallingfod, Oxon, United Kingdom: CAB International.

Woods, Christopher. 1992. *Encyclopedia of Perennials: A Gardener's Guide.* New York: Facts on File.

Nursery Sources

This is a partial list, limited to nurseries in the United States and the United Kingdom that have a specialty in ornamental grasses or bamboos, or that offer grasses that are generally hard to find. Catalogs or lists are available from most. No endorsement is intended, nor is criticism implied of sources not mentioned. An asterisk before a name indicates the nursery sells wholesale only.

The spades shown on page 128 are manufactured by and may be ordered from: W. W. Manufacturing, 60 Rosenhayn Avenue, Bridgeton, New Jersey 08302.

American Ornamental Perennials
29977 SE Weitz Lane
Eagle Creek, Oregon 97022

André Viette Farm & Nursery
P.O. Box 1109
Fishersville, Virginia 22939

Apple Court
Hordle Lane
Hordle
Lymington, Hampshire
United Kingdom

*Babikow Greenhouses
7838 Babikow Road
Baltimore, Maryland 21237

Bald Eagle Nursery
18510 Sand Road
Fulton, Illinois 61252

Bernardo Beach Native Plant Farm
1 Sanchez Road
Veguita, New Mexico 87062

Beth Chatto Gardens Ltd.
Elmstead Market
Colchester CO7 7DB
United Kingdom

Blooms of Bressingham
Bressingham, Diss
Norfolk, IP22 2AB
United Kingdom

Bluebird Nursery
P.O. Box 460
Clarkson, Nebraska 68629

*Bluemount Nurseries
2103 Blue Mount Road
Monkton, Maryland 21111

*Carolina Nurseries
739 Gaillard Road
Moncks Corner, South Carolina
29461

Carroll Gardens
444 East Main Street
P.O. Box 310
Westminster, Maryland 21157

Comstock Seed
8520 W. 4th Street
Reno, Nevada 89523

*Conard-Pyle Company
372 Rose Hill Road
West Grove, Pennsylvania 19390

Crystal Palace Perennials
P.O. Box 154
St. John, Indiana 46373

Digging Dog Nursery
P.O. Box 471
Albion, California 95410

*Emerald Coast Growers
7400 Klondike Road
Pensacola, Florida 32526

Garden Treasure Nursery
P.O. Box 1935
East Hampton, NY 11937

Glasshouse Works
Church Street
P.O. Box 97
Stewart, Ohio 45778

Granite Seed
1697 West 2100 North
Lehi, Utah 84043

Greenlee Nursery
301 E. Franklin Ave.
Pomona, California 91766

Four Seasons Seed Company
P. O. Box 6293
Albany, California 94706

Hedgerow Farms
21740 County Road 88
Winters, California 95694

Heronswood Nursery
7530 NE 288th Street
Kingston, Washington 98346

*Hines Nurseries
P.O. Box 1449
Vacaville, California 95696

Hoffman Nursery
5520 Bahama Road
Rougemont, North Carolina 27572

Jelitto Perennial Seeds
125 Chenoweth Lane
Louisville, Kentucky 40207

Kurt Bluemel Inc.
2740 Greene Lane
Baldwin, Maryland 21013

Larner Seeds
P.O. Box 407
Bolinas, California 94924

Limerock Ornamental Grasses
R.D. 1, Box 111-C
Port Matilda, Pennsylvania 16870

Maryland Aquatic Nurseries
3427 North Furnace Road
Jarrettsville, Maryland 21084

Mileager's Gardens
4838 Douglas Avenue
Racine, Wisconsin 53402

*Monrovia Nursery
18331 E. Foothill Blvd.
Azusa, California 91702

*Mountain States Wholesale Nursery
10020 W. Glendale Avenue
Glendale, Arizona 85307

The Natural Garden
38W443 Highway 64
St. Charles, Illinois 60175

New England Bamboo Company
P.O. Box 358
Rockport, Massachusetts 01966

Niche Gardens
1111 Dawson Road
Chapel Hill, North Carolina 27516

North American Prairies Company
11754 Jarvis Avenue
Annandale, Minnesota 55302

*North Creek Nurseries
R.R. 2, Box 33
Landenberg, Pennsylvania 19350

Plant Delights Nursery
9241 Sauls Road
Raleigh, North Carolina 27603

Plants of the Southwest
Agua Fria, Rt. 6
Box 11A
Santa Fe, New Mexico 87501

Prairie Moon Nursery
Route 3, Box 163
Winona, Minnesota 55987

Prairie Nursery
P.O. Box 306
Westfield, Wisconsin 53964

Prairie Ridge Nursery
R.R. 2
9738 Overland Road
Mt. Horeb, Wisconsin 53572

Prairie Seed Source
P.O. Box 83
North Lake, Wisconsin 53064

*Russell Gardens
P.O. Box 702
Richboro, Pennsylvania 18954

*San Marcos Growers
125 S. San Marcos Road
P.O. Box 6827
Santa Barbara, California 93160

Southwestern Native Seeds
P.O. Box 50503
Tucson, Arizona 85703

Stock Seed Farms
Rt. 1
P.O. Box 112
Murdock, Nebraska 68407

Sunlight Gardens
174 Golden Lane
Andersonville, Tennessee 37705

Terra Nova Nursery
4309 SW. Cullen Boulevard
Portland, Oregon 97221

Theodore Payne Foundation
10459 Tuxford Street
Sun Valley, California 91352

Tornello Nursery (Bamboo)
P.O. Box 788
Ruskin, Florida 33570

Tradewinds Bamboo Nursery
28446 Hunter Creek Loop
Gold Beach, Oregon 97444

Tree of Life Nursery
33201 Ortega Highway
P.O. Box 635
San Juan Capistrano, California
92693

Wayside Gardens
1 Garden Lane
Hodges, South Carolina 29695

Weiss Brothers Perennial Nursery
11690 Colfax Highway
Grass Valley, California 95945

White Flower Farm
P.O. Box 50
Litchfield, Connecticut 06759

Wild Earth Native Plant Nursery
49 Mead Avenue
Freehold, New Jersey 07728

Wild Seed
P.O. Box 27751
Tempe, Arizona 85285

Yucca Do Nursery at Peckerwood
Gardens
P.O. Box 450
Waller, Texas 77484

USDA Hardiness Zone Map

European Hardiness Zone Map

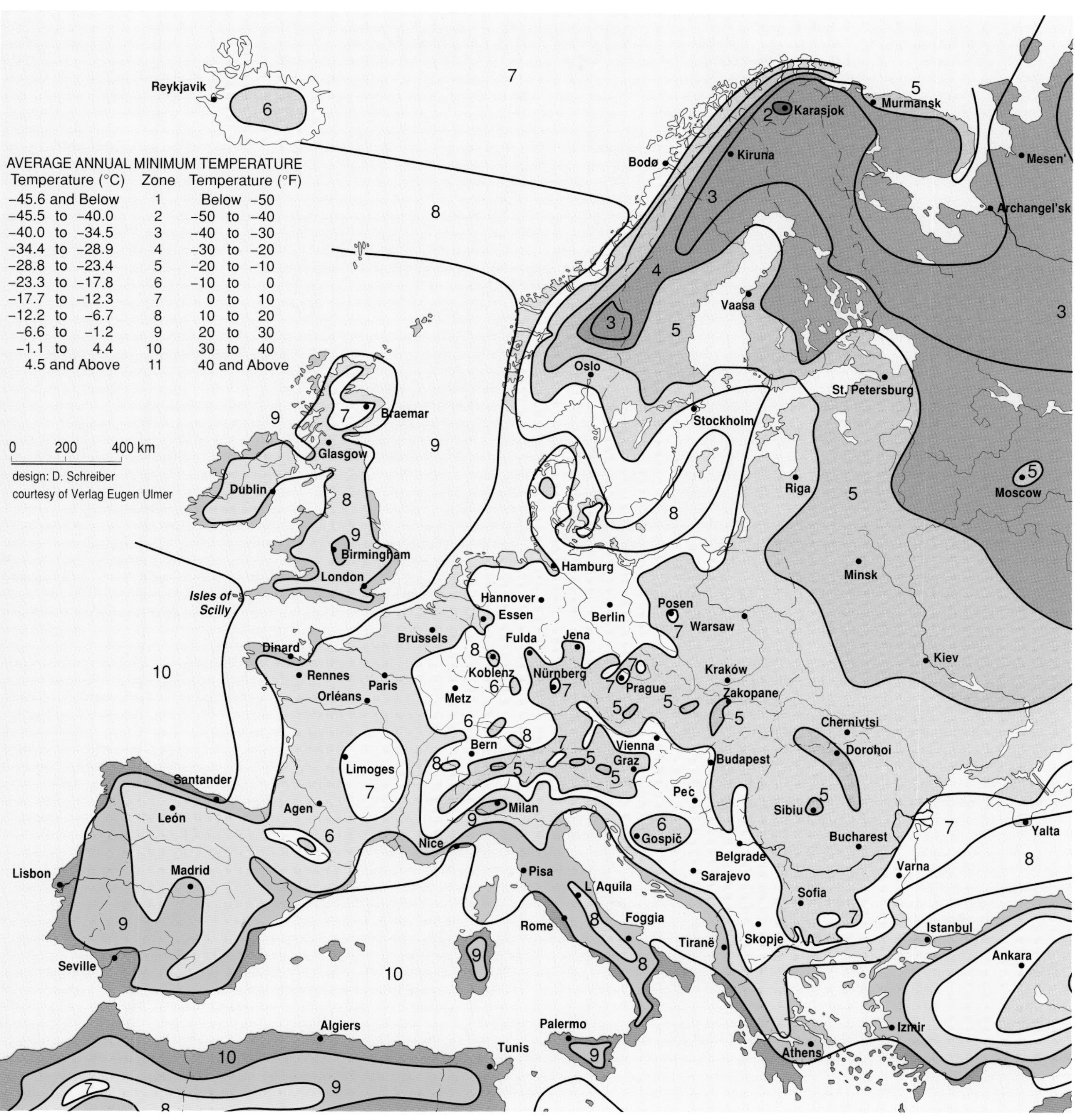

Index of Common Names

Index of Botanical Names

Page numbers in **boldface** indicate a main text entry. Page numbers in *italic* indicate photographs.